PSYCHOANALYSIS AND CINEMA

LANGUAGE, DISCOURSE, SOCIETY

Editors: Stephen Heath and Colin MacCabe

PSYCHOANALYSIS AND CINEMA
The Imaginary Signifier

Christian Metz

*Translated by Celia Britton, Annwyl Williams,
Ben Brewster and Alfred Guzzetti*

MACMILLAN

First edition 1982
Reprinted 1983, 1985

Published by
THE MACMILLAN PRESS LTD
Houndmills, Basingstoke, Hampshire RG21 2XS
and London
Companies and representatives
throughout the world

Printed in Hong Kong

ISBN 0-333-27805-4 (hardcover)
ISBN 0-333-36640-9 (paperback)

Contents

v

Acknowledgements

The four texts which make up this book were written between 1973 and 1976, the first in 1974, the second and third in 1973 and the fourth in 1975–6. They first appeared in book form under the title *Le Signifiant imaginaire. Psychanalyse et cinéma* (Paris: Union Générale d'Éditions, 10/18) in 1977.

Part I, 'Le signifiant imaginaire', and Part III, 'Le film de fiction et son spectateur', were first published in *Communications*, 23 (1975), pp. 3–55 and pp. 108–35. Part II, 'Histoire/discours', was first published in *Langue, Discours, Société – Pour Emile Benveniste* (Paris: Editions du Seuil) 1975, pp. 301–6. 'Métaphose/ Métonymie ou le référent imaginaire' appeared for the first time in *Le Signifiant imaginaire*.

Part I, 'The Imaginary Signifier', is translated by Ben Brewster; Part II, 'Story/Discourse (A Note on Two Kinds of Voyeurism)', by Celia Britton and Annwyl Williams; Part III, 'The Fiction Film and its Spectator: a Metapsychological Study', by Alfred Guzzetti; and Part IV, 'Metaphor/Metonymy, or the Imaginary Referent', by Celia Britton and Annwyl Williams. The index was compiled by Ben Brewster.

Part I, 'The Imaginary Signifier', was first published in *Screen*, vol. 16, no. 2 (1975) pp. 14–76; Part III, 'The Fiction Film and its Spectator: a Metapsychological Study', in *New Literary History*, vol. VIII, no. 1 (1976) pp. 75–105. Both of these translations appear here in a marginally revised form.

Part I
The Imaginary Signifier

Translated by Ben Brewster

Part 1

1

The Imaginary and the 'Good Object' in the Cinema and in the Theory of the Cinema

Reduced to its most fundamental procedures, any psychoanalytic reflection on the cinema might be defined in Lacanian terms as an attempt to disengage the cinema-object from the imaginary and to win it for the symbolic, in the hope of extending the latter by a new province:[1] an enterprise of displacement, a territorial enterprise, a symbolising advance; that is to say, in the field of films as in other fields, the psychoanalytic itinerary is *from the outset a semiological one,* even (above all) if in comparison with the discourse of a more classical semiology it shifts its point of focus from the statement [the *énoncé*] to the enunciation [the *énonciation*].[2]

Those who look superficially or who share the ritual eagerness to detect 'changes' as often as possible will perhaps think that I have abandoned certain positions or turned away from them when in fact, more simply – less simply, of course – I am accepting the temptation (the attempt) to drive a little deeper into the very procedures of knowledge, which constantly symbolises new fragments of the 'real' in order to annex them to 'reality'. 'There are formulae that are not imagined. For a time, at least, they range themselves with the real.'[3] For a time, at least: let us therefore attempt to imagine some of them.

It has very often, and rightly, been said that the cinema is a technique of the imaginary. A technique, on the other hand, which is peculiar to a historical epoch (that of capitalism) and a state of society, so-called industrial civilisation.

A technique of the imaginary, but in two senses. In the ordinary sense of the word, as a whole critical tendency culminating

3

in the work of Edgar Morin[4] has demonstrated, because most films consist of fictional narratives and because all films depend even for their signifier on the primary imaginary of photography and phonography. In the Lacanian sense, too, in which the imaginary, opposed to the symbolic but constantly imbricated with it, designates the basic lure of the ego, the definitive imprint of a stage *before* the Oedipus complex (which also continues after it), the durable mark of the mirror which alienates man in his own reflection and makes him the double of his double, the subterranean persistence of the exclusive relation to the mother, desire as a pure effect of lack and endless pursuit, the initial core of the unconscious (primal repression). All this is undoubtedly reactivated by the play of that *other mirror*, the cinema screen, in this respect a veritable psychical substitute, a prosthesis for our primally dislocated limbs. But our difficulty – the same one as everywhere else – will be that of grasping in any detail the intimately ramifying articulation of this imaginary with the feats of the signifier, with the semiotic imprint of the Law (here, the cinematic codes) which also marks the unconscious, and thereby man's productions, including films.

The symbolic is at work not only in these films but equally in the discourse of anyone who discusses them, and hence in the article I am just beginning. This certainly does not mean that the symbolic is enough to produce a knowledge,[5] since the uninterpreted dream, the phantasy, the symptom, are all symbolic operations. Nevertheless, it is in its wake that we can find hope for a little more knowledge, it is one of its avatars that introduces 'understanding', whereas the imaginary is the site of an unsurpassable opacity, almost by definition. Thus as a beginning it is absolutely essential to tear the symbolic from its own imaginary and to return it to it as a look. To tear it from it, but not completely, or at least not in the sense of ignoring it and fleeing from it (fearing it): the imaginary is also what has to be *rediscovered* precisely in order to avoid being swallowed up by it: a never-ending task. If here I could manage a small part of this task (in the cinematic field), I should by no means be displeased.

For the problem of the cinema is always reduplicated as a problem of the theory of the cinema and we can only extract knowledge from what we are (what we are as persons, what we are as culture and society). As in political struggles, our only weapons are those of the adversary, as in anthropology, our only source is the native, as in the analytical cure, our only knowledge is that of the analysand, who is also (current French usage tells us so) the analyser [*analysant*]. The posture which inaugurates knowledge is defined by a *backward turn* and by it alone – a backward turn is the movement common to my three examples, which are more than examples. If the effort of science is constantly threatened by a relapse into the very thing against which it is constituted, that is because it is constituted as much *in* it as *against* it, and because the two prepositions are here in some sense synonymous (in a very similar way, the neurotic defences set to work against anxiety themselves become anxiogenic because they originate in anxiety). The work of the symbolic, in the theoretician who would delimit the share of the imaginary and that of the symbolic in the cinema, is always in danger of being swallowed up in the very imaginary which is sustained by the cinema, which makes the film likeable, and which is thus the instigation for the theoretician's very existence (= 'the desire to study the cinema', to use more ordinary terms): to sum up, the objective conditions that give rise to the theory of the cinema are one and the same as those that make that theory precarious and permanently threaten it with sliding into its opposite, in which the *discourse of the object* (the native discourse of the cinematic institution) insidiously comes to occupy the place of *discourse about the object*.

This is the risk that has to be run, there is no choice; anyone who does not run it has already fallen victim to it: like certain cinema journalists, he gossips about films in order to *prolong* their affective and social incidence, their imaginary, that is, perfectly real power.

In Part III, 'The Fiction Film and its Spectator', I attempt to show that the cinema spectator has veritable 'object relations' with films. In Part II, 'Story/Discourse', my aim is to specify, following Jean-Louis Baudry, but obliquely with respect to his remarkable analyses,[6] what the voyeurism of the spectator has to do with the primordial experience of the mirror, and also with the primal scene (with a unilateral voyeurism without exhibitionism on the part of the object looked at).

This is thus the moment to recall certain given facts which will be very important for the rest of this study, facts that pre-exist my intervention and belong to the history of the psychoanalytic movement. The very notion of an 'object relation' – a phantasy relation, quite distinct from real relations to real objects and yet contributing to their construction – constitutes one of Melanie Klein's unique contributions to the Freudian field, and is inscribed entirely within what was to become for Lacan the dimension of the imaginary. Lacan's discourse in fact 'skirts' certain Kleinian themes without coinciding with them (= partial objects, role of the breast, importance of the oral stage, persecution phantasies of fragmentation, depressive positions of loss, etc.), but this only on the side of the imaginary. And the main grounds for Lacan's criticism of Melanie Klein will be familiar: her reduction of the psyche to only one of its axes, the imaginary, the absence of a theory of the symbolic, 'incapable of even so much as suspecting the existence of the category of the signifier'.[7] On the other hand, the experience of the mirror as it is described by Lacan[8] is essentially situated on the side of the imaginary (= formation of the ego by identification with a phantom, an image), even if the mirror also makes possible a first access to the symbolic by the mediation of the mother holding the child to the glass whose reflection, functioning here as the capitalised Other,[9] necessarily appears in the field of the mirror alongside that of the child.

To sum up, what I analyse, or attempt to analyse in Parts II and III (written in fact several months before this first part, and constituting my first two Freudian inspired studies) turns out, without my having precisely intended it, to be already established on one of the flanks of the ridge-line, that of the imaginary: cinematic fiction as a semi-dreamlike instance, in Part III, and in Part II, the spectator-screen relationship as a mirror identification. That is why I should now like to approach my object from its symbolic flank, or rather along the ridge-line itself. My dream today is to speak of the cinematic dream in terms of a code: the code of this dream.

'GOING TO THE CINEMA'

For the spectator, the film can on occasion be a 'bad object':[10] then we have *filmic unpleasure*, which I deal with elsewhere (see pp. 111 and 112) and which defines the relation of certain spectators to certain films, or of certain groups of spectators to certain groups of films. Nevertheless, the 'good object' relation is more basic from the standpoint of a socio-historical critique of the cinema, for it is this relation and not the opposite one (which thus appears as a local failure of the former) that constitutes the aim of the cinematic institution and that the latter is constantly attempting to maintain or re-establish.

Let me insist once again, the cinematic institution is not just the cinema industry (which works to fill cinemas, not to empty them), it is also the mental machinery – another industry – which spectators 'accustomed to the cinema' have internalised historically and which has adapted them to the consumption of films. (The institution is outside us and inside us, indistinctly collective and intimate, sociological and psychoanalytic, just as the general prohibition of incest has as its individual corollary the Oedipus complex, castration or perhaps in other states of society different psychical configurations, but ones which still *imprint* the institution in us in their own way.) The second machine, i.e. the social regulation of the spectator's metapsychology, like the first, has as its function to set up good object relations with films if at all possible; here too the 'bad film' is a failure of the institution: one goes to the cinema because one wants to and not because one has to force oneself, in the hope that the film will please and not that it will displease. Thus filmic pleasure and filmic unpleasure, although they correspond to the two imaginary objects shaped by the persecutory splitting described by Melanie Klein, are not in my view arranged in positions of antithetic symmetry, since the institution as a whole has filmic pleasure alone as its aim.

In a social system in which the spectator is not forced physically to go to the cinema but in which it is still important that he should go so that the money he pays for his admission makes it possible to shoot other films and thus ensures the auto-reproduction of the institution – and it is the specific characteristic of every true institution that it takes charge of the mechanisms of its own perpetuation – there is no other solution than to set up arrangements whose aim and effect is to give the spectator the 'spontaneous' desire to visit the cinema and pay for his ticket. The outer machine (the cinema as industry) and the inner machine (the spectator's psychology) are not just metaphorically related, the latter a facsimile of the former, 'internalising' it as a reversed mould, a receptive hollow of identical form, but also metonymically related as complementary segments: 'wanting to go to the cinema' is a kind of reflection shaped by the film industry, but it is also a real link in the chain of the overall mechanism of that industry. It occupies one of the essential positions in the circulation of money, the turnover of capital without which films could no longer be made: a privileged position since it intervenes just after the 'outward' movement (which includes the financial investment in cinematic undertakings, the material manufacture of the films, their distribution, their hire to the cinemas) and inaugurates the circuit of return which brings the money back eventually, if possible with a profit, from the pockets of the individual spectators to those of the production companies or the banks supporting them, thus giving the go-ahead for new films to be made. In this way, the libidinal economy (filmic pleasure in its historically constituted form) reveals its 'correspondence' with the political economy (the current cinema as a commercial enterprise), and it is, moreover – as the very existence of 'market research' shows – one of the specific elements of that economy: this is what is euphemistically translated by the term *'motivation'* in socio-psychological surveys directly geared to sales.

If I am concerned to define the cinematic institution as a wider instance than the cinema industry (or than the ambiguous commonplace notion of the 'commercial cinema') it is because of this *dual kinship* – mould and segment, facsimile and component – between the psychology of the spectator (which is only apparently 'individual'; as everywhere else, only its most minute variations can be described as such) and the financial mechanisms of the cinema. My insistence on this point may be irritating, but imagine what would occur in the absence of such a state of affairs: we should have to suppose the existence of some special police force (no less) or some statutory system of *a posteriori* inspection (= a stamp in one's identity card on admission to a cinema) to force people to go to the cinema: a little piece of science fiction which is of course absurd, but does at least have the paradoxically dual advantage that it both corresponds to a situation which is not quite without real examples of an attenuated and localised kind (such as those political regimes in which certain direct propaganda films are practically 'obligatory' for members of the movement or of the official youth organisations), and yet clearly designates a modality of *regular* cinema attendance very different from that on which the institution depends in the vast majority of cases, i.e. in what one would (for that very reason) call its 'normal' forms. Here I am touching on political analysis, and the difference there is between a cinema-institution which would be of a fascist type (and has hardly ever existed on a large scale, even in regimes which might have made a greater call on it) and a cinema-institution which is capitalist and liberal in inspiration, and is broadly dominant almost everywhere, even in countries otherwise more or less socialist.

'TALKING ABOUT THE CINEMA'

In the register of the imaginary (= Klein's object relation), the institution thus depends on the good object, although it may happen that it manufactures bad ones. At this point we perhaps glimpse the existence within the cinema of a *third machine* which I have so far only mentioned pp. 4–5, and even then not named. I shall now leave the industry and the spectator to consider the *cinematic writer* (critic, historian, theoretician, etc.), and I am struck by the extreme concern he often reveals – a concern which gives him an odd resemblance to producer and consumer – to maintain a good object relation with as many films as possible, and at any rate with the cinema as such.

This proposition will immediately 'arouse' a host of counter-examples, but I shall not stop for them since I accept them entirely. All the same, let me recall one of them, chosen at random: the representatives of the French 'new wave', when they had not yet made any films and were working as critics for *Cahiers du cinéma*, based a broad sector of their theory on the denunciation of a certain type of film, the 'French quality' film; this attack was no pretence, it went much further than a mere disagreement at the intellectual level, it conveyed a real and profound antipathy for the films denounced: it constituted them as bad objects, for the denouncers themselves first of all, then for the audience that attached itself to them and a little later guaranteed the success of *their* films (thus restoring a 'good' cinema). Besides, cinematic literature, taken as a whole, is not sparing in passages where a film, a film-maker, a genre, some general aspect of the cinema itself, are taken briskly to task. Settling accounts is as frequent, probably more so and certainly rougher, in cinema criticism than in literary criticism, for example.

It might be enough, and it would not be false, to say that the very violence of these reactions confirms the broadly projective character of the relation the cinema writer often maintains to his 'object' (very aptly named here). But it is essential to go further. What I should like to emphasise is the fact that despite these hostilities which come to be 'imprinted' in cinematic writings and are neither uncommon nor simulated, there is a more fundamental and opposite tendency in cinema writers, an intention to establish, maintain or re-establish the cinema (or films) in the position of good object. Thus cinema criticism is imaginary in both its two main movements, linked together by the bond of a true reaction-formation: in the persecutory aspects of blind polemic, in the great depressive plunge in which the cinema-object is restored, repaired, protected.

It is very often for the purpose of exalting one kind of cinema that another has been violently attacked: the oscillation between 'good' and 'bad', the immediacy of the restoration mechanism, then appear in all their clarity.

Another case, and just as frequent a one, is that of conceptions of the cinema which aim to be theoretical and general but in fact consist of justifying a given type of film that one has first liked, and rationalising this liking after the event. These 'theories' are often author aesthetics (aesthetics of taste); they may contain insights of considerable theoretical importance, but the writer's posture is not theoretical: the statement is sometimes scientific, the enunciation never. A rather similar but more ingenuous phenomenon, varying in the extent to which it is caricatural, can often be observed in certain young cinephiles who substantially change their basic opinion of the cinema, sometimes in an exuberant or dramatic way, after each film they have seen which has strongly attracted them: the new theorisation is tailored each time to the precise measure of this unique and delicious film, and yet it is indispensable that it be sincerely experienced as 'general' to prolong and amplify, to *sanction* the vivid momentary pleasure they obtained on seeing the film: the id does not bring its own super-ego with it,[11] it is not enough to be happy, or rather one cannot be perfectly happy, unless one is sure one has a right to be happy. (In the same way some men can only fully live their present love by projecting it into a mental temporality and persuading themselves that it will last throughout their lives: the contradiction of experience, the precise renewal of the same inflation vis-à-vis the next love are incapable of shaking the disposition they carry with them: for its real mechanism is almost the diametrical opposite of its apparent result: far from the strength of their love guaranteeing it a real future, the psychical representation of that future is the prior condition for the establishment of their full amorous potency in the present; the institution of marriage answers to this need and reinforces it.) To return to the cinema, the rationalisation of a taste into a theory in its numerous and commonplace forms obeys an objective law which hardly varies in its broad lines. It could be described in Lacanian terms as a slight wavering between the functions of the imaginary, the symbolic and the real; in Kleinian terms as a slight overflow of the unconscious phantasies; in Freudian terms as a slight inadequacy of secondarisation.[12] The real object (here the film *which has pleased*) and the truly theoretical discourse by which it might have been symbolised have been more or less confused with the imaginary object (= the film *such as it has pleased*, i.e. something which owes a great deal to its spectator's own phantasy), and the virtues of the latter have been conferred on the former by projection. Thus a simultaneously internal and external love object is constituted, at once comforted by a justificatory theory which only goes beyond it (occasionally even silently ignoring it) the better to surround and protect it, according to the cocoon principle. The general discourse is a kind of advanced structure of the phobic (and also counter-phobic) type, a proleptic reparation of any harm which might come to the film, a depressive procedure occasionally breached by persecutory returns, an unconscious protection against a possible change in the taste of the lover himself, a defence more or less intermingled with pre-emptive counter-attack. To adopt the outward marks of theoretical discourse is to occupy a strip of territory *around* the adored film, all that really counts, in order to bar all the roads by which it might be attacked. The cinematic rationaliser, locking himself up in his system, is gripped by a kind of siege psychosis;

he protects the film, but also, within the shelter of the ramparts of theory, organises his dual relationship with it for a more integral pleasure [*jouissance*].[13] The traits of the symbolic are convoked, since the texture of the discourse is often sufficiently close, but they are taken over by the imaginary and work to its advantage alone. The question never posed is precisely the one which would overthrow the whole construction: 'Why did I like this film (I rather than another, this film rather than another)?' A true theory is recognisable among other things by the fact that it would see a problem here, whereas many cinematic conceptions depend, on the contrary, on the redoubtable effectivity of the fact itself, and hence on a silence established with respect to it: these are *deproblematisation* techniques and to that extent the exact opposite of the procedures of knowledge, even when they contain some authentically scientific break-throughs.

This 'sanctioning construction' built on to a film and a taste is not the only manifestation of the powers of the imaginary in cinematic writings. There are several others, some of which are so striking that I am amazed not to have thought of them sooner, at least in this light (it would be better were I less amazed: I am myself a victim of what I am criticising). Consider cinematic historians: they very often act – and this is not to be regretted, for without this cast of mind we should have no cinematic documentation – as real cinema archivists, the keepers of an imaginary archive, in the sense in which Malraux's *Museum* was imaginary. Their wish is to *save* as many films as possible; not *qua* copies, *qua* celluloid, but the social memory of those films and hence a by no means unfavourable image of them. The history of the cinema often presents the appearance of an easy-going theodicy, a vast Last Judgement in which indulgence will be the rule. Its real aim is to annex to the category of the 'interesting' (a subtly valorising variant of that of the 'notable' as defined by Roland Barthes[14]) the maximum number of tracks. To this end various and sometimes contradictory criteria are called on, in a disparate and gossipy gathering: one film is 'retained' for its aesthetic value, another as a sociological document, a third as a typical example of the bad films of a period, a fourth is the minor work of a major film-maker, a fifth the major work of a minor film-maker, a further one owes its inscription in the catalogue to its place in a particular chronology (it is the first film shot with a certain type of lens, or else the last film made in Tsarist Russia): one is reminded of the similarly heteroclite justifications unfailingly offered by Proust's Françoise for her choice of each day's menus for the meals at Combray: 'A brill, because the fishwoman had guaranteed its freshness; a turkey, because she had seen a beauty in the market at Roussainville-le-Pin; cardoons with marrow, because she had never done them for us in that way before; a roast leg of mutton, because the fresh air made one hungry and there would be plenty of time for it to "settle down" in the seven hours before dinner; spinach by way of a change; apricots, because they were still hard to get . . . etc.'[15] The true function of this *accumulation of criteria* practised by many historians of the cinema is to mention as many films as possible (hence the usefulness of their works), and to this end to multiply as often as can be the number of points of view from which a film may be felt to be 'good' in one respect or another.

Like critics, like historians, but in slightly different ways, theoreticians often help to maintain the cinema in the imaginary enclosure of a pure love. Thus it is rather rare for the *properties* of cinematic language to be presented as such, i.e. precisely as properties, which would be to appeal before all else to an existential judgement (= 'there is a type of montage called accelerated montage') and to an inclusive judgement (= 'the sequence shot is one of the possibilities of the cinema'): to those two forms of judgement whose inaugural importance for all thought of a rational and logical kind was demonstrated by Freud along with their affective roots.[16] Much more frequently, the properties are offered to us straightaway as 'resources', 'riches', 'means of expression', and this vocabulary insinuates into the apparently analytic account the invisible and permanent thread of a very different procedure which is really a *plea*, a claim for legitimacy and an appeal for recognition (even before cognition), a declaration of rivalry or candidature with respect to the older, more accepted arts. These movements were more clearly apparent in the theoreticians of the earliest days of the cinema, sometimes quite explicitly so.

'LOVING THE CINEMA'

What is it in the end that I want to say about these writings whose approach is that of a love? Certainly not that their authors are 'wrong' all the time, or that what they say is always false. That is not the point. Wishing to get rid of the affective gets one nowhere, nor would it get this article anywhere. Even less is it my purpose to forget that these *assertive affects* are the reversed consequence of the opposite cultural prejudice, still alive today, that sees in the cinema a low-level distraction (and which thus starts by thinking in levels). In a history of contemporary culture the concern for the good object which I have tried to bring out can only be understood in relation to the bad-object status that society initially conferred on the cinema and to which it still confines it to some extent. In doing so it has considerably set back the possibility of a knowledge of the cinematic fact: directly (by neglect or disdain), but also by reaction (which concerns me here), by exacerbating in those concerned with the cinema the persistent drama of an *adherence* that sometimes becomes a kind of entanglement – the revolt against an enforced marginalisation.

Discourse about the cinema is too often part of the institution, whereas it should be studying it and believes or pretends that it is doing so. It is, as I have said, its third machine: after the one that manufactures the films, and the one that consumes them, the one that *vaunts* them, that valorises the product. Often, by unexpected paths, unperceived by those who have quite unintentionally taken them, paths which manifest the radical exteriority of effects to conscious intentions, writings on film become another form of cinema advertising and at the same time a linguistic appendage of the institution itself. Like those alienated sociologists who unknowingly repeat the pronouncements of their society, it extends the object, it *idealises* it instead of turning back on to it, it makes explicit the film's inaudible murmuring to us of 'Love me': a mirror reduplication of the film's own ideological inspiration, already based on the mirror identification of the spectator with the camera (or secondarily with the characters, if any).

Discourse about the cinema then becomes a dream: an uninterpreted dream. This is what constitutes its symptomatic value; it has already said everything. But it is also what makes it obligatory to turn it inside out like a glove, to return it like the gauntlet on accepting a challenge; it does not know what it is saying.

Knowledge of the cinema is obtained via a *reprise* of the native discourse, in two senses of the word: taking it into consideration and re-establishing it.

The turning I am discussing is never anything but a return. In the cinema, too, the product presents us with a reversed image of the production, as it does in the materialist conception of ideologies, or in neurotic rationalisations, as in the *camera obscura* which, with its 180-degree-turned optical image, is the very starting-point of cinematic technique. The effort towards knowing is necessarily sadistic insofar as it can only grasp its object against the grain, re-ascend the slopes of the institution (whereas the latter is designed for one to 'follow' them, to descend them), like the interpretation that goes back along the path of the dream-work,[17] acting by nature in the manner of a counter-current.

To be a theoretician of the cinema, one should ideally no longer love the cinema and yet still love it: have loved it a lot and only have detached oneself from it by taking it up again from the other end, taking it as the target for the very same scopic drive which had made one love it. Have broken with it, as certain relationships are broken, not in order to move on to something else, but in order to return to it at the next bend in the spiral. Carry the institution inside one still so that it is in a place accessible to self-analysis, but carry it there as a distinct instance which does not over-infiltrate the rest of the ego with the thousand paralysing bonds of a tender unconditionality. Not have forgotten what the cinephile one used to be was like, in all the details of his affective inflections, in the three dimensions of his living being, and yet no longer be invaded by him: not have lost sight of him, but be keeping an eye on him. Finally, be him and not be him, since all in all these are the two conditions on which one can speak of him.

This balance may seem a somewhat acrobatic one. It is and it is not. Of course no one can be sure to attain it perfectly, everyone is in danger of slipping off on one side or the other. And yet, in principle, considering the very possibility of *maintaining* such a position, it is not true that it is so very acrobatic, or rather it is no more so than the other (really very similar) mental postures required for tasks more ordinarily evoked. This is forgotten because it is not customary (it is one of the great taboos of scien-

tism, one of its terrors) to mention the metapsychological preconditions of scientific work. But for anyone who is prepared to
consider them, the kind of deliberate ambivalence I am trying to
describe, this special variety of splitting, at once salutary and
fragile, this minimum of flexibility in one's relations to oneself,
this economic conversion by which a strong object cathexis[18]
(here attraction to the cinema), initially molar and opaque, subsequently undergoes an instinctual vicissitude that bifidates it
and arranges it like a pair of pliers, one pincer (voyeuristic
sadism sublimated into epistemophilia) coming to meet the other
in which the original imaginary of the dual effusion with the
object is retained as a (living, surviving) witness – in short, this
itinerary and the present configuration that results from it are not
in the end especially exceptional or contorted (even if for some
'scientists' they are among those things that must not be stated).
It is itineraries and economies of the same kind (tendentially,
still, never as a finished result) that also define the objective conditions of the subjective possibility of the ethnologist's work, or
that of the analysand in the cure, ultimately of all work of *interpré-
tance* in the semiotic and Peircean sense of the word (= translation from one system into another). What really is uncommon
is not the thing itself, but simply the idea that cinematic studies
are not in themselves blessed with any special privilege of exemp-
tion, any *magical extra-territoriality*, any adolescent immunity from
the common requirements of knowledge and symbolic cathexis
which are (sometimes) more clearly perceived in other fields.

2

The Investigator's Imaginary

I ask myself: what in fact is the object of this text? What is the *driving uncertainty* without which I should not have the desire to write it, and thus would not be writing it? What is my imaginary at this moment? What is it that I am trying, even without illusions, to bring to a conclusion?

It seems to me that it is a *question*, in the material sense of the word – a sentence terminating in a question mark – and that, as in dreams, it is inscribed right there in front of me, armed from head to toe. I shall unfold it here, with, of course, that slightly obsessional coefficient which is party to any aspiration to rigour.

So let me spell it out: 'What contribution can Freudian psychoanalysis make to the study of the cinematic signifier?'

This is, in other words, the manifest content of my dream, and its interpretation will (I hope) constitute my text. I can already see three vital points, three nodal points in it. Let me examine them separately (*The Interpretation of Dreams* invites us to do so, as does the minimal necessity of having a 'plan'), and associate freely from each of them. They are the words 'contribution', 'Freudian psychoanalysis' and above all 'cinematic signifier'.

PSYCHOANALYSIS, LINGUISTICS, HISTORY

'Contribution', then, first of all: this term tells me that psychoanalysis cannot be the only discipline concerned in the study of the cinematic signifier, and that its offering has to be articulated with others. To begin with, and fairly directly, with that of classical semiology – based on linguistics – a guiding principle in my earliest filmic investigations and today in those of several others.

17

Why 'directly'? Because linguistics and psychoanalysis are both sciences of the symbolic and are even, come to think of it, the only two sciences whose immediate and sole object is the fact of signification as such (obviously all sciences are concerned with it, but never so frontally or exclusively). To be slightly cavalier, linguistics – together with its close relations, notably modern symbolic logic – can be regarded as taking for its share the exploration of the secondary process, and psychoanalysis that of the primary process:[1] that is to say, between them they cover the whole field of the *signification-fact* taken in itself. Linguistics and psychoanalysis are the two main 'sources' of semiology, the only disciplines that are semiotic through and through.

That is why both in turn have to be set within the horizon of a *third perspective*, which is as it were their common and permanent background: the direct study of societies, historical criticism, the examination of infrastructures. This time the junction is much less easy (if the other one can be described as easy), for the signifier has its own laws (primary and secondary), and so does political economy. Even technically, if one thinks of the daily work of the investigator, of his reading, his documentation, etc., the 'dual competence' which was not impossible a moment ago now becomes a bit of a gamble: thus in the case of the cinema, where is the semiotician who could seriously claim, given his education and his specialised conceptual tools, to be able to explain the role of capitalist monopolies in the film industry in as pertinent and rigorous a way as economists like Henri Mercillon and his disciples have? In cinematic studies as in others, semiology (or semiologies) cannot replace the various disciplines that discuss the social fact itself (the source of all symbolism), with its laws that determine those of the symbolic without being identical with them: sociology, anthropology, history, political economy, demography, etc. It cannot replace them, nor must it repeat them (danger of ritual repetition or 'reductionism'). It must take them into account, move forward on its own front (it too is materialist in its own way) and mark the anchorage points in all the cases in which the state of research already makes this possible (for example the spectator's psychism as a factor of historical adjustment and a link in the chain of the money circuit). In other words, it must be inscribed in advance, by a kind of epistemological anticipation (but one which must not become the pretext for a voluntary paralysis), in the perspective of a true knowledge of man – a perspective still only present as a dotted line in most of its circuit, and a knowledge in the singular, very different from today's 'human sciences', so often gnawed by scientism and yet necessary, for today is not tomorrow – of a state of knowing in which the way the development of technologies and balances of social forces (society in its physical state, as it were) finally comes to influence inflections peculiar to the work of the symbolic such as the order of 'shots' or the role of 'sound off' in some cinematic sub-code, in some genre of films, for example, would be *known* in all the reality of the intermediate mechanisms without which only a global inkling and postulation of causality is possible.

Here I am touching on the famous problem of 'relative autonomies' but not necessarily (although the two things are often confused) on a simple distinction between infrastructures and superstructures. For if it is clear that the cinema as an industry, its modes of financing, the technological development of film stock, the average income of the spectators (enabling them to go more or less often to the cinema), the price of seats and many other things belong fully to infrastructural studies, it does not follow that, by some mechanical symmetry, the symbolic (primary or secondary) is exclusively superstructural in its order. It is partly so, of course, and even largely so in its most apparent strata, in its manifest content, in those of its features that are directly related to precise social facts and change when the latter change: e.g. in linguistics broad sectors of the lexicon (but already much less of phonology or syntax), in psychoanalysis the various historical variants of the Oedipus complex – or perhaps the Oedipus complex itself, which is far from being the whole of psychoanalysis – which are clearly linked to the development of the institution of the family. But signification also has more buried and permanent springs (ones by definition less visible, less striking to the mind) whose validity extends, in our present state of knowledge, to the whole of humanity, i.e. to man as a biological 'species'. Not that the symbolic is something 'natural', non-social; on the contrary, in its deepest foundations (which are always structures and not 'facts'), signification is no longer just a consequence of social development, it becomes, along with the infrastructures, a party to the constitution of sociality itself, which in its turn defines the human race. The partial 'uncoupling' of the laws of signification from short-term historical developments does not mean a naturalisation of the semiotic (its *psychologisation*), but on the contrary re-emphasises its radical, as it were definitional, sociality. There is always a moment after the obvious observation that it is man who makes the symbol when it is also clear that the symbol makes man: this is one of the great lessons of psychoanalysis,[2] anthropology[3] and linguistics.[4]

Abstracting from the immense sector in which it is specifically *cultural* (varying in a time scale which is of the same order as that of history), the symbolic is thus not precisely a superstructure.[5] This does not make it an infrastructure, unless one departs from the strict (Marxist) sense of the term, and there is nothing to be gained from such a mélange. Rather, in its deeper strata it represents a kind of *juxtastructure*, to use a term which has already been put forward[6] for other phenomena of the same kind, a juxtastructure in which are expressed, in the last analysis, certain characteristics of man as an animal (and as an animal different from all other animals, i.e. as a non-animal too). I shall only recall two well-known examples of these 'laws' (of these aspects of 'The Law' as Lacan would say) that help underpin all significatory work. In linguistics, in all known idioms, double articulation, the paradigm/syntagm opposition, the necessary duplication of the logical generation of sentences into a categorial component and a transformational component. In psychoanalysis, in all known societies, the prohibition of incest (and yet sexual procreation, as in all the higher animals) along with the inevitable corollary of these two as it were contradictory facts, the very remarkable relationship (whether or no it consists of an Oedipus complex of the classical type) which each human offspring must definitively enter into with respect to its father and its mother (or to a more diffuse world of kin) and thus a variety of major consequences such as repression, the division of the psychical apparatus into several systems which are relatively ignorant of one another, hence the permanent coexistence in human productions (such as films) of two irreducible 'logics', one of which is 'illogical' and opens permanently on to a multiplicity of overdeterminations, etc.

To sum up, the influence of linguistics and of psychoanalysis may lead gradually, in combination, to a relatively autonomous science of the cinema (= 'semiology of the cinema'), but the latter will deal *simultaneously* with facts which are superstructural and others which are not, without for all that being specifically infrastructural. In both these aspects its relation to truly infrastructural studies (cinematic and general) will continue to hold. It is on these three levels that the symbolic is social (hence it is entirely social). But, like the society which creates it and which it creates, it too has a materiality, a kind of *body*: it is in this almost physical state that it concerns semiology and that the semiologist desires it.

FREUDIAN PSYCHOANALYSIS AND OTHER PSYCHOANALYSES

In the 'formula' occupying my mind at the moment of writing and that I am unwinding as I write, I feel another point of insistence: 'Freudian psychoanalysis' ('How can it contribute to the study of the cinematic signifier?'). Why this word, or rather why these two words? Because as is well known, psychoanalysis is not entirely Freudian, far from it, and the vigorous 'return to Freud' imposed by Lacan has its origin and its necessity in this very situation. But this return has not affected the world psychoanalytic movement as a whole. Even independently of this influence, psychoanalysis and Freudianism are inter-related in a manner varying from region to region (in France psychoanalysis is as a whole more Freudian than it is in the USA, etc.), so anyone claiming to make any use of psychoanalysis, as I do at this moment for the cinema, is necessarily called on to say what psychoanalysis he is talking about. There are plenty of examples of 'psychoanalytic' practices, and more or less explicit accompanying theories, in which all that is vital in Freud's discovery, everything that makes it (should make it) an irreversible achievement, a decisive moment in knowledge, is smoothed out, pared down, 'recuperated' as a new variant of ethical psychology or medical psychiatry (humanism and medicine: two great evasions of Freudianism). The most striking example (but far from the only one) is that provided by certain 'American-style' therapeutic doctrines, solidly installed more or less everywhere,[7] which are in large part techniques for the standardisation or banalisation of character, for avoidance of conflict at any price.

What I shall call psychoanalysis will be the tradition of Freud and its still continuing developments, with original extensions such as those that revolve around the contributions of Melanie Klein in England and Jacques Lacan in France.

Our distance in time from Freud's work enables us without too much difficulty or arbitrariness to distinguish even within it, for it is not only immense by virtue of its quality, certain fairly individualised 'sectors' which are unequal in their intrinsic interest (at least in the sense that some are more 'obsolete' than others) and also unequal – and it is this that is of importance for me – in the contribution they can make outside their original field (the study of the cinema is basically one of the branches of what Freud and psychoanalysts sometimes call 'applied psychoanalysis': which is a curious term because here, as in linguistics, nothing is ever applied, or if it is, so much the worse; it is a question of something else: certain phenomena that psychoanalysis has illuminated or can illuminate occur in the cinema, they play a real part there). To return to the various writings of Freud, I shall (somewhat hastily) distinguish six main groups:

1. His metapsychological and theoretical works, from *The Interpretation of Dreams* to *Inhibitions, Symptoms and Anxiety* via the *Papers on Metapsychology*, including the 'major articles' such as 'On Narcissism: an Introduction', *Beyond the Pleasure Principle*, *The Ego and the Id*, 'The Economic Problem of Masochism', '"A Child is Being Beaten"', 'Negation', 'Fetishism', etc.

2. The more strictly clinical works: the five *Case Studies* and also the *Studies on Hysteria* (with Breuer), articles such as 'On the Beginning of Treatment', etc.

3. Works of popularisation: *Introductory Lectures on Psycho-Analysis* and various others (*New Introductory Lectures on Psycho-Analysis*, *An Outline of Psycho-Analysis, On Dreams*, a 'didactic' version of *The Interpretation of Dreams*, etc.).

4. Studies of art and literature: *Delusions and Dreams in Jensen's 'Gradiva'*, 'The Moses of Michelangelo', *Leonardo da Vinci and a Memory of his Childhood*, etc.

5. Studies with an anthropological or socio-historical aim, such as *Totem and Taboo, Civilization and its Discontents, Group Psychology and the Analysis of the Ego*, etc.

6. There is a last group, less clearly outlined than the others and

perhaps half-way between the fourth and fifth, which would include e.g. *The Psychopathology of Everyday Life* and *Jokes and their Relation to the Unconscious*; in other words, investigations which focus especially on the psychology of the preconscious and whose object is cultural but not strictly speaking aesthetic (unlike those in the fourth category), and social but not strictly speaking historical or anthropological (unlike those in the fifth category).[8]

Having thus arranged the books in several piles, what am I going to do with them? Some of them pose no special problems. For example, the didactic pile: it retains precisely its didactic interest, but for the same reason it is inadequate. Or the 'clinical' pile: by definition, neither directly nor on every page could we expect it to concern the analysis of cultural productions such as the cinema, but it is clear that it does concern it nonetheless, through the great wealth of very varied insights it contains, and also because without it it is not really possible to understand the books of theory. Or the sixth group of works, on parapraxes, verbal slips, humour, the comic: they will be especially useful to us in the study of the corresponding cinematic phenomena, the comic, the burlesque, the gag, etc. (see for instance the contributions of Daniel Percheron and Jean-Paul Simon[9]).

The situation is more unexpected, on the other hand, though it has often been signalled in the conversations of specialists and no doubt also in written form, when we turn to the works Freud saw as plainly sociological or ethnological, such as *Totem and Taboo*. Their very object might seem to make such studies more important to our semiological perspective, at any rate more pertinent to my present purposes, than the works of 'pure' metapsychology. However, ethnologists often say that the opposite is the case (and I think so too); even if Freud's general theory is one of the great permanent inspirations of their labours, the specifically ethnological works are those least useful to them. Basically this is not all that surprising: Freud's discovery in its breadth is of concern to virtually all fields of knowledge, but only if it is suitably articulated with the data and exigencies peculiar to each of them, and notably to those whose object is directly social; nothing guarantees that the 'discoverer' (the father), just because he is the discoverer, should be best placed to carry out this readjustment in domains of which he sometimes had no fundamental knowledge. (I have noticed the same thing where the linguistic import of Freud's work is concerned: it is potentially very considerable, and Jacques Lacan has brought this out very forcefully, but it is not to be found, or only very rarely, in Freud's explicit allusions to linguistic facts; these passages are sometimes a disappointment for the linguist.) It is well known that the 'phylogenetic hypothesis' which forms the background to *Totem and Taboo* (= the primal horde, the *real* murder of the father in the remote past, etc.) is not acceptable to today's anthropologists. It is obviously difficult to decide quite what status Freud himself attributed to it, for the precise extent of Freud's 'realism', here as in other cases (premature seductions of future hysterics, etc.) is always a problem: hypothesis of a true prehistory or mythical parable to be understood in a symbolic sense? However, there can be no doubt that in many passages Freud opted at least in part for the first (realist) interpretation, and it has been Lacan's work to 'transfer' into the register of the second (which anthropologists are more prepared to accept) the whole of psychoanalytic thought about castration, the murder of the father, the Oedipus complex and the Law. More generally, it seems to me that the weakness of Freud's sociological efforts lies, in the last analysis, in a certain misrecognition, easily explicable given his own objective situation, of the intrinsic importance of socioeconomic factors and of the irreducibility of their specific mechanisms. It is at this weak point that the 'psychologism' to be found in Freud (but not in his central discoveries) and for which he has been justly criticised, bursts through.

The situation is rather similar, although in fact a bit more muddled, when one considers Freud's aesthetic studies. Sometimes one feels a need in them for less biography and more psychoanalysis; at others for less 'psychoanalyticalness' in the interests precisely of a more psychoanalytic illumination; also for a greater concern for the specificities of each art and the autonomy of the signifier, problems which were clearly by no means central to Freud's thought. One is tempted to exclaim that the general works contained in germ the possibility of finer 'applications' and above all of ones centred more on the text: this is true, and besides it is in this sense that attempts are being made today to deploy the potentialities of the analytical tool. But we should not be surprised that Freud himself did not go further in this direction, although he is its inspiration. His was a different period, Freud was a very cultured man in the sense that adjective had for the bourgeoisie at the turn of the century, and not a theoretician of art; above all (this is often forgotten because it seems no more than a truism) he was the first to try out a psychoanalytic approach to literature and art, alone and already with brilliance: a new enterprise cannot be expected to achieve its full precision at the first attempt.

In insisting on these perhaps rather boring bibliographical divisions, my intention – on the threshold of a period in which I hope to see psychoanalytic studies of the cinema develop – has been to make explicit a state of affairs more familiar to ethnologists than to ourselves, but one which concerns us too: we should not be surprised if overall the semiology of the cinema turns out to rely more on those texts of Freud's that do not appear to be its special concern (the theoretical and metapsychological studies) than on those that would seem more directly related to the undertaking in its two aspects, aesthetic and socio-historical.

VARIOUS KINDS OF PSYCHOANALYTIC STUDY OF THE CINEMA

I now return to my question: in what way can psychoanalysis cast light on the cinematic signifier? Its third vital point is the word 'signifier': why especially the signifier of films, or in other words, why not their signified?

The fact is that psychoanalytic studies of the cinema are of various kinds, already exemplified or clearly conceivable. We should try to avoid confusing them (try to 'put them into place') in order to be able to designate more precisely the one I have in view myself.

First of all there is the *nosographic* approach.[10] It would treat films as symptoms or as secondary manifestations that have been partially symptomatised, from which it is possible to 'work back' to the neurosis of the film-maker (or the script-writer, etc.). An undertaking necessarily in the classificatory spirit of medicine, even if in a less rigid form: there will be obsessional, hysterical or perverse film-makers, and so on. This approach breaks the textual fabric of the film on principle and accords no intrinsic importance to its manifest content, which becomes simply a kind of (discontinuous) reservoir of more or less isolated clues whose immediate purpose is to reveal the latent. Here it is not the film that interests the analyst but the film-maker. Hence everything depends on two postulates, that of the biographical and that of the pathological; I use the term 'nosography' in order to cover them both.

This theme has a variation in which everything remains the same except the sharp distinction between the normal and the pathological (in this the variation is closer to Freud's teachings). The concern for classification remains, but it is demedicalised; the result is a kind of psychoanalytically inspired characterology which no longer divides up neuroses but rather metapsychological and economic types which are 'normal' or else common to the normal and the pathological (someone's 'character' is his potential neurosis: moreover, this neurosis is always capable of being actualised). The 'biographism' remains intact, and with it the indifference to the filmic text as such.

We have not yet had to 'choose' between a study of the signifier and a study of the signified, but rather between a study of the text and a study of the non-text. The two approaches I have just rapidly outlined are not defined by their orientation towards the 'pure signified', or at least not so immediately as to reveal any naïvety, inexperience or blindness about the specific work of the signifier. They are open to such a criticism, but in other directions: they run the risk of freezing and impoverishing the signification of films insofar as they constantly threaten to relapse into a belief in an ultimate signified (unique, static and definitive), here the *typological membership* by the film-maker of a category, whether pathological or merely psychical; they also contain another inherent threat of reduction issuing directly from this first one: psychologising reduction and the ideology of pure 'creation'; they tend to neglect everything in a film which escapes the conscious and unconscious psychism of the film-maker as an individual, everything that is a direct social imprint and ensures that no one is ever the 'author' of his 'works': influences and pressures of an ideological kind, the objective state of the cinematic codes and techniques at the moment of shooting, etc. Thus they only have validity (and I think they do have validity) if their purpose is strictly signalled from the beginning (= principle of pertinence) and then checked en route: if they are clearly presented as attempts at *diagnosis* (nosographic or characterological) applied to *persons* (film-makers), thus explicitly proclaiming their indifference both to the textual and to the social.

But it would be inaccurate to speak of their indifference to the signifier, although this is sometimes done when their literary equivalents are under discussion. Inaccurate in two ways. Not only is it a principle of these investigations to set up certain aspects of the film as so many signifiers (manifest signifiers of a less apparent psychism), but it may turn out that the filmic features thus selected themselves belong within the film to what the semiologist would rank on the 'plane of the signifier'. The habitual themes of a film-maker, his characters, the period in which he likes to situate his plots, can tell us about his individual nature, but so can the way he moves (or does not move) the camera, or cuts and edits his sequences.[11] These two approaches are thus not exactly 'studies of the signified'. What is peculiar to them is the fact that they are interested in persons and not in *discursive facts* (= filmic texts or cinematic codes): the latter do not concern them in their internal logic but rather as a neutral milieu in which they seek the sporadic indications that improve their understanding of the former.

PSYCHOANALYSIS OF THE FILM SCRIPT

This leads me to a third orientation which this time attains the film as discourse. It is not so easy to delineate as the first two, and I am not yet sure that I am very clear about it in my own mind; therefore, as a somewhat simplifying first step, I shall call it the *psychoanalytic study of film scripts*. Of course, it does not always confine itself to the script in the narrowest sense of the term (the written sheets followed in shooting the film); it also extends to a large number of features that do not appear in that written skeleton (which is more or less absent in the making of certain films anyway) and yet form part of the script in the broad sense – in the true sense: a script if need be implicit, a definitive script after editing – insofar as it is still a question of elements with something to do with the plot, 'situations', characters, landscapes, possibly 'period details', etc.; in short, the manifest thematic complex of the film, envisaged if necessary in extreme detail. So defined, the script represents a rather ambiguous, fleeting instance, and an all the more interesting one for that.[12] In certain respects it is on the side of the signified: this is clear if we set opposite it, by a kind of commutation, the various codes via which it is grasped by the spectator, cinematic codes (i.e. visual and auditory analogy, editing, etc.) or non-cinematic codes such as that of verbal language in talking films: so many systems which serve to *communicate* the script, which should not be confused with it and with respect to which it becomes a signified. A signified that is defined as the set of apparent themes of the film, as its most literal purport (= circumstantial denotation). Obviously it is not the most important signification of the film, but it remains indispensable if one wishes to go further, as psychoanalytic studies of the script do. So the first effect of such studies is to transform the script into a signifier and from it to disengage some less immediately visible significations. To disengage them, or rather to *open on to them* (I should almost say: engage them). For there can be no claim to unveil *a* hidden meaning, a kind of second script, armed from head to toe, as clear and peremptory as the first, distinguished from it only by its hidden status; this would turn into a preposterous and childish 'hide-and-seek', with the hidden having the same texture, the same facture as the unhidden (hence it would have to have been hidden deliberately! Dreams themselves have no latent meaning in this sense: there is no second dream beneath the dream, there is only one dream which is manifest and opens on to a never ending series of non-apparent significations). Nor is it a question of wishing to endow the film (to swell it, to make it big) with three or four more and more 'profound' levels of meaning, retaining the notion of a fixed and finite number and the conception of each as an instance with the same order of relationship to explicitness (with differences of degree) as the true script (the script as such: there is only one): this would still be to believe, at a lower gear, in a closure of the signified and so to block the infinite *pursuit* of the symbolic which, in a sense (like the imaginary from which it is spun), lies entirely in its flight.

On this point I have partly changed my mind – or if you prefer, this is something I regard as a contribution of psychoanalysis to linguistics: I refer to the corresponding passages in my book *Language and Cinema* [*Langage et cinéma*],[13] and especially to the notion of a 'textual system' as I presented it there. There certainly is textual system, meaning thereby something always of a structural and relational (but not necessarily exhaustible) order, and peculiar to a given film, not to the cinema, distinct from every code and combining several of them. But I no longer believe that each film has *a* textual system (the one I suggested in *Language and Cinema* (pp. 107–11) for a film of Griffith's, *Intolerance*, is only one of the systems possible, a stage in the work of interpretation, a stage inadequately presented as such at the time), nor even, a possibility I foresaw in a special chapter (Chapter VI. 4), a fixed number of quite distinct textual systems (several 'readings' of the same film). In this (or these) system(s), I now see working conveniences – that is precisely why they impressed themselves upon me in the first place: one needs to examine one's tools at each and every stage – sorts of 'blocs of interpretation' already foreseen or established by the analysis, sectors of signification (or in some cases a single vast sector) that the analysis has already *selected* at different moments in its in fact interminable movement from the indefinite thickness of the textual system as I now see it, that is, as this perpetual possibility of a finer, or else less apparent structuration, of a grouping of the elements into a new configuration, of the registration of a new *significatory pressure* which does not annul the preceding ones (as in the unconscious, where everything is accumulated), but complements or in other cases distorts and complicates them, at any rate points in a slightly different direction, a little to one side (a little or more than a little). In *Language and Cinema*, I already attached great importance to the dynamic aspect of the textual system – a production rather than a product – which distinguishes it from the static character proper to the codes; at present I feel that this pressure, this 'activity', comes into play not only inside a textual system but for any one film between each and the next one to be discovered; or, if it is thought that there is only one such system in all, then the analyst will never complete his exploration of it and should not seek any 'end'.

Thus analyses of scripts – the script is one aspect among others in the textual system – wish to go further than the script itself, than what is occasionally called the 'plot pure and simple' (inaccurately, however, for this manifest level also includes the characters, their social positions, the diegetic locations, the indicators of period and many other factors that go beyond the action). The instance of the script, in the wide sense I am giving it, now shifts to the side of the signifier, since it is no longer related to the codes of expression that communicate it, but to the interpretations on to which it opens. In order to show, as a recent doctoral thesis[14] does, that one of the 'meanings' of Howard Hawks's *Red River* is to present a justification of private property and the right of conquest, and that another of its meanings is to be found in a misogynist variant of male homosexuality, it is the film script above all that has to be examined for the corresponding clues (signifiers). The script has ceased to be a signified: nowhere in the film is what I have just said plainly inscribed. To study the script from a psychoanalytic (or more broadly semiotic) viewpoint is to constitute it as a signifier.

In this the script is like a dream, as are many human products. The manifest dream, i.e. the dream as such – 'dream content' for Freud, in opposition to 'dream-thoughts' – is a signifier for the interpretation, and yet it has itself had to be *established* (narrated, and to begin with communicated to the conscious apperception of the dreamer) as the signified of different codes of expression, including that of verbal language (one does not dream in languages one does not know). There would be no manifest dream, and hence no interpretation, if for example the dreamer failed to identify any of the visual objects in the dream, i.e. if he was unfamiliar with the code of socialised perception; it is because he recognises some of them that others he is unable to identify take on their true value of enigmas, or that composite objects (= condensations) appear as such, presupposing some idea, or suspicion, of the different objects superimposed into one, or at least of the fact that there are several of them. The imaginary itself needs to be symbolised, and Freud noted[15] that without secondary revision (without codes) there would be no dreams, for the secondary process is the condition on which access to perception and consciousness is possible. For the same reason, the script, a conscious and perceived instance, must first be a signified before it can be made to signify anything else at all.

Analyses of scripts, then, are not studies of the signified. What strikes me is rather the fact that they are sometimes considered as such. An error which is part of another more general one; it is easy to forget that every signifier itself needs to be a signified and that every signified, in turn, can but be a signifier (this constant back and forth is precisely the work of the symbolic; it is not possible to constitute some elements as 'pure' signifiers and others as 'pure' signifieds — the adjective 'pure' is a very tiresome one anyway — except with respect to a precise code, a given investigation; to one segment and one only in the indefinite chain of signification). The result, for the script, is that two different things are confused: its place *in the text*, in the film (everywhere a manifest instance), in which it is the apparent signified of apparent signifiers, and its place *in the textual system*, a non-manifest instance whose apparent signifier it is (or at any rate one of its apparent signifiers). At this point the suggestions of linguistics and those of psychoanalysis coincide perfectly. Relying solely on the former I had carefully distinguished between the text, an *attested* progression, and the textual system, which is never given and does not pre-exist the semiologist's work of construction:[16] this was already to define the gap between them as that between a manifest content and its interpretation. The textual system shares the status Freud sometimes called *latent*[17] and which includes both the unconscious and the preconscious.

Certain studies of scripts are directed above all at unconscious significations, and thus correspond to what is normally expected of a psychoanalytically inspired approach. Others work principally at the level of preconscious significations: e.g. most of those studies described as 'ideological' (I gave an example a moment ago *vis-à-vis Red River*), turned towards 'layers of meaning' which do not feature directly in the film but constitute its implicit rather than its unconscious part. It does not follow that studies of the preconscious of the script are necessarily 'less psychoanalytic': it all depends on the way they are conducted, and psychoanalysis includes a theory of the preconscious (Freud did not regard this instance as an accessory one, he showed great interest in it, notably in *The Psychopathology of Everyday Life*; he reckoned that a kind of 'second censorship' dynamically linked to the first divided the preconscious topographically from the conscious.[18] Nor does it follow that ideology is an exclusively preconscious production: more probably, like many other things, it has its preconscious strata and its unconscious strata, even if the latter have hardly been explored as yet (not at all before Deleuze, Guattari and Lyotard)[19] and differ more or less from ideology in its classical conception. It is just that ideological studies have tended so far (as a point of fact, not one of principle) to limit themselves to preconscious ideology. As is well known, it is for this reason that Deleuze and Guattari criticise them, anxious as they are to trace the imprint of history in the unconscious itself and hence rather sceptical about the very notion of ideology, at least in its current forms.

PSYCHOANALYSIS OF THE TEXTUAL SYSTEM

At any rate, once analyses of scripts are at all profound and do more than state the obvious, they posit the perspective of a 'latent' region which they wish to approach. That is surely why in certain cases they are hard to distinguish from another – fourth – possible kind of psychoanalytic studies of films: those that have the textual system and interpretation as their aim, like the preceding ones, but set out for it from the manifest filmic material as a whole (signifieds and signifiers), not from the manifest signified (the script) alone. It is the film as a whole that is now constituted as a signifier. Thus what is striking in the both ideological and psychoanalytic interpretation proposed by Jean-Paul Dumont and Jean Monod for Stanley Kubrick's film *2001: a Space Odyssey*[20] is that the elements they take as clues come not only from the thematics of the film but also from the specifically cinematic signifier, or at least from the use the film studied makes of it; in the structural grids of occurrences and co-occurrences that the authors establish, we find for example (p. 149) the items 'Track forward', 'Track back', as well as 'Weight', 'Weightlessness', 'Spaceship', 'Bone thrown in the air by an ape', etc. This approach raises difficulties insofar as the cinematic elements and the script elements are not revealing *in the same way* (the authors are too inclined to 'diegeticise' the signifier), and what is most revealing, what gives us the most central access to the textual system, is no doubt the relation between the two sets of elements rather than one or other of them or their addition. But in one point, and a very important one, the method has to be approved: the filmic signifier is as indicative as its signified of the latent significations of the film, the entire apparent material is open to a symptomatic reading (here we recognise the banal but true observation usually rather badly expressed as 'the "form" of a film tells us as much as its "content" about its "true meaning"'').

Raymond Bellour's impressive study of Hitchcock's *North by North-West*, in *Communications*,[21] shows, I believe, what is to be expected of a psychoanalytic approach to films which is at once attentive to the signifier, to the script, and to their mutual articulation; the Oedipal structure this analysis brings to light informs the script (as it were on the large scale) but also the editing schemes in the sequence, on a smaller scale, so that the (non-manifest) relation between the manifest signifier and the manifest signified of the film is that of a mirror reduplication or an insistence, a metaphor of microcosm and macrocosm: the latent is doubly anchored in the apparent, it can be read in it twice over, in two sizes, in a spiral movement. With this movement, which is not precisely cinematic and does not only concern the story told but is installed just between the two (and would be different in other films), we are really getting close to the order of the textual system as I understand it.

Investigations of this kind (the fourth kind on my list) are thus *studies of textual systems*. Those of the third group, for which I shall retain the name studies of scripts, are also studies of textual systems, but from a narrower angle of incidence: the script is part of the apparent data, but not all of it, one of the elements that leads up to interpretation, but not the only one. Artificially isolating it from the others one runs the risk of falsifying the textual system overall, since the latter forms a whole, and this might be enough to invalidate analyses of scripts on principle. But for many films, and not always uninteresting ones, this disadvantage is less than it might seem, since the script dimension plays a considerable part in them while the work of the cinematic signifier is not very great. With other films, on the contrary (I shall return to this point), the analysis of the script is from the start an inadequate approach, inadequate to different degrees moreover, as different as the relative importance of the script in the textual system, which varies greatly from film to film.

PSYCHOANALYSIS OF THE CINEMA-SIGNIFIER

The more I unfold (for the moment only at the preconscious level) the scientific imaginary initially expressed in a single sen-

tence, the closer I get to the problems presented to a psychoanalytic study by the signifier of the cinema as such, by the level
of 'cinematic specificity'. It is a characteristic of analyses of
scripts that they disregard this level: the Freudian inspiration
finds a place in them as it would in aesthetic studies outside the
cinema (and with the same difficulties, which I shall leave aside
here because they are so familiar). These investigations may be
psychoanalytic but they are not basically cinematic (though very
well suited to certain films for that very reason). What they 'psy-
choanalyse' is not the cinema but a story which happens to have
been told by it (and there are many such stories). The script of a
film may be treated just like a novel and the already classical
dossier of the relations between psychoanalysis and literary criticism could be introduced here en bloc (the absence of the couch
and hence of real transference, the precise scope of the method
proposed by Mauron, etc.). To sum up, what distinguishes
studies of scripts (and also nosographic or characterological
studies) from the approach I am trying to define here, and
towards which I am slowly making my way via everything which
is not that approach, is, as I have tried to show by this traversal,
not so much that they are indifferent to the signifier as that they
are indifferent to the *cinematic* signifier.

It will perhaps be thought astonishing that in this lengthy discussion of studies of scripts I have not even thought of recalling
that they become impossible in the case of certain films, *films
without scripts*, 'abstract' films, the 'avant-garde' films of the
1920s, current experimental films, etc. Or else (an attenuated
version of the same observation) that when these studies are possible, their interest declines to the extent that (even if it retains a
'plot') the film they apprehend escapes the full regime of
narration-representation (every possible intermediate case
exists; Eisenstein's films are diegetic, but they are less so than
most Hollywood productions). What is peculiar to these films is
the fact that in them to one degree or another the cinematic signifier abandons the status of a neutral and transparent vehicle at
the direct behest of a manifest signified which alone is important
(=the script), and that on the contrary it tends to inscribe its own
action in them, to take over a more and more important part of
the overall signification of the film, thus more and more invali-
dating studies of scripts, to the point of making them impossible.

As for studies in the fourth category (complete studies of the textual system), they are marked on the contrary by their concern for the signifier. They even cast a particularly effective light on how it works insofar as, like every textual study, they visualise it within the bounds of a limited *corpus* (one film, several films by the same author or in the same genre) that can be explored in great detail. However, psychoanalytic knowledge of the signifier of the cinema (the *cinema-signifier*) is not their sole and specific object (that object is the structure of a film, hence the name I have given them). I have attempted elsewhere[22] to show that the textual system, the interpretation of each film in its uniqueness, constitutes by definition a kind of *mixed site* in which specific codes (codes more or less peculiar to the cinema and only the cinema) and non-specific codes (codes more or less common to various 'languages' and a state of culture) meet and combine one with another; indeed, although the figures of the cinema, considered in their most immediate signification, can themselves be analysed into a signifier and a signified, and the cultural figures, too, the former are all ranked with the signifier and the latter with the (manifest) signified once less instantaneous and *proximate* significations are envisaged, in other words once it is the whole film that is taken into consideration (as in studies of the textual system precisely) rather than the 'value' of a given camera movement or sentence of the dialogue.[23] The latent signification of a singular 'work' in any art always has something to do with this *coupling* of a global signifier with a global signified, or rather of a specificity and a generality both of which signify; it is an instance – a *pressure*, rather – which is always profoundly and intimately reversible and mixed: what it 'tells' us touches on the particular art itself but also on something else (man, society, the author) and it tells us all this together, at a stroke as it were. The work of art steals the art from us at the same time as it presents it to us, because it is both less and more than it. Every film shows us the cinema, and is also its death.

That is why there is room for a special kind of psychoanalytic reflection on the cinema specifically devoted to the cinema itself (and not to films), to the signifier as such. Of course there will be overlapping phenomena here as everywhere else, and care must be taken to avoid aggressively (fearfully) erecting this orientation of work into a fortified sector, solitary and cut off from the others.

The psychoanalytic knowledge of the cinematic signifier can advance on a broad front thanks to textual studies particularly attentive to the peculiar play of the cinema in their texts, and also thanks to the analysis of certain films in which the work of the cinema is more important than it is in others (it is in these two respects in particular that I believe investigations like those of Thierry Kuntzel[24] are of great interest). Another approach – the one I have had in view and have now reached – consists of a direct examination, outside any particular film, of the psycho-analytic implications of the *cinematic*; I shall undertake this exam-ination, or begin to, in the second half of this text (Part I, Chapters 3, 4 and 5), and in the rest of the book.

In France during the years following 1968, the *Cahiers du Cinéma* team played an important part in the emergence of this new line of investigation: I am thinking in particular (but not only: there was a whole group of them) of Jean-Louis Comolli or Pascal Bonitzer's contributions. Studies of this kind have some-times been criticised for their obscurity or fashionable preten-tiousness; or again because they are so to speak *raids*, somewhat elliptical, not systematic enough, covering the ground at great speed without really consolidating their position. In some cases (though not always by any means) these criticisms are not altogether beside the point. But they cannot detract from the in-terest and the pertinence of the breakthrough, the *gesture*, the orientation: how often, after all, in cinematic theory up until then, had people been concerned to illuminate in Freudian terms phenomena such as off-screen space, framing, rapid cutting or depth of field?

It is indeed well known that different 'languages' (painting, music, cinema, etc.) are distinguished from one another – and are first *several* – by means of their signifiers, in the physical and per-ceptual definition of those signifiers as well as in the formal and structural features that flow from them, and not by means of their signifieds, or at any rate, not immediately.[25] There is no signified which is peculiar to literature or on the contrary to the cinema, no 'great global signified' that might be attributed to painting itself, for example (= one more mythical avatar of the belief in an ultimate signified). Each means of expression allows everything to be said: by 'everything' I mean an indefinite number of 'things' (?), very broadly coinciding from one language to another. Obviously each one says them in its own way, and that is precisely why it sometimes seems there should be such a great signified. But a signified which is still very badly named, since it can only be approached in terms of a signifier: the cinematic does not consist of some static list of themes or subjects which are supposed to be especially apt for the cinema and for which the other arts have a lesser 'vocation' (a truly metaphysical conception, proceeding by *essences*), it can only be defined, or rather foreseen, as a special way of saying anything (or nothing), i.e. as a *signifier effect*: a specific coefficient of signification (and not a signified) linked to the intrinsic workings of the cinema and to its very adoption rather than that of another machine, another apparatus. In linguistic terms, I shall say that what calls for psychoanalytic illumination is not just each film (not just films) but also the pertinent features of the matter of the signifier in the cinema, and the specific codes that these features allow: the matter of the signifier and the form of the signifier, in Hjelmslev's sense.

THE MAJOR REGIMES OF THE SIGNIFIER

A study of the signifier, but not necessarily of the cinema 'in general' (= stating propositions each of which applies to all films). For there are many intermediate stages. Relatively narrow groupings such as the set of all films by one film-maker or belonging to one very historically circumscribed 'genre' give rise to investigations which remain very close to textual analyses. But there are also wider categories, sorts of 'super-genres', which I would rather describe as so many *major cinematic regimes*: each one still corresponds to a group of films, but only virtually, for the group is vast and allows of no explicit enumeration (and also because these regimes are very often intermingled, so that one and the same film belongs to several of them at once). What is paradoxical about these regimes, which correspond to the main *cinematic formulae* so far, is that quite often they are evanescent and uncertain in their boundaries, which break into an indefinite series of special cases, and yet they are very clear and sharply defined in their centres of gravity: that is why they can be defined in comprehension but not in extension. Hazily outlined, but by no means empty institutions. The spectator accustomed to the cinema (the native) is quite at home with them, they are mental categories he has and can handle. He may have seen many so-called 'fictional documentaries' (and the expression already bears witness to a mixture of genres, hence to two genres which are distinct in principle), but he has no doubt that the documentary and the 'story film' remain autonomous in their definitions and that on other occasions they are each manifested in a pure, or at any rate purer, state.

It is not my aim here to list these major genres exhaustively; I am interested in their status, not in their enumeration. There are a number of them, some of which are arranged in series. Each series forms a paradigm (in logical terms a sum of complementary classes) the set of which coincides with cinematic production as a whole, but divides it up differently from the other series. Thus the series 'Newsreel/documentary film/trailer/advertising film/"main" film'. Or 'Colour film/black-and-white film', 'Silent film/sound film'. (It is clear that some categories have clearer boundaries than others.) In other cases no real series is constituted; instead there is a certain 'sort' of films, felt socially to be slightly separate (precisely a sort), and opposed en bloc to all other films; the latter become 'ordinary films' (= *unmarked* films from the point of view considered). There are 3-D films and the rest, cinemascope films and the rest, cinerama films and the rest, etc.

One of the most important of these various divisions for any study of the cinematic signifier (inaugurator of these classifications), and particularly for a psychoanalytic one, is also, as so often happens, one of the most blurred in its external contours, one of the most difficult (the most impossible) to establish by enumeration. This is the division that puts on one side the films I call diegetic (narrative-representational films) and on the other those that do not tell a story, this pair being connected by a particularly impressive gradation of specific or mixed positions.[26] The importance of this distinction, what makes it so real in all types of reflection from the most 'naïve' to the most theoretical, despite its fleeting nature, has to do with factors which are essentially historical (i.e. industrial, ideological, psychoanalytic, etc.), which are independent of each spectator's taste or distaste for the fiction film (on the contrary, this taste is dependent on a factual situation which is, moreover, a complex one). Since its birth at the end of the nineteenth century the cinema has, as it were, been snapped up by the Western, Aristotelian tradition of the fictional and representational arts, of *diegesis* and *mimesis*, for which its spectators were prepared – prepared in spirit, but also instinctually – by their experience of the novel, of theatre, of figurative painting, and which was thus the most profitable tradition for the cinema industry. Most films made today still belong in some degree to the fictional formula; I attempt to explain why and how in Part III.

It should also be noted that the fictional division, in its (historically rather revealing) formal mechanism, acts in a manner opposite to that of the other paradigms I have cited. It distinguishes the narrative films from all the rest, i.e. the 'positive' pole, the one that is given a definition, corresponds to the majority of films and not to the minority, as it does when cinerama films are opposed to 'ordinary' films. Now it is the film felt ideologically to be ordinary (the fiction film) that serves as a reference point and opens the paradigm, and on the contrary the category of 'all the rest' groups fewer films and ones society regards as slightly strange (at any rate when they are full-length films claiming to count as 'main films'). The *marking* is troubled here: it would seem that it should be the non-fiction film that would be offered as the marked term since it is more uncommon and more 'special', and yet (and this is rather uncommon) it is the unmarked term, the fiction film, that is posed first and with respect to which the *rest* can be defined. This peculiar disposition of the mark can be seen whenever society opposes a normality to a marginality: the marginal (as the word suggests) comes 'after', it is a residue, it could not function as a primary, positive term; but as the positive is also in a majority (and the term 'normal' contains both these notions at once), the more uncommon marginal is marked while remaining the 'rest'. Here we see once again that formal configurations are fully socio-ideological in scope (the objectively dominant position of the fiction film has repercussions in ordinary mental divisions), and that the latter open on to something latent which in this passage I have only designated at its preconscious level; there are regions of the preconscious which are kept apart from consciousness in a fairly regular way but without access to them needing an analytic cure or a true removal of repression. One should not be in too much of a hurry to attribute everything implicit or unspoken, even when it is fairly permanently so, to the unconscious. However, this marginal status of the non-fiction film might be traced to unconscious roots; so long as these two stages are not confused.

The fiction film is the film in which the cinematic signifier does not work on its own account but is employed entirely to remove the traces of its own steps, to open immediately on to the transparency of a signified, of a story, which is in reality manufactured by it but which it pretends merely to 'illustrate', to transmit to us after the event, as if it had existed previously (= referential illusion): another example of a product which is its own production in reverse. This *previous existence effect* – this gentle hum of a 'once-upon-a-time', of an essential childhood – is surely one of the great (and largely unconscious) charms of all fiction in the very many cultures where fiction is found. Thus the fiction film represents both the negation of the signifier (an attempt to have it forgotten) and a certain working regime of that signifier, a very precise one, just the one that is required to get it forgotten (more or less forgotten, according to whether the film is more or less submerged in its script). Hence what distinguishes fiction films is not the 'absence' of any specific work of the signifier; but *its presence in the mode of denegation*, and it is well known that this type of presence is one of the strongest there are. It is important to study this play of presence-absence, which André Bazin already foresaw in his notion of 'classical editing', it is important to explore the cinematic signifier in its fictional regime. On the other hand, as I have said, the more a film can be reduced to its diegesis, the less the study of its signifier is important for the textual system. This is not contradictory: the diegetic formula of the signifier is a complex mechanism which is not as yet well understood, but whatever precisely it turns out to be, it concerns a very large number of films and hence none of them in particular.

Thus there are broad categories (fiction film, colour film, cinemascope film, etc.) which seem not to be enumerable sets of films (even if they sometimes are to a certain extent) so much as the different faces of the cinema itself, or at least those of its faces that it has already shown us, for it has others in reserve for us in the future. One can concern oneself with them as such, and still be studying the cinema-signifier via one or other of its major institutional modes. The most pertinent methodological distinction in a semiological perspective is not the opposition between the singular film (= one film and it alone) and the cinema as a whole (= all existing films), but that between studies of texts and studies of codes. In either case one may be dealing with groups of films, reducible to one only for textual analyses, extendable to the whole cinema for analyses of codes. The incidence of the gap which remains is to separate groups which can be mastered in extension from those that cannot be approached by way of text (i.e. as a *corpus*) because of their indefinite character or their enormous size, and can only be grasped by the direct study of certain pertinent features of the signifier (immediately common to an indeterminate number of films), and are besides, from the moment of their historical or sociological definition, less groups of films than aspects of the cinema. Their analysis is related to those that bear on the entire cinema and thus belongs to the same kind of investigation.

3

Identification, Mirror

'What contribution can Freudian psychoanalysis make to the knowledge of the cinematic signifier?': that was the question-dream I posed (the scientific imaginary wishing to be symbolised), and it seems to me that I have now more or less *unwound* it; unwound but no more; I have not given it an answer. I have simply paid attention to what it was I wished to say (one never knows this until one has written it down), I have only questioned my question: this unanswered character is one that has to be deliberately accepted, it is constitutive of any epistemological procedure.

Since I have wished to mark the places (as empty boxes some of which are beginning to fill without waiting for me, and so much the better), the places of different directions of work, and particularly of the last, the psychoanalytic exploration of the signifier, which concerns me especially, I must now begin to inscribe something in this last box; must take further, and more plainly in the direction of the unconscious, the analysis of the investigator's desire that makes me write. And to start with, of course, this means asking a new question: among the specific features of the cinematic signifier that distinguish the cinema from literature, painting, etc. which ones by nature call most directly on the type of knowledge that psychoanalysis alone can provide?

PERCEPTION, IMAGINARY

The cinema's signifier is *perceptual* (visual and auditory). So is that of literature, since the written chain has to be *read*, but it involves a more restricted perceptual register: only graphemes,

42

writing. So too are those of painting, sculpture, architecture, photography, but still within limits, and different ones: absence of auditory perception, absence in the visual itself of certain important dimensions such as time and movement (obviously there is the time of the look, but the object looked at is not inscribed in a precise and ordered time sequence forced on the spectator from outside). Music's signifier is perceptual as well, but, like the others, less 'extensive' than that of the cinema: here it is vision which is absent, and even in the auditory, extended speech (except in song). What first strikes one then is that the cinema is *more perceptual*, if the phrase is allowable, than many other means of expression; it mobilises a larger number of the axes of perception. (That is why the cinema has sometimes been presented as a 'synthesis of all the arts'; which does not mean very much, but if we restrict ourselves to the quantitative tally of the registers of perception, it is true that the cinema contains within itself the signifiers of other arts: it can present pictures to us, make us hear music, it is made of photographs, etc.)

Nevertheless, this as it were numerical 'superiority' disappears if the cinema is compared with the theatre, the opera and other spectacles of the same type. The latter too involve sight and hearing simultaneously, linguistic audition and non-linguistic audition, movement, real temporal progression. Their difference from the cinema lies elsewhere: they do not consist of *images*, the perceptions they offer to the eye and the ear are inscribed in a true space (not a photographed one), the same one as that occupied by the public during the performance; everything the audience hear and see is actively produced in their presence, by human beings or props which are themselves present. This is not the problem of fiction but that of the definitional characteristics of the signifier: whether or no the theatrical play mimes a fable, its *action*, if need be mimetic, is still managed by real persons evolving in real time and space, *on the same stage or 'scene' as the public*. The 'other scene', which is precisely not so called, is the cinematic screen (closer to phantasy from the outset): what unfolds there may, as before, be more or less fictional, but the unfolding itself is fictive: the actor, the 'décor', the words one hears are all absent, everything is *recorded* (as a memory trace which is immediately so, without having been something else before), and this is still true if what is recorded is not a 'story' and does not aim for the fictional illusion proper. For it is the signifier itself, and as

a whole, that is recorded, that is absence: a little rolled up perfo-
rated strip which 'contains' vast landscapes, fixed battles, the
melting of the ice on the River Neva, and whole life-times, and
yet can be enclosed in the familiar round metal tin, of modest
dimensions, clear proof that it does not 'really' contain all that.

At the theatre, Sarah Bernhardt may tell me she is Phèdre or, if
the play were from another period and rejected the figurative
regime, she might say, as in a type of modern theatre, that she is
Sarah Bernhardt. But at any rate, I should see Sarah Bernhardt.
At the cinema, she could make the same two kinds of speeches
too, but it would be her shadow that would be offering them to
me (or she would be offering them in her own absence). Every
film is a fiction film.

What is at issue is not just the actor. Today there are a theatre
and a cinema without actors, or in which they have at least
ceased to take on the full and exclusive function which characterises them in classical spectacles. But what is true of Sarah
Bernhardt is just as true of an object, a prop, a chair for example.
On the theatre stage, this chair may, as in Chekhov, pretend to
be the chair in which the melancholy Russian nobleman sits
every evening; on the contrary (in Ionesco), it can explain to me
that it is a theatre chair. But when all is said and done it is a chair.
In the cinema, it will similarly have to choose between two atti-
tudes (and many other intermediate or more tricky ones), but it
will not be there when the spectators see it, when they have to recognise the choice; it will have delegated its reflection to them.

What is characteristic of the cinema is not the imaginary that it
may happen to represent, but the imaginary that it *is* from the
start, the imaginary that constitutes it as a signifier (the two are
not unrelated; it is so well able to represent it because it is it;
however it is it even when it no longer represents it). The (possible) reduplication inaugurating the intention of fiction is preceded in the cinema by a first reduplication, always-already
achieved, which inaugurates the signifier. The imaginary, by
definition, combines within it a certain presence and a certain
absence. In the cinema it is not just the fictional signified, if there
is one, that is thus made present in the mode of absence, it is from
the outset the signifier.

Thus the cinema, 'more perceptual' than certain arts according to the list of its sensory registers, is also 'less perceptual' than others once the status of these perceptions is envisaged rather than their number or diversity; for its perceptions are all in a sense 'false'. Or rather, the activity of perception which it involves is real (the cinema is not a phantasy), but the perceived is not really the object, it is its shade, its phantom, its double, its *replica* in a new kind of mirror. It will be said that literature, after all, is itself only made of replicas (written words, presenting absent objects). But at least it does not present them to us with all the really perceived detail that the screen does (giving more and taking as much, i.e. taking more). The unique position of the cinema lies in this dual character of its signifier: unaccustomed perceptual wealth, but at the same time stamped with unreality to an unusual degree, and from the very outset. More than the other arts, or in a more unique way, the cinema involves us in the imaginary: it drums up all perception, but to switch it immediately over into its own absence, which is nonetheless the only signifier present.

THE ALL-PERCEIVING SUBJECT

Thus film is like the mirror. But it differs from the primordial mirror in one essential point: although, as in the latter, everything may come to be projected, there is one thing and one thing only that is never reflected in it: the spectator's own body. In a certain emplacement, the mirror suddenly becomes clear glass.

In the mirror the child perceives the familiar household objects, and also its object par excellence, its mother, who holds it up in her arms to the glass. But above all it perceives its own image. This is where primary identification (the formation of the ego) gets certain of its main characteristics: the child sees itself as an other, and beside an other. This other other is its guarantee that the first is really it: by her authority, her sanction, in the register of the symbolic, subsequently by the resemblance between her mirror image and the child's (both have a human form). Thus the child's ego is formed by identification with its like, and this in two senses simultaneously, metonymically and metaphorically: the other human being who is in the glass, the own reflection which is and is not the body, which is like it. The child identifies with itself as an object.

In the cinema, the object remains: fiction or no, there is always something on the screen. But the reflection of the own body has disappeared. The cinema spectator is not a child and the child really at the mirror stage (from around six to around eighteen months) would certainly be incapable of 'following' the simplest of films. Thus, what *makes possible* the spectator's absence from the screen – or rather the intelligible unfolding of the film despite that absence – is the fact that the spectator has already known the experience of the mirror (of the true mirror), and is thus able to constitute a world of objects without having first to recognise himself within it. In this respect, the cinema is already on the side of the symbolic (which is only to be expected): the spectator knows that objects exist, that he himself exists as a subject, that he becomes an object for others: he knows himself and he knows his like: it is no longer necessary that this similarity be literally *depicted* for him on the screen, as it was in the mirror of his childhood. Like every other broadly 'secondary' activity, the practice of the cinema presupposes that the primitive undifferentiation of the ego and the non-ego has been overcome.

But *with what*, then, does the spectator identify during the projection of the film? For he certainly has to identify: identification in its primal form has ceased to be a current necessity for him, but he continues, in the cinema – if he did not the film would become incomprehensible, considerably more incomprehensible than the most incomprehensible films – to depend on that permanent play of identification without which there would be no social life (thus, the simplest conversation presupposes the alternation of the *I* and the *you*, hence the aptitude of the two interlocutors for a mutual and reversible identification). What form does this *continued* identification, whose essential role Lacan has demonstrated even in the most abstract reasoning[1] and which constituted the 'social sentiment' for Freud[2] (= the sublimation of a homosexual libido, itself a reaction to the aggressive rivalry of the members of a single generation after the murder of the father), take in the special case of one social practice among others, cinematic projection?

Obviously the spectator has the opportunity to identify with the *character* of the fiction. But there still has to be one. This is thus only valid for the narrative-representational film, and not for the psychoanalytic constitution of the signifier of the cinema as such. The spectator can also identify with the actor, in more or less 'a-fictional' films in which the latter is represented as an actor, not a character, but is still offered thereby as a human being (as a perceived human being) and thus allows identification. However this factor (even added to the previous one and thus covering a very large number of films) cannot suffice. It only designates secondary identification in certain of its forms (secondary in the cinematic process itself, since in any other sense all identification except that of the mirror can be regarded as secondary).

An insufficient explanation, and for two reasons, the first of which is only the intermittent, anecdotal and superficial consequence of the second (but for that reason more visible, and that is why I call it the first). The cinema deviates from the theatre on an important point that has often been emphasised: it often presents us with long sequences that can (literally) be called 'inhuman' – the familiar theme of cinematic 'cosmomorphism' developed by many film theorists – sequences in which only inanimate objects, landscapes, etc. appear and which for minutes at a time offer no human form for spectator identification: yet the latter must be supposed to remain intact in its deep structure, since at such moments the film *works* just as well as it does at others, and whole films (geographical documentaries, for example) unfold intelligibly in such conditions. The second, more radical reason is that identification with the human form appearing on the screen, even when it occurs, still tells us nothing about the *place of the spectator's ego* in the inauguration of the signifier. As I have just pointed out, this ego is already formed. But since it exists, the question arises precisely of *where it is* during the projection of the film (the true primary identification, that of the mirror, forms the ego, but all other identifications presuppose, on the contrary, that it has been formed and can be 'exchanged' for the object or the fellow subject). Thus when I 'recognise' my like on the screen, and even more when I do not recognise it, where am I? Where is that someone who is capable of self-recognition when need be?

It is not enough to answer that the cinema, like every social practice, demands that the psychical apparatus of its participants be fully constituted, and that the question is thus the concern of general psychoanalytic theory and not that of the cinema proper. For my *where is it?* does not claim to go so far, or more precisely tries to go slightly further: it is a question of the *point* occupied by this already constituted ego, occupied during the cinema showing and not in social life in general.

The spectator is absent from the screen: contrary to the child in the mirror, he cannot identify with himself as an object, but only with objects which are there without him. In this sense the screen is not a mirror. The perceived, this time, is entirely on the side of the object, and there is no longer any equivalent of the own image, of that unique mix of perceived and subject (of other and I) which was precisely the figure necessary to disengage the one from the other. At the cinema, it is always the other who is on the screen; as for me, I am there to look at him. I take no part in the perceived, on the contrary, I am *all-perceiving*. All-perceiving as one says all-powerful (this is the famous gift of 'ubiquity' the film makes its spectator); all-perceiving, too, because I am entirely on the side of the perceiving instance: absent from the screen, but certainly present in the auditorium, a great eye and ear without which the perceived would have no one to perceive it, the instance, in other words, which *constitutes* the cinema signifier (it is I who make the film). If the most extravagant spectacles and sounds or the most unlikely combination of them, the combination furthest removed from any real experience, do not prevent the constitution of meaning (and to begin with do not *astonish* the spectator, do not really astonish him, not intellectually: he simply judges the film as strange), that is because he knows he is at the cinema.

In the cinema the *subject's knowledge* takes a very precise form without which no film would be possible. This knowledge is dual (but unique). I know I am perceiving something imaginary (and that is why its absurdities, even if they are extreme, do not seriously disturb me), and I know that it is I who am perceiving it. This second knowledge divides in turn: I know that I am really perceiving, that my sense organs are physically affected, that I am not phantasising, that the fourth wall of the auditorium (the screen) is really different from the other three, that there is a projector facing it (and thus it is not I who am projecting, or at least not all alone), and I also know that it is I who am perceiving all this, that this perceived-imaginary material is deposited in me as if on a second screen, that it is in me that it forms up into an organised sequence, that therefore I am myself the place where this really perceived imaginary accedes to the symbolic by its inauguration as the signifier of a certain type of institutionalised social activity called the 'cinema'.

In other words, the spectator *identifies with himself*, with himself as a pure act of perception (as wakefulness, alertness): as the condition of possibility of the perceived and hence as a kind of transcendental subject, which comes before every *there is*.

A strange mirror, then, very like that of childhood, and very different. Very like, as Jean-Louis Baudry has emphasised,[3] because during the showing we are, like the child, in a sub-motor and hyper-perceptive state; because, like the child again, we are prey to the imaginary, the double, and are so paradoxically through a real perception. Very different, because this mirror returns us everything but ourselves, because we are wholly outside it, whereas the child is both in it and in front of it. As an *arrangement* (and in a very topographical sense of the word), the cinema is more involved on the flank of the symbolic, and hence of secondariness, than is the mirror of childhood. This is not surprising, since it comes long after it, but what is more important to me is the fact that it is inscribed in its wake with an incidence at once so direct and so oblique, which has no precise equivalent in other apparatuses of signification.

IDENTIFICATION WITH THE CAMERA

The preceding analysis coincides in places with others which have already been proposed and which I shall not repeat: analyses of *quattrocento* painting or of the cinema itself which insist on the role of monocular perspective (hence of the *camera*) and the 'vanishing point' that inscribes an empty emplacement for the spectator-subject, an all-powerful position which is that of God himself, or more broadly of some ultimate signified. And it is true that as he identifies with himself as look, the spectator can do no other than identify with the camera, too, which has looked before him at what he is now looking at and whose stationing (= framing) determines the vanishing point. During the projection this camera is absent, but it has a representative consisting of another apparatus, called precisely a 'projector'. An apparatus the spectator has behind him, *at the back of his head*,[4] that is, precisely where phantasy locates the 'focus' of all vision. All of us have experienced our own look, even outside the so-called *salles obscures* [= cinemas], as a kind of searchlight turning on the axis of our own necks (like a pan) and shifting when we shift (a tracking shot now): as a cone of light (without the microscopic dust scattered through it and streaking it in the cinema) whose vicariousness draws successive and variable slices of obscurity from nothingness wherever and whenever it comes to rest. (And in a sense that is what perception and consciousness are, a *light*, as Freud put it,[5] in the double sense of an illumination and an opening, as in the arrangement of the cinema, which contains both, a limited and wandering light that only attains a small part of the real, but on the other hand possesses the gift of casting light on it.) Without this identification with the camera certain facts could not be understood, though they are constant ones: the fact, for example, that the spectator is not amazed when the image 'rotates' (= a pan) and yet he knows he has not turned his head. The explanation is that he has no need to turn it really, he has turned it in his all-seeing capacity, his identification with the movement of the camera being that of a transcendental, not an empirical subject.

All vision consists of a double movement: projective (the 'sweeping' searchlight) and introjective: consciousness as a sensitive recording surface (as a screen). I have the impression at once that, to use a common expression, I am 'casting' my eyes on things, and that the latter, thus illuminated, come to be deposited within me (we then declare that it is these things that have been 'projected', on to my retina, say). A sort of stream called the look, and explaining all the myths of magnetism, must be sent out over the world, so that objects can come back up this stream in the opposite direction (but using it to find their way), arriving at last at our perception, which is now soft wax and no longer an emitting source.

The technology of photography carefully conforms to this (banal) phantasy accompanying perception. The camera is 'trained' on the object like a fire-arm (= projection) and the object arrives to make an imprint, a trace, on the receptive surface of the film-strip (= introjection). The spectator himself does not escape these pincers, for he is part of the apparatus, and also because pincers, on the imaginary plane (Melanie Klein), mark our relation to the world as a whole and are rooted in the primary figures of orality. During the performance the spectator is the searchlight I have described, duplicating the projector, which itself duplicates the camera, and he is also the sensitive surface duplicating the screen, which itself duplicates the film-strip. There are two cones in the auditorium: one ending on the screen and starting both in the projection box and in the spectator's vision insofar as it is projective, and one starting from the screen and 'deposited' in the spectator's perception insofar as it is introjective (on the retina, a second screen). When I say that 'I see' the film, I mean thereby a unique mixture of two contrary currents: the film is what I receive, and it is also what I release, since it does not pre-exist my entering the auditorium and I only need close my eyes to suppress it. Releasing it, I am the projector, receiving it, I am the screen; in both these figures together, I am the camera, which points and yet which records.

Thus the constitution of the signifier in the cinema depends on a series of mirror-effects organised in a chain, and not on a single reduplication. In this the cinema as a topography resembles that other 'space', the technical equipment (camera, projector, film-strip, screen, etc.), the objective precondition of the whole insti-tution: as we know, the apparatuses too contain a series of mirrors, lenses, apertures and shutters, ground glasses, through which the cone of light passes: a further reduplication in which the equipment becomes a metaphor (as well as the real source) for the mental process instituted. Further on we shall see that it is also its fetish.

In the cinema, as elsewhere, the constitution of the symbolic is only achieved through and above the play of the imaginary: projection-introjection, presence-absence, phantasies accom-panying perception, etc. Even when acquired, the ego still depends in its underside on the fabulous figures thanks to which it has been acquired and which have marked it lastingly with the stamp of the lure. The secondary process does no more than 'cover' (and not always hermetically) the primary process which is still constantly present and conditions the very possibility of what covers it.

Chain of many mirrors, the cinema is at once a weak and a robust mechanism: like the human body, like a precision tool, like a social institution. And the fact is that it is really all of these at the same time.

And I, at this moment, what am I doing if not to add to all these reduplications one more whereby theory is attempting to set itself up? Am I not looking at myself looking at the film? This *passion for seeing* (and also hearing), the foundation of the whole edifice, am I not turning it, too, on (against) that edifice? Am I not still the voyeur I was in front of the screen, now that it is this voyeur who is being seen, thus postulating a second voyeur, the one writing at present, myself again?

ON THE IDEALIST THEORY OF THE CINEMA

The place of the ego in the institution of the signifier, as transcendental yet radically deluded subject, since it is the institution (and even the equipment) that give it this place, surely provides us with an appreciable opportunity the better to understand and judge the precise epistemological import of the idealist theory of the cinema which culminates in the remarkable works of André Bazin. Before thinking directly about their validity, but simply reading texts of this kind, one cannot but be struck by the great precision, the acute and immediately sensitive intelligence that they often demonstrate; at the same time they give the diffuse impression of a permanent ill-foundedness (which affects nothing and yet affects everything), they suggest that somewhere they contain something like a weak point at which the whole might be overturned.

It is certainly no accident that the main form of idealism in cinematic theory has been phenomenology. Bazin and other writers of the same period explicitly acknowledged their debt to it, and more implicitly (but in a more generalised fashion) all conceptions of the cinema as a mystical revelation, as 'truth' or 'reality' unfolding by right, as the apparition of what is [*l'étant*], as an epiphany, derive from it. We all know that the cinema has the gift of sending some of its lovers into prophetic trances. However, these cosmophanic conceptions (which are not always expressed in an extreme form) register rather well the 'feeling' of the *deluded ego* of the spectator, they often give us excellent descriptions of this feeling and to this extent there is something scientific about them and they have advanced our knowledge of the cinema. But the *lure of the ego* is their blind spot. These theories are still of great interest, but they have, so to speak, to be put the other way round, like the optical image of the film.

For it is true that the topographical apparatus of the cinema resembles the conceptual apparatus of phenomenology, with the result that the latter can cast light on the former. (Besides, in any domain, a phenomenology of the object to be understood, a 'receptive' description of its appearances, must be the starting-point; only afterwards can *criticism* begin; psychoanalysts, it should be remembered, have their own phenomenology.) The *'there is'* of phenomenology proper (philosophical phenomenology) as an ontic revelation referring to a perceiving-subject (='perceptual *cogito*'), to a subject for which alone there can be anything, has close and precise affinities with the installation of the cinema signifier in the ego as I have tried to define it, with the spectator withdrawing into himself as a pure instance of perception, the whole of the perceived being 'out there'. To this extent the cinema really is the 'phenomenological art' it has often been called, by Merleau-Ponty himself, for example.[6] But it can only be so because its objective determinations make it so. The ego's position in the cinema does not derive from a miraculous resemblance between the cinema and the natural characteristics of all perception; on the contrary, it is foreseen and marked in advance by the institution (the equipment, the disposition of the auditorium, the mental system that internalises the two), and also by more general characteristics of the psychical apparatus (such as projection, the mirror structure, etc.), which although they are less strictly dependent on a period of social history and a technology, do not therefore express the sovereignty of a 'human vocation', but inversely are themselves shaped by certain specific features of man as an animal (as the only animal that is not an animal): his primitive *Hilflosigkeit*, his dependence on another's care (the lasting source of the imaginary, of object relations, of the great oral figures of feeding), the motor prematurity of the child which condemns it to an initial self-recognition by sight (hence outside itself) anticipating a muscular unity it does not yet possess.

In other words, phenomenology can contribute to knowledge of the cinema (and it has done so) insofar as it happens to be like it, and yet it is on the cinema *and* phenomenology in their common illusion of *perceptual mastery* that light must be cast by the real conditions of society and man.

ON SOME SUB-CODES OF IDENTIFICATION

The play of identification defines the cinematic situation in its generality, i.e. *the* code. But it also allows more specific and less permanent configurations, 'variations' on it, as it were; they intervene in certain coded figures which occupy precise segments of precise films.

What I have said about identification so far amounts to the statement that the spectator is absent from the screen *as perceived*, but also (the two things inevitably go together) present there and even 'all-present' as *perceiver*. At every moment I am in the film by my look's caress. This presence often remains diffuse, geographically undifferentiated, evenly distributed over the whole surface of the screen; or more precisely *hovering*, like the psychoanalyst's listening, ready to catch on preferentially to some motif in the film, according to the force of that motif and according to my own phantasies as a spectator, without the cinematic code itself intervening to govern this anchorage and impose it on the whole audience. But in other cases, certain articles of the cinematic codes or sub-codes (which I shall not try to survey completely here) are made responsible for suggesting to the spectator the vector along which his permanent identification with his own look should be extended temporarily inside the film (the perceived) itself. Here we meet various classic problems of cinematic theory, or at least certain aspects of them: subjective images, out-of-frame space, looks (looks and no longer the look, but the former are articulated to the latter).

There are various sorts of subjective image and I have tried elsewhere (following Jean Mitry) to distinguish between them.[7] Only one of them will detain me for the moment, the one which 'expresses the viewpoint of the film-maker' in the standard formula (and not the viewpoint of a character, another traditional sub-case of the subjective image): unusual framings, uncommon shot-angles, etc. as for example in one of the sketches which make up Julien Duvivier's film *Carnet de bal* (the sketch with Pierre Blanchar, shot continuously in tilted framings). In the standard definitions one thing strikes me: I do not see why these uncommon angles should express the viewpoint of the film-

maker any more than perfectly ordinary angles, closer to the horizontal. However, the definition is comprehensible even in its
inaccuracy: precisely because it is uncommon, the uncommon
angle makes us more aware of what we had merely forgotten to
some extent in its absence: an identification with the camera
(with 'the author's viewpoint'). The ordinary framings are
finally felt to be non-framings: I espouse the film-maker's look
(without which no cinema would be possible), but my consciousness is not too aware of it. The uncommon angle reawakens me
and (like the cure) teaches me what I already knew. And then, it
obliges my look to stop wandering freely over the screen for the
moment and to scan it along more precise lines of force which are
imposed on me. Thus for a moment I become directly aware of
the *emplacement* of my own presence-absence in the film simply
because it has changed.

Now for looks. In a fiction film, the characters look at one
another. It can happen (and this is already another 'notch' in the
chain of identifications) that a character looks at another who is
momentarily out-of-frame, or else is looked at by him. If we have
gone one notch further, this is because everything out-of-frame
brings us closer to the spectator, since it is the peculiarity of the latter
to be out-of-frame (the out-of-frame character thus has a point in
common with him: he is looking at the screen). In certain cases
the out-of-frame character's look is 'reinforced' by recourse to
another variant of the subjective image, generally christened the
'character's point of view': the framing of the scene corresponds
precisely to the angle from which the out-of-frame character
looks at the screen. (The two figures are dissociable moreover: we
often know that the scene is being looked at by someone other
than ourselves, by a character, but it is the logic of the plot, or an
element of the dialogue, or a previous image that tells us so, not
the position of the camera, which may be far from the presumed
emplacement of the out-of-frame onlooker.)
    In all sequences of this kind, the identification that founds the
signifier is *twice relayed,* doubly duplicated in a circuit that leads it
to the heart of the film along a line which is no longer hovering,
which follows the inclination of the looks and is therefore
governed by the film itself: the spectator's look (= the basic
identification), before dispersing all over the surface of the screen

in a variety of intersecting lines (= looks of the characters in the frame = second duplication), must first 'go through' – as one goes through a town on a journey, or a mountain pass – the look of the character out-of-frame (= first duplication), himself a spectator and hence the first delegate of the true spectator, but not to be confused with the latter since he is inside, if not the frame, then at least the fiction. This invisible character, supposed (like the spectator) to be seeing, will collide obliquely with the latter's look and play the part of an obligatory intermediary. By offering himself as a crossing for the spectator, he inflects the circuit followed by the sequence of identifications and it is only in this sense that he is himself seen: as we see through him, we see ourselves not seeing him.

Examples of this kind are much more numerous and each of them is much more complex than I have suggested here. At this point textual analysis of precise film sequences is an indispensable instrument of knowledge. I just wished to show that in the end there is no break in continuity between the child's game with the mirror and, at the other extreme, certain localised figures of the cinematic codes. The mirror is the site of primary identification. Identification with one's own look is secondary with respect to the mirror, i.e. for a general theory of adult activities, but it is the foundation of the cinema and hence primary when the latter is under discussion: it is *primary cinematic identification* proper ('primary identification' would be inaccurate from the psychoanalytic point of view; 'secondary identification', more accurate in this respect, would be ambiguous for a cinematic psychoanalysis). As for identifications with characters, with their own different levels (out-of-frame character, etc.), they are secondary, tertiary cinematic identifications, etc.; taken as a whole in opposition to the identification of the spectator with his own look, they constitute secondary cinematic identification in the singular.[8]

'SEEING A FILM'

Freud noted, *vis-à-vis* the sexual act[9] that the most ordinary practices depend on a large number of psychical functions which are distinct but work consecutively, so that all of them must be intact if what is regarded as a normal performance is to be possible (it is because neurosis and psychosis dissociate them and put some of them out of court that a kind of commutation is made possible whereby they can be listed retrospectively by the analyst). The apparently very simple act of *seeing a film* is no exception to this rule. As soon as it is subjected to analysis it reveals to us a complex, multiply interconnected imbrication of the functions of the imaginary, the real and the symbolic, which is also required in one form or another for every procedure of social life, but whose cinematic manifestation is especially impressive since it is played out on a small surface. (To this extent the theory of the cinema may some day contribute something to psychoanalysis, even if, through force of circumstances, this 'reciprocation' remains very limited at the moment, the two disciplines being very unevenly developed.)

In order to understand the fiction film, I must both 'take myself' for the character (= an imaginary procedure) so that he benefits, by analogical projection, from all the schemata of intelligibility that I have within me, and not take myself for him (= the return to the real) so that the fiction can be established as such (= as symbolic): this is *seeming-real*. Similarly, in order to understand the film (at all), I must perceive the photographed object as absent, its photograph as present, and the presence of this absence as signifying. The imaginary of the cinema presupposes the symbolic, for the spectator must first of all have known the primordial mirror. But as the latter instituted the ego very largely in the imaginary, the second mirror of the screen, a symbolic apparatus, itself in turn depends on reflection and lack. However, it is not phantasy, a 'purely' symbolic-imaginary site, for the absence of the object and the codes of that absence are really produced in it by the *physis* of an equipment: the cinema is a body (a *corpus* for the semiologist), a fetish that can be loved.

4

The Passion for Perceiving

The practice of the cinema is only possible through the perceptual passions: the desire to see (= scopic drive, scopophilia, voyeurism), which was alone engaged in the art of the silent film, the desire to hear which has been added to it in the sound cinema (this is the *pulsion invocante*, the invocatory drive, one of the four main sexual drives for Lacan;[1] it is well known that Freud isolated it less clearly and hardly deals with it as such).

These two sexual drives are distinguished from the others in that they are more dependent on a lack, or at least dependent on it in a more precise, more unique manner, which marks them from the outset, even more than the others, as being on the side of the imaginary.

However, this characteristic is to a greater or lesser degree proper to all the sexual drives insofar as they differ from purely organic instincts or needs (Lacan), or in Freud from the self-preservation drives (the 'ego drives' which he tended subsequently to annex to narcissism, a tendency he could never quite bring himself to pursue to its conclusion). The sexual drive does not have so stable and strong a relationship with its 'object' as do for example hunger and thirst. Hunger can only be satisfied by food, but food is quite certain to satisfy it; thus instincts are simultaneously more and less difficult to satisfy than drives; they depend on a perfectly real object for which there is no substitute, but they depend on nothing else. Drives, on the contrary, can be satisfied up to a point outside their objects (this is sublimation, or else, in another way, masturbation) and are initially capable of doing without them without putting the organism into immediate danger (hence repression). The needs of self-preservation can neither be repressed nor sublimated; the sexual drives are more

58

labile and more accommodating, as Freud insisted[2] (more radically perverse, says Lacan[3]). Inversely, they always remain more or less unsatisfied, even when their object has been attained; desire is very quickly reborn after the brief vertigo of its apparent extinction, it is largely sustained by itself as desire, it has its own rhythms, often quite independent of those of the pleasure obtained (which seemed nonetheless its specific aim); the lack is what it wishes to fill, and at the same time what it is always careful to leave gaping, in order to survive as desire. In the end it has no object, at any rate no real object; through real objects which are all substitutes (and all the more numerous and interchangeable for that), it pursues an imaginary object (a 'lost object') which is its truest object, an object that has always been lost and is always desired as such.

How, then, can one say that the visual and auditory drives have a stronger or more special relationship with the absence of their object, with the infinite pursuit of the imaginary? Because, as opposed to other sexual drives, the 'perceiving drive' – combining into one the scopic drive and the invocatory drive – *concretely represents the absence of its object* in the distance at which it maintains it and which is part of its very definition: distance of the look, distance of listening. Psychophysiology makes a classic distinction between the 'senses at a distance' (sight and hearing) and the others all of which involve immediate proximity and which it calls the 'senses of contact' (Pradines): touch, taste, smell, cœnaesthetic sense, etc. Freud notes that voyeurism, like sadism in this respect, always keeps apart the *object* (here the object looked at) and the *source* of the drive, i.e. the generating organ (the eye); the voyeur does not look at his eye.[4] With orality and anality, on the contrary, the exercise of the drive inaugurates a certain degree of partial fusion, a coincidence (= contact, tendential abolition of distance) of source and aim, for the aim is to obtain pleasure at the level of the source organ (= 'organ pleasure'[5]): e.g. what is called 'pleasure of the mouth'.[6]

It is no accident that the main socially acceptable arts are based on the senses at a distance, and that those which depend on the senses of contact are often regarded as 'minor' arts (e.g. the culinary arts, the art of perfumes, etc.). Nor is it an accident that the visual or auditory imaginaries have played a much more im-

portant part in the histories of societies than the tactile or olfac-
tory imaginaries.

The voyeur is very careful to maintain a gulf, an empty space,
between the object and the eye, the object and his own body: his
look fastens the object at the right distance, as with those cinema
spectators who take care to avoid being too close to or too far
from the screen. The voyeur represents in space the fracture
which forever separates him from the object; he represents his
very dissatisfaction (which is precisely what he needs as a
voyeur), and thus also his 'satisfaction' insofar as it is of a
specifically voyeuristic type. To fill in this distance would
threaten to overwhelm the subject, to lead him to consume the
object (the object which is now too close so that he cannot see it
any more), to bring him to orgasm and the pleasure of his own
body, hence to the exercise of other drives, mobilising the senses
of contact and putting an end to the scopic arrangement. *Retention*
is fully part of perceptual pleasure, which is thereby often coloured with anality. Orgasm is the object rediscovered in a state of
momentary illusion; it is the phantasy suppression of the gap
between object and subject (hence the amorous myths of
'fusion'). The looking drive, except when it is exceptionally well
developed, is less directly related to orgasm than are the other
component drives; it favours it by its excitatory action, but it is
not generally sufficient to produce it by its figures alone, which
thus belong to the realm of 'preparatives'. In it we do not find
that illusion, however brief, of a lack filled, of a non-imaginary, of
a full relation to the object, better established in other drives. If it
is true of all desire that it depends on the infinite pursuit of its
absent object, voyeuristic desire, along with certain forms of
sadism, is the only desire whose principle of distance symbolically and spatially evokes this fundamental rent.

The same could be said, making the necessary modifications of
course, about the invocatory (auditory) drive, less closely studied
by psychoanalysis hitherto, with the exception of writers like
Lacan and Guy Rosolato. I shall merely recall that of all hallucinations – and what reveals the dissociation of desire and real
object better than the hallucination? – the main ones by far are
visual and auditory hallucinations, those of the senses at a
distance (this is also true of the dream, another form of hallucination).

THE SCOPIC REGIME OF THE CINEMA

However, although this set of features seems to me to be important, it does not yet characterise the signifier of the cinema proper,
but rather that of all means of expression based on sight or
hearing, and hence, among other 'languages', that of practically
all the arts (painting, sculpture, architecture, music, opera,
theatre, etc.). What distinguishes the cinema is an extra reduplication, a supplementary and specific turn of the screw bolting
desire to the lack. First because the spectacles and sounds the
cinema 'offers' us (offers us at a distance, hence as much *steals*
from us) are especially rich and varied: a mere difference of
degree, but already one that counts: the screen presents to our
apprehension, but absents from our grasp, more 'things'. (The
mechanism of the perceiving drive is identical for the moment
but its object is more endowed with matter; this is one of the
reasons why the cinema is very suited to handling 'erotic scenes'
which depend on direct, non-sublimated voyeurism.) In the
second place (and more decisively), the specific affinity between
the cinematic signifier and the imaginary persists when film is
compared with arts such as the theatre in which the audio-visual
given is as rich as it is on the screen in the number of perceptual
axes involved. Indeed, the theatre really does 'give' this given, or
at least slightly more really: it is physically present, in the same
space as the spectator. The cinema only gives it in effigy, inaccessible from the outset, in a primordial *elsewhere*, infinitely desirable (= never possessible), on another scene which is that of
absence and which nonetheless represents the absent in detail,
thus making it very present, but by a different itinerary. Not only
am I at a distance from the object, as in the theatre, but what
remains in that distance is now no longer the object itself, it is a
delegate it has sent me while itself withdrawing. A double withdrawal.

What defines the specifically cinematic *scopic regime* is not so
much the distance kept, the 'keeping' itself (first figure of the
lack, common to all voyeurism), as the absence of the object seen.
Here the cinema is profoundly different from the theatre as also
from more intimate voyeuristic activities with a specifically erotic
aim (there are intermediate genres, moreover: certain cabaret
acts, strip-tease, etc.): cases where voyeurism remains linked to

exhibitionism, where the two faces, active and passive, of the component drive are by no means so dissociated; where the object seen is present and hence presumably complicit; where the perverse activity – aided if need be by a certain dose of bad faith and happy illusion, varying from case to case, moreover, and sometimes reducible to very little, as in true perverse couples – is rehabilitated and reconciled with itself by being as it were undividedly taken in charge by two actors assuming its constitutive poles (the corresponding phantasies, in the absence of the actions, thus becoming interchangeable and shared by the play of reciprocal identification). In the theatre, as in domestic voyeurism, the passive actor (the one seen), simply because he is bodily present, because he does not go away, is presumed to consent, to cooperate deliberately. It may be that he really does, as exhibitionists in the clinical sense do, or as, in a sublimated fashion, does that oft noted triumphant exhibitionism characteristic of theatrical acting, counterposed even by Bazin to cinematic representation. It may also be that the object seen has only accepted this condition (thus becoming an 'object' in the ordinary sense of the word, and no longer only in the Freudian sense) under the pressure of more or less powerful external constraints, economic ones for example with certain poor strippers. (However, they must have consented at some point; rarely is the degree of acceptance zero, except in the case of *victimisation*, e.g. when a fascist militia strips its prisoners: the specific characteristics of the scopic arrangement are then distorted by the overpowerful intervention of another element, sadism.) Voyeurism which is not too sadistic (there is none which is not so at all) rests on a kind of *fiction*, more or less justified in the order of the real, sometimes institutionalised as in the theatre or strip-tease, a fiction that stipulates that the object 'agrees', that it is therefore exhibitionist. Or more precisely, what is necessary in this fiction for the establishment of potency and desire is presumed to be sufficiently guaranteed by the physical presence of the object: 'Since it is there, it must like it', such, hypocritical or no, deluded or no, is the retrenchment needed by the voyeur so long as sadistic infiltrations are insufficient to make the object's refusal and constraint necessary to him. Thus, despite the distance instituted by the look – which transforms the object into a *picture* (a '*tableau vivant*') and thus tips it over into the imaginary, even in its real presence – that presence, which persists, and the active consent which is its real or mythical correlate (but always real as myth) re-establish in the scopic space, momentarily at least, the illusion of a fullness of the object relation, of a state of desire which is not just imaginary.

It is this last recess that is attacked by the cinema signifier, it is in its precise emplacement (*in its place*, in both senses of the word) that it installs a new figure of the lack, the physical absence of the object seen. In the theatre, actors and spectators are present at the same time and in the same location, hence present one to another, as the two protagonists of an authentic perverse couple. But in the cinema, the actor was present when the spectator was not (= shooting), and the spectator is present when the actor is no longer (= projection): a failure to meet of the voyeur and the exhibitionist whose approaches no longer coincide (they have 'missed' one another). The cinema's voyeurism must (of necess-ity) do without any very clear mark of consent on the part of the object. There is no equivalent here of the theatre actors' final 'bow'. And then the latter could see their voyeurs, the game was less unilateral, slightly better distributed. In the darkened hall, the voyeur is really left alone (or with other voyeurs, which is worse), deprived of his other half in the mythical hermaphrodite (a hermaphrodite not necessarily constituted by the distribution of the sexes but rather by that of the active and passive poles in the exercise of the drive). Yet still a voyeur, since there is some-thing to see, called the film, but something in whose definition there is a great deal of 'flight': not precisely something that hides, rather something that *lets* itself be seen without *presenting* itself to be seen, which has gone out of the room before leaving only its trace visible there. This is the origin in particular of that 'recipe' of the classical cinema which said that the actor should never look directly at the audience (= the camera).

Thus deprived of rehabilitatory agreement, of a real or sup-posed consensus with the other (which was also the Other, for it had the status of a sanction on the plane of the symbolic), cine-matic voyeurism, *unauthorised* scopophilia, is from the outset more strongly established than that of the theatre in direct line from the primal scene. Certain precise features of the institution con-tribute to this affinity: the obscurity surrounding the onlooker, the aperture of the screen with its inevitable keyhole effect. But

the affinity is more profound. It lies first in the spectator's solitude in the cinema: those attending a cinematic projection do
not, as in the theatre, constitute a true 'audience', a temporary
collectivity; they are an accumulation of individuals who, despite
appearances, more closely resemble the fragmented group of
readers of a novel. It lies on the other hand in the fact that the
filmic spectacle, the object seen, is more radically ignorant of its
spectator, since he is not there, than the theatrical spectacle can
ever be. A third factor, closely linked to the other two, also plays a
part: the *segregation of spaces* that characterises a cinema performance and not a theatrical one. The 'stage' and the auditorium are
no longer two areas set up in opposition to each other within a
single space; the space of the film, represented by the screen, is
utterly heterogeneous, it no longer communicates with that of the
auditorium: one is real, the other perspective: a stronger break
than any line of footlights. For its spectator the film unfolds in
that simultaneously very close and definitively inaccessible 'elsewhere' in which the child *sees* the amorous play of the parental
couple, who are similarly ignorant of it and leave it alone, a pure
onlooker whose participation is inconceivable. In this respect the
cinematic signifier is not only 'psychoanalytic'; it is more precisely Oedipal in type.

In this set of differences between the cinema and the theatre, it is
difficult to be precise about the relative importance of two types
of conditioning, and yet they are definitely distinct: on the one
hand the characteristics of the signifier (alone envisaged here),
i.e. the supplementary degree of absence that I have tried to
analyse, and on the other the socio-ideological circumstances
that marked the historical birth of the two arts in a divergent
manner. I have broached the latter topic elsewhere in my contribution to the *Hommage à Emile Benveniste* (= Part II of this book)
and I shall only recall that the cinema was born in the midst of
the capitalist epoch in a largely antagonistic and fragmented
society, based on individualism and the restricted family (=
father–mother–children), in an especially super-egotistic bour-
geois society, especially concerned with 'elevation' (or façade),
especially opaque to itself. The theatre is a very ancient art, one
which saw the light in more authentically ceremonial societies, in
more integrated human groups (even if sometimes, as in Ancient

Greece, the cost of this integration was the rejection into a non-human exterior of a whole social category, that of the slaves), in cultures which were in some sense closer to their desire (= paganism): the theatre retains something of this deliberate civic tendency towards ludico-liturgical 'communion', even in the degraded state of a fashionable rendez-vous around those plays known as *'pièces de boulevard'*.

It is for reasons of this kind too that theatrical voyeurism, less cut off from its exhibitionist correlate, tends more towards a reconciled and community-orientated practice of the scopic perversion (of the component drive). Cinematic voyeurism is less accepted, more 'shame-faced'.

But it is not just a question of global determinations (by the signifier or by history), there are also the personal efforts of the writers, producers and actors. Like all general tendencies, the ones I have signalled are unevenly manifest from work to work. There is no need to be surprised that certain films accept their voyeurism more plainly than do certain plays. It is at this point that the problems of political cinema and political theatre would come in, and also those of a politics of the cinema and the theatre. The militant use of the two signifiers is by no means identical. In this respect the theatre is clearly at a great advantage, thanks to its 'lesser degree of imaginariness', thanks to the direct contact it allows with the audience. The film which aims to be a film of intervention must take this into account in its self-definition. As we know, this is by no means easy.

The difficulty also lies in the fact that cinematic scopophilia, which is 'non-authorised' in the sense I have just pointed out, is at the same time authorised by the mere fact of its institutionalisation. The cinema retains something of the prohibited character peculiar to the vision of the primal scene (the latter is always surprised, never contemplated at leisure, and the permanent cinemas of big cities, with their highly anonymous clientele entering or leaving furtively, in the dark, in the middle of the action, represent this transgression factor rather well) – but also, in a kind of inverse movement which is simply the 'reprise' of the imaginary by the symbolic, the cinema is based on the legalisation and generalisation of the prohibited practice. Thus it shares in miniature in the special regime of certain activities (such as the frequentation of '*maisons de tolérance*', very well named in this respect) that are both official and clandestine, and in which neither of these two characteristics ever quite succeeds in obliterating the other. For the vast majority of the audience, the cinema (rather like the dream in this) represents a kind of enclosure or 'reserve' which escapes the fully social aspect of life although it is accepted and prescribed by it: going to the cinema is one lawful activity among others with its place in the admissible pastimes of the day or the week, and yet that place is a 'hole' in the social cloth, a *loophole* opening on to something slightly more crazy, slightly less approved than what one does the rest of the time.

THEATRE FICTION, CINEMA FICTION

Cinema and theatre do not have the same relation to fiction. There is a fictional cinema, just as there is a fictional theatre, a 'non-fiction' cinema just as there is a non-fiction theatre, because fiction is a great historical and social figure (particularly active in our Western tradition and perhaps in others), endowed with a force of its own which leads it to invest various signifiers (and inversely, to be more or less expelled from them on occasion). It does not follow that these signifiers have an even and uniform affinity with it (that of music, after all, finds it particularly uncongenial, and yet there is such a thing as programme music). The cinematic signifier lends itself the better to fiction in that it is itself fictive and 'absent'. Attempts to 'defictionalise' the spectacle, notably since Brecht, have gone further in the theatre than in the cinema, and not by chance.

But what interests me here is rather the fact that this unevenness is still apparent if one compares only the fictional theatre with the fictional cinema. They are not 'fictional' in quite the same way, and it was this that I had been struck by in 1965 when I compared the 'impression of reality' produced by these two forms of spectacle.[8] At that time my approach was a purely phenomenological one, and it owed very little to psychoanalysis. However, the latter confirms me in my earlier opinion. Underlying all fiction there is the dialectical relationship between a real instance and an imaginary instance, the former's job being to *mimic* the latter: there is the representation, involving real materials and actions, and the represented, the fictional properly speaking. But the balance established between these two poles and hence the precise nuance of the *regime of belief* that the spectator will adopt varies tolerably from one fictional technique to the other. In the cinema as in the theatre, the represented is by definition imaginary; that is what characterises fiction as such, independently of the signifiers in charge of it. But the representation is fully real in the theatre, whereas in the cinema it too is imaginary, the material being already a reflection. Thus the theatrical fiction is experienced more – it is only a matter of a different 'dosage', of a difference of economy, rather, but that is precisely why it is important – as a set of real pieces of behaviour actively directed at the evocation of something unreal, whereas cinematic fiction is experienced rather as the quasi-real presence of that unreal itself; the signifier, already imaginary in its own way, is less palpably so, it plays more into the hands of the diegesis, it tends more to be swallowed up by it, to be credited to its side of the balance-sheet by the spectator. The balance is established slightly closer to the represented, slightly further from the representation.

For the same reason, fictional theatre tends to depend more on the actor (representer), fictional cinema more on the character (represented). This difference has often been emphasised by the theory of the cinema, where it constitutes an already classical theme. In the psychoanalytic field it has also been noted, by Octave Mannoni in particular.[9] Even when the cinema spectator does identify with the actor rather than with the part (somewhat as he does in the theatre), it is with *the actor as 'star'*, i.e. still as a character, and a fabulous one, itself fictional: with the best of his parts.

It may be said that there are much simpler reasons for this difference, that in the theatre the same part can be interpreted by various actors from one production to another, that the actor thus becomes 'detached' from the character, whereas in the cinema there are never several productions (several 'casts') for one film, so the part and its unique interpreter are definitively associated with one another. This is quite true, and it does affect the very different balance of forces between actor and character in theatre and cinema. But it is not a 'simple' fact, nor is it independent of the distance between the respective signifiers, on the contrary, it is but one aspect of that distance (merely a very striking one). If the theatrical part can have a variety of interpreters, that is because its representation is real and mobilises people who are really present each evening (and who are not therefore necessarily always the same). If the cinematic part is fastened once and for all to its interpreter, it is because its representation involves the reflection of the actor and not the actor himself, and because the reflection (the signifier) is *recorded* and is hence no longer capable of change.

5

Disavowal, Fetishism

As can be seen, the cinema has a number of roots in the unconscious and in the great movements illuminated by psychoanalysis, but they can all be traced back to the specific characteristics of the institutionalised signifier. I have gone a little way in tracing some of these roots, that of mirror identification, that of voyeurism and exhibitionism. There is also a third, that of fetishism.

Since the famous article by Freud that inaugurated the problem,[1] psychoanalysis has linked fetish and fetishism closely with castration and the fear it inspires. Castration, for Freud, and even more clearly for Lacan, is first of all the mother's castration, and that is why the main figures it inspires are to a certain degree common to children of both sexes. The child who sees its mother's body is constrained by way of perception, by the 'evidence of the senses', to accept that there are human beings deprived of a penis. But for a long time – and somewhere in it for ever – it will not interpret this inevitable observation in terms of an anatomical difference between the sexes (= penis/vagina). It believes that all human beings originally have a penis and it therefore understands what it has seen as the effect of a mutilation which redoubles its fear that it will be subjected to a similar fate (or else, in the case of the little girl after a certain age, the fear that she has already been subjected to it). Inversely, it is this very terror that is projected on to the spectacle of the mother's body, and invites the reading of an absence where anatomy sees a different conformation. The scenario of castration, in its broad lines, does not differ whether one understands it, like Lacan, as an essentially symbolic drama in which castration takes over in a decisive metaphor all the losses, both real and imaginary, that the child has already suffered (birth trauma, maternal breast, excrement, etc.), or whether on the contrary one tends, like Freud, to take that scenario slightly more literally. Before this *unveiling of a lack* (we are already close to the cinema signifier), the child, in order to avoid too strong an anxiety, will have to double up its belief (another cinematic characteristic) and from then on forever hold two contradictory opinions (proof that in spite of everything the real perception has not been without effect): 'All human beings are endowed with a penis' (primal belief) and 'Some human beings do not have a penis' (evidence of the senses). In other words, it will, perhaps definitively, retain its former belief *beneath* the new one, but it will also hold to its new perceptual observation while *disavowing* it on another level (= denial of perception, disavowal, Freud's '*Verleugnung*'). Thus is established the lasting matrix, the affective prototype of all the splittings of belief which man will henceforth be capable of in the most varied domains, of all the infinitely complex unconscious and occasionally conscious interactions which he will allow himself between 'believing' and 'not believing' and which will on more than one occasion be of great assistance to him in resolving (or denying) delicate problems. (If we were all a little honest with ourselves, we would realise that a truly integral belief, without any 'underside' in which the opposite is believed, would make even the most ordinary everyday life almost impossible.)

At the same time, the child, terrified by what it has seen or glimpsed, will have tried more or less successfully in different cases, to *arrest* its look, for all its life, at what will subsequently become the fetish: at a piece of clothing, for example, which masks the frightening discovery, or else precedes it (underwear, stockings, boots, etc.). The fixation on this 'just before' is thus another form of disavowal, of retreat from the perceived, although its very existence is dialectical evidence of the fact that the perceived has been perceived. The fetishistic prop will become a precondition for the establishment of potency and access to orgasm [*jouissance*], sometimes an indispensable precondition (true fetishism); in other developments it will only be a favourable condition, and one whose weight will vary with respect to the other features of the erotogenic situation as a whole. (It can be observed once again that the defence against desire itself becomes erotic, as the defence against anxiety itself becomes anxiogenic; for an analogous reason: what arises 'against' an affect also arises 'in' it and is not easily separated from it, even if that is its aim.) Fetishism is generally regarded as the 'perversion' par excellence, for it intervenes itself in the 'tabulation' of the others, and above all because they, like it (and this is what makes it their model), are based on the avoidance of castration. The fetish always represents the penis, it is always a substitute for it, whether metaphorically (= it masks its absence) or metonymically (= it is contiguous with its empty place). To sum up, the fetish signifies the penis as absent, it is its negative signifier; supplementing it, it puts a 'fullness' in place of a lack, but in doing so it also affirms that lack. It resumes within itself the structure of disavowal and multiple belief.

These few reminders are intended above all to emphasise the fact that the dossier of fetishism, before any examination of its cinematic extensions, contains two broad aspects which coincide in their depths (in childhood and by virtue of structure) but are relatively distinct in their concrete manifestations, i.e. the problems of belief (= disavowal) and that of the fetish itself, the latter more immediately linked to erotogenicity, whether direct or sublimated.

STRUCTURES OF BELIEF

I shall say very little about the problems of belief in the cinema. First because they are at the centre of the third part of this book. Second because I have already discussed them in this part apropos of identification and the mirror (Chapter 3): I have tried to describe, outside the special case of fiction, a few of the many and successive twists, the 'reversals' (reduplications) that occur in the cinema to articulate together the imaginary, the symbolic and the real; each of these twists presupposes a division of belief; in order to work, the film does not only require a splitting, but a whole series of stages of belief, imbricated together into a chain by a remarkable machinery. In the third place, because the subject has already been largely dealt with by Octave Mannoni in his remarkable studies of the theatrical illusion,[2] with reference to the fictional theatre. Of course, I have said above that theatrical fiction and cinematic fiction are not fictional in the same way; but this deviation concerned the representation, the signifying material and not the represented, i.e. the fiction-fact as such, in which the deviation is much smaller (at any rate so long as one is dealing with *spectacles* such as theatre and cinema – written fiction obviously presents somewhat different problems). Mannoni's analyses are just as valid for the fiction film, with the single reservation that the divergences in representation that I have already discussed (at the end of Chapter 4) are borne in mind.

I shall rest content to adapt these analyses to a cinematic perspective, and not feel obliged to repeat them (not so well) in detail. It is understood that the audience is not duped by the diegetic illusion, it 'knows' that the screen presents no more than a fiction. And yet, it is of vital importance for the correct unfolding of the spectacle that this make-believe be scrupulously respected (or else the fiction film is declared 'poorly made'), that everything is set to work to make the deception effective and to give it an air of truth (this is the problem of *verisimilitude*). Any spectator will tell you that he 'doesn't believe it', but everything happens as if there were nonetheless someone to be deceived, someone who really would 'believe in it'. (I shall say that behind any fiction there is a second fiction: the diegetic events are fictional, that is the first; but everyone pretends to believe that they are true, and that is the second; there is even a third: the general refusal to admit that somewhere in oneself one believes they are genuinely true.) In other words, asks Mannoni, since it is 'accepted' that the audience is incredulous, *who is it who is credulous* and must be maintained in his credulousness by the perfect organisation of the machinery (of the machination)? This credulous person is, of course, another part of ourselves, he is still seated *beneath* the incredulous one, or in his heart, it is he who continues to believe, who disavows what he knows (he for whom all human beings are still endowed with a penis). But by a symmetrical and simultaneous movement, the incredulous person disavows the credulous one; no one will admit that he is duped by the 'plot'. That is why the instance of credulousness is often projected into the outer world and constituted as a separate person, a person completely abused by the diegesis: thus in Corneille's *L'Illusion comique*, a play with a significant title, the character Pridamant, the *naïf*, who does not know what theatre is, and *for whom*, by a reversal foreseen in Corneille's plot itself, the representation of the play is given. By a partial identification with this character, the spectators can sustain their credulousness in all incredulousness.

This instance which believes and also its personified projection have fairly precise equivalents in the cinema: for example, the credulous spectators at the '*Grand Café*' in 1895, frequently and complacently evoked by the incredulous spectators who have come *later* (and are no longer children), those spectators of 1895 who fled their seats in terror when the train entered La Ciotat station (in Lumière's famous film), because they were afraid it would run them down. Or else, in so many films, the character of the 'dreamer' – the sleeping dreamer – who during the film believed (as we did!) that it was true, whereas it was he who saw it all in a dream and who wakes up at the end of the film (as we do again). Octave Mannoni compares these switches of belief with those the ethnologist observes in certain populations in which his informers regularly declare that 'long ago we used to believe in the masks' (these masks are used to deceive children, like our Father Christmas, and adolescents learn at their initiation ceremonies that the 'masks' were in fact adults in disguise); in other words, these societies have always 'believed' in the masks, but have always relegated this belief to a 'long ago': they still believe in them, but always in the aorist tense (like everyone). This 'long ago' is childhood, when one really was duped by masks; among adults, the beliefs of 'long ago' irrigate the unbelief of today, but irrigate it by denegation (one could also say: *by delegation*, by attributing credulity to the child and to former times).

Certain cinematic sub-codes inscribe disavowal into the film in the form of less permanent and more localised figures. They should be studied separately in this perspective. I am not thinking only of films which have been 'dreamt' in their entirety by one of their characters, but also of all the sequences accompanied by a 'voice-off' commentary, spoken sometimes by a character, sometimes by a kind of anonymous 'speaker'. This voice, precisely a voice 'off', beyond jurisdiction, represents the rampart of unbelief (hence it is the opposite of the Pridamant character, yet has the same effect in the last analysis). The distance it establishes between the action and ourselves comforts our feeling that we are not duped by that action: thus reassured (behind the rampart), we can allow ourselves to be duped by it a bit longer (it is the speciality of naïve distanciations to resolve themselves into alibis). There are also all those 'films within a film' which downgear the mechanism of our belief-unbelief and anchor it in several stages, hence more strongly: the included film was an illusion, so the including film (the film as such) was not, or was somewhat less so.[3]

THE CINEMA AS TECHNIQUE

As for the fetish itself, in its cinematic manifestations, who could fail to see that it consists fundamentally of the equipment of the cinema (= its 'technique'), or of the cinema as a whole as equipment and as technique, for fiction films and others? It is no accident that in the cinema some cameramen, some directors, some critics, some spectators demonstrate a real 'fetishism of technique', often noted or denounced as such ('fetishism' is taken here in its ordinary sense, which is rather loose but does contain within it the analytical sense that I shall attempt to disengage). As strictly defined, the fetish, like the apparatus of the cinema, is a *prop*, the prop that disavows a lack and in doing so affirms it without wishing to. A prop, too, which is as it were placed on the body of the object; a prop which is the penis, since it negates its absence, and hence a partial object that makes the whole object lovable and desirable. The fetish is also the point of departure for specialised practices, and as is well known, desire in its modalities is all the more 'technical' the more perverse it is.

Thus with respect to the desired body – to the body of desire rather – the fetish is in the same position as the technical equipment of the cinema with respect to the cinema as a whole. A fetish, the cinema as a technical performance, as prowess, as an *exploit*, an exploit that underlines and denounces the lack on which the whole arrangement is based (the absence of the object, replaced by its reflection), an exploit which consists at the same time of making this absence forgotten. The cinema fetishist is the person who is enchanted at what the machine is capable of, at the *theatre of shadows* as such. For the establishment of his full potency for cinematic enjoyment [*jouissance*] he must think at every moment (and above all *simultaneously*) of the force of presence the film has and of the absence on which this force is constructed.[4] He must constantly compare the result with the means deployed (and hence pay attention to the technique), for his pleasure lodges in the gap between the two. Of course, this attitude appears most clearly in the 'connoisseur', the cinephile, but it also occurs, as a partial component of cinematic pleasure, in those who just go to the cinema: if they do go it is partly in order to be carried away by the film (or the fiction, if there is one), but also in order to *appreciate* as such the machinery that is carrying them away: they will say, precisely when they have been carried away, that the film was a 'good' one, that it was 'well made' (the same thing is said in French of a harmonious body).

It is clear that fetishism, in the cinema as elsewhere, is closely linked to the good object. The function of the fetish is to restore the latter, threatened in its 'goodness' (in Melanie Klein's sense) by the terrifying discovery of the lack. Thanks to the fetish, which covers the wound and itself becomes erotogenic, the object as a whole can become desirable again without excessive fear. In a similar way, the whole cinematic institution is as it were *covered* by a thin and omni-present garment, a stimulating prop through which it is consumed: the ensemble of its equipment and its tricks – and not just the celluloid strip, the *'pellicule'* or 'little skin' which has been rightly mentioned in this connection[5] – of the equipment which *needs* the lack in order to stand out in it by contrast, but which only affirms it insofar as it ensures that it is forgotten, and which lastly (its third twist) needs it also not to be forgotten, for fear that at the same stroke the fact that *it* caused it to be forgotten will be forgotten.

The fetish is the cinema in its *physical* state. A fetish is always material: insofar as one can make up for it by the power of the symbolic alone one is precisely no longer a fetishist. At this point it is important to recall that of all the arts the cinema is the one that involves the most extensive and complex equipment; the 'technical' dimension is more obtrusive here than elsewhere. Along with television, it is the only art that is also an industry, or at least is so from the outset (the others become industries subsequently: music through the gramophone record or the cassette, books by mass printings and publishing trusts, etc.). In this respect only architecture is a little like it; there are 'languages' that are *heavier* than others, more dependent on 'hardware'.

At the same time as it localises the penis, the fetish represents by synecdoche the whole body of the object as desirable. Similarly, interest in the equipment and technique is the privileged representative of *love for the cinema*.

The Law is what permits desire: the cinematic equipment is the instance thanks to which the imaginary turns into the symbolic, thanks to which the lost object (the absence of what is filmed) becomes the law and the principle of a specific and instituted signifier, which it is legitimate to desire.

For in the structure of the fetish there is another point on which Mannoni quite rightly insists and which directly concerns my present undertaking. Because it attempts to disavow the evidence of the senses, the fetish is evidence that this evidence has indeed been *recorded* (like a tape stored in the memory). The fetish is not inaugurated because the child still believes its mother has a penis (= order of the imaginary), for if it still believed it completely, as 'before', it would no longer need the fetish. It is inaugurated because the child now 'knows very well' that its mother has no penis. In other words, the fetish not only has disavowal value, but also *knowledge value*.

That is why, as I said a moment ago, the fetishism of cinematic technique is especially well developed among the 'connoisseurs' of the cinema. That is also why the theoretician of the cinema necessarily retains within him – at the cost of a new backward turn that leads him to interrogate technique, to symbolise the fetish, and hence to maintain it as he dissolves it – an interest in the equipment without which he would not be motivated to study it.

Indeed, the equipment is not just physical (= the fetish proper); it also has its discursive imprints, its extensions in the very text of the film. Here is revealed the specific movement of theory: when it shifts from a fascination with technique to the critical study of the different *codes* that this equipment authorises. *Concern for the signifier* in the cinema derives from a fetishism that has taken up a position as far as possible along its cognitive flank. To adapt the formula by which Octave Mannoni defines disavowal (= 'I know very well, but all the same...'), the study of the signifier is a libidinal position which consists in weakening the 'but all the same' and profiting by this saving of energy to dig deeper into the 'I know very well', which thus becomes 'I know nothing at all, but I desire to know'.

FETISH AND FRAME

Just like the other psychical structures that constitute the foundation of the cinema, fetishism does not intervene only in the constitution of the signifier, but also in certain of its more particular configurations. Here we have *framings* and also certain *camera movements* (the latter can anyway be defined as progressive changes in framing).

Cinema with directly erotic subject matter deliberately plays on the edges of the frame and the progressive, if need be incomplete revelations allowed by the camera as it moves, and this is no accident. Censorship is involved here: censorship of films and censorship in Freud's sense. Whether the form is static (framing) or dynamic (camera movements), the principle is the same; the point is to gamble simultaneously on the excitation of desire and its non-fulfilment (which is its opposite and yet favours it), by the infinite variations made possible precisely by the studios' technique on the exact emplacement of the *boundary* that bars the look, that puts an end to the 'seen', that inaugurates the downward (or upward) tilt into the dark, towards the unseen, the guessed-at. The framing and its displacements (that determine the *emplacement*) are in themselves forms of 'suspense' and are extensively used in suspense films, though they retain this function in other cases. They have an inner affinity with the mechanisms of desire, its postponements, its new impetus, and they retain this affinity in other places than erotic sequences (the only difference lies in the *quantum* which is sublimated and the *quantum* which is not). The way the cinema, with its wandering framings (wandering like the look, like the caress), finds the means to reveal space has something to do with a kind of permanent undressing, a generalised strip-tease, a less direct but more perfected strip-tease, since it also makes it possible to dress space again, to remove from view what it has previously shown, to *take back* as well as to retain (like the child at the moment of the birth of the fetish, the child who has already seen, but whose look beats a rapid retreat): a strip-tease pierced with 'flash-backs', inverted sequences that then give new impetus to the forward movement. These veiling-unveiling procedures can also be compared with certain cinematic 'punctuations', especially slow ones strongly marked by a concern for control and expectation (slow fade-ins and fade-outs, irises, 'drawn out' lap-dissolves like those of Sternberg).[6]

'Theorise', he says ...
(Provisional Conclusion)

The psychoanalytic constitution of the cinema signifier is a very wide problem, one containing, so to speak, a number of 'panels'. I cannot examine them all here, and there will surely be some that I have not even mentioned.

However, something tells me that (for the present) I can stop here. I wanted to give a first idea of the field I perceive and, to begin with, to assure myself that I was indeed perceiving it (I was not certain of it all at once).

Now I shall turn back on this study itself as an unfolding of my initial dream. Psychoanalysis does not illuminate only the film, but also the conditions of desire of whoever makes himself its theoretician. Interwoven into every analytical undertaking is the thread of a self-analysis.

I have loved the cinema, I no longer love it. I still love it. What I have wished to do in these pages is to keep at a distance, as in the scopic practice I have discussed, that which in me (= in everyone) *can* love it: to retain it as *questioned*. As questioning, too, for in wishing to construct the film into an object of knowledge one extends, by a supplementary degree of sublimation, the passion for seeing that made the cinephile and the institution themselves. Initially an undivided passion, entirely occupied in preserving the cinema as a good object (imaginary passion, passion for the imaginary), it subsequently splits into two diverging and reconverging desires, one of which 'looks' at the other; this is the theoretical break, and like all breaks it is also a link: that of theory with its object.

I have used words like 'love of the cinema'. I hope I will have been understood. The point is not to restrict them to their usual meaning, the meaning suggested by 'archive rats' or fanatical

'Macmahonites' (who provide no more than exaggerated examples). Nor is the point to relapse into the absurd opposition between the affective and the intellectual. The point is to ask why many people go to the cinema when they are not obliged to, how they manage to 'assimilate' the rules of this game which is exceedingly complex and historically fairly new, how they themselves become cogs of the institution. For anyone who asks this question, 'loving the cinema' and 'understanding film' are no more than two closely mingled aspects of one vast socio-psychical machinery.

As for the person who looks at this machine itself (the theoretician who desires to know it), I have said that he was necessarily sadistic. There is no sublimation, as Freud himself insisted, without 'defusion of the drives'. The good object has moved to the side of knowledge and the cinema becomes a bad object (a dual displacement which makes it easy for 'science' to stand back). The cinema is 'persecuted', but this persistence is also a reparation (the knowing posture is both aggressive and depressive), a reparation of a specific kind, peculiar to the semiologist; the *restoration* to the theoretical body of what has been taken from the *institution*, from the code which is being 'studied'.

To study the cinema: what an odd formula! How can it be done without 'breaking' its beneficial image, all that idealism about film as an 'art' full and simple, the seventh of the name? By breaking the toy one loses it, and that is the position of the semiotic discourse; it feeds on this loss, it puts in its place the hoped for advance of knowledge: it is an inconsolable discourse that consoles itself, that takes itself by the hand and goes to work. Lost objects are the only ones one is afraid to lose, and the semiologist is he who rediscovers them *from the other side: 'Il n'y a de cause que de ce qui cloche'* – 'there is a cause only in something that doesn't work'.[1]

Notes and References to Part I

CHAPTER 1: THE IMAGINARY AND THE 'GOOD OBJECT' IN THE CINEMA AND IN THE THEORY OF THE CINEMA

Translators' notes are given in square brackets, the author's own notes without brackets.

1 [The symbolic, the imaginary and the real: for these key terms in Lacan's reading of Freud, see the entries 'Imaginary' and 'Symbolic' in J. Laplanche and J.-B. Pontalis, *The Language of Psychoanalysis*, trans. D. Nicholson-Smith (London: The Hogarth Press, 1973), a dictionary which can usefully be con- • sulted for all the psychoanalytic terminology to be found in this book.]

2 [The French terms *énonciation* and *énoncé*, referring respectively to the act of speaking (or writing, or constructing a sequence of images, etc.) and to what is said (written, etc.) are here translated throughout as 'enunciation' and 'statement'.]

3 J. Lacan, 'Radiophonie', *Scilicet*, 2–3 (1970) p. 75.

4 E. Morin, *Le Cinéma ou l'homme imaginaire* (Paris: Ed. de Minuit, 1956).

5 J. Lacan, 'Sur la théorie du symbolisme d'Ernest Jones', *Ecrits* (Paris: Ed. du Seuil, 1966) p. 711.

6 'Cinéma: effets idéologiques produits par l'appareil de base', *Cinéthique*, 7–8, pp. 1–8 (translated as 'Ideological Effects of the Basic Cinematographic Apparatus', *Film Quarterly*, XXVIII, 2 (1974–5) 39–47), 'Le dispositif: approches métapsychologiques de l'impression de réalité', *Communications*, 23 (1975) 56–72, (translated as 'The Apparatus', *Camera Obscura*, 1 (1976) 104–26).

7 J. Lacan, 'The direction of the treatment and the principles of its power', *Ecrits. A Selection*, trans. A. Sheridan (London: Tavistock Publications, 1977) p. 272.

8 [Lacan's conception of the mirror stage is discussed in more detail in Part I, ch. 3, below. See Laplanche and Pontalis, op.cit., and J. Lacan, 'The Mirror Stage' in *Ecrits*, trans. Sheridan, pp. 1–7.]

9 [The capitalised Other: the mirror stage establishes a dual relation between the child and its mirror image, internalised as the ego; this produces the register of what Lacan calls the imaginary, which constitutes a

81

moment of any relation to an other (with a small o) or object later in life. However, the imaginary relation of ego and other is immediately marked by and subordinated to the symbolic order through the set of introjections of the ego that culminate in the ego ideal, and the relativisation of any other or object with respect to a primordially lost object which a real object or other can only represent metonymically. Ego and other are then subordinated to an order that is always elsewhere, more radically Other than any other and hence unconscious, *the* unconscious. The absolute character of this otherness is marked in Lacan's writings by the use of an initial capital. The establishment of this subordination culminates in the resolution of the Oedipus complex, but it begins immediately after, or even during, the mirror stage itself, in the presence of a third party (the mother) in the mirror with the child's image, and in the *fort-da* game, the child's discovery through repetition of presence and absence.]

10 [In Melanie Klein's account of the pre-Oedipal development of the child, its earliest drives, particularly the oral drives associated with feeding and the breast, are primordially ambivalent, both loving and destructive; in one of the earliest phases of development, called the 'paranoid-schizoid position' (position – *Einstellung* – because these phases structure unconscious phantasy and can therefore recur at any age), the child's weak ego handles this ambivalence by splitting the object (e.g. the breast) into a good and a bad object, projecting its own love and hate on to its two aspects (gratifying, frustrating); at a later phase, the 'depressive position', the two objects are reunited, the ego being reconciled to the ambivalence by inhibition of the aggression and reparation (*Wiedergutmachung*) of the object.]

11 [Ego, super-ego and id: from around 1920, Freud distinguished three psychic instances, the id or instinctual pole of the personality, the ego, representing the interests of the total personality and cathected (see note 18 below) with narcissistic libido, and the super-ego, corresponding roughly to the earlier concept of the ego ideal, a critical instance resulting from the internalisation of parental demands and prohibitions. This second topography does not contradict the earlier division between unconscious, preconscious and conscious, but nor do its divisions correspond to those of the first topography; in particular, more than the id is unconscious.]

12 [Primary process and secondary process: Freud distinguished two modes of functioning of the psychical apparatus, an unconscious primary process, dominated by the pleasure principle, i.e. allowing a free flow of psychical energy from representation to representation and fully recathecting (see note 18 below) desired representations, and a preconscious and conscious secondary process, dominated by the reality principle, in which psychical energy is bound, flowing only in a controlled fashion, with representations more stably cathected, satisfaction postponed, allowing rational thought and the testing of the various possible ways to satisfaction. 'Secondarisation' is the binding process that the making conscious of a representation or desire involves.]

13 [*Jouissance*: the French term means both 'orgasm' and simple 'enjoyment' or 'pleasure'. It has been translated as seemed best from the context, but the ambiguity should always be borne in mind.]

14 In 'L'effet du réel', *Communications*, 11 (1968) p. 85; translated as 'The Real-

istic Effect', *Film Reader*, 3 (1978) 131–5.
15 *Remembrance of Things Past*, vol. i, *Swann's Way*, Part One, trans. C.K. Scott Moncrieff (London: Chatto and Windus, 1941), pp. 93–4.
16 'Negation' (1925) in J. Strachey (ed.), *Standard Edition of the Complete Psychological Works of Sigmund Freud*, 24 volumes (London: The Hogarth Press, 1953–66) vol. xix, pp. 235–9.
   [Unless otherwise stated, references to Freud's work in the rest of this book will be references to the *Standard Edition*.]
17 [Dream-work: the manifest content of the dream is the product of the dream-work which transforms (and distorts in the interests of censorship) the materials of the dream: dream-thoughts, day's residues and bodily stimuli. Analysis works backwards from the analysand's account of his manifest dream to the materials of the dream. The main mechanisms of the dream-work are condensation (accumulation of a number of dream-thoughts, etc. into a single manifest representation), displacement (shift of cathexis – see note 18 – from one representation to an associated one, or replacement of the former by the latter), considerations of representability (translation of abstract thoughts into concrete images) and secondary revision (assembly of the result of the other three mechanisms into a relatively coherent and comprehensible whole).]
18 [Cathexis: the term adopted in English (e.g. in the *Standard Edition*) to translate Freud's *Besetzung*, in French usually (as here) *investissement*, meaning the attachment of psychical energy deriving from the drives to a representation or object.]

CHAPTER 2: THE INVESTIGATOR'S IMAGINARY

1 If I see this division as a deliberate simplification (but perhaps that is precisely why it is useful), this is for various reasons, two of which are more important than the rest: (i) psychoanalysis has not introduced only the idea of the primary process, but also the very distinction between the primary and the secondary (hence it has 're-founded' the secondary); (ii) inversely, certain linguists, such as Emile Benveniste, for example, in his studies of the personal pronouns, go beyond the study of the pure 'statement' and through their reflections on the enunciation enter on a road which leads closer to the 'primary', to the constitution of the subject, etc.
2 Lacan: 'The order of the symbol can no longer be conceived as constituted by man, but rather as constituting him', translated from 'Le séminaire sur "La Lettre volée"', *Ecrits*, p. 46.
3 E.g. Lévi-Strauss: myths think themselves out among themselves.
4 See Benveniste's notion that, in a sense, it is *langue* that 'contains' society rather than the reverse ('Sémiologie de la langue', *Problèmes de linguistique générale*, vol. ii (Paris: Gallimard, 1974) p. 62).
5 It will be remembered that this is what Stalin said of language. Lacan recalls it maliciously ('The Agency of the Letter in the Unconscious', *Ecrits*, trans. Sheridan, p. 176, note 7).
6 L. Sève, *Marxisme et théorie de la personnalité* (Editions Sociales, 1969). See especially p. 200. A juxtastructural phenomenon differs from a superstruc-

tural phenomenon in two respects: (i) it is not exactly a *consequence* of the 'base' since it forms part of it, in addition to the strictly infrastructural determinations; and (ii) it represents the biological element in man: as such it is distinct from the 'social base' and 'as it were *laterally engaged* with it'.

7 In many Hollywood film scripts, for instance, cf. Marc Vernet's article 'Mise en scène: U.S.A. – Freud: effets spéciaux' in *Communications*, 23 (1975) 223–34.

8 Raymond Bellour, when he read this article in manuscript, pointed out to me that this paragraph is debatable, and at all events incomplete: indeed, as Lacan emphasises, the *Psychopathology of Everyday Life* and *Jokes* are in a sense the direct 'sequel' to *The Interpretation of Dreams*; these books constitute a kind of single demonstration in three parts, and a highly coherent one, which (in some respects) already contains the totality of Freud's discovery. All three works, more so than others, deal directly, via numerous concrete examples, and not just in the specific region of the 'pathological', with the very movements of the mind, its trajectories, its 'processes', its modes of progress and ordering. In other words, the essentials of the discovery of the unconscious, along with its consequences in the preconscious (= the problem of the 'second censorship', which Freud held to be identical to the first from the dynamic viewpoint; cf. p. 31).

For this reason, the *Psychopathology* and *Jokes* ought not to be listed separately; they belong, as prime candidates even, to the first category, that of the 'theoretical' works.

And yet (and this is not, I think, contradictory) there is something which sets them apart, and stresses what they have in common with each other. This is what I was trying to define, and I have not changed my mind. But I was only seeing one aspect of the question, and Raymond Bellour was right to remind me about the other.

9 D. Percheron, 'Rire au cinéma', *Communications*, 23 (1975) 190–201. J.-P. Simon, *Trajets de sémiotique filmique A la recherche des Marx Brothers*) (Editions Albatros, 1977); on the metapsychology of the comic film see in particular the section headed 'Le film comique entre la "transgression" du genre et le "genre" de la transgression'.

10 Things never happen in isolation when an idea or a research tendency is 'in the air', called for by the general development of the intellectual field. When this article first appeared in the spring of 1975 I was becoming interested in the possibility of the 'nosographic' approach, and was keen to locate it, as it were in advance, in the varied field of the research undertakings which might link the cinema-object and the tools of psychoanalysis. But there did not seem to be a fully developed example, nothing in the way of a detailed study say of a whole film or a major film-maker. By a striking convergence it was in autumn 1975 that Dominique Fernandez' *Eisenstein* appeared (Paris: Ed. Grasset), a study applying the psychocritical method to the life and work of the great Soviet film-maker.

11 Thus, in the book by Dominique Fernandez I referred to a moment ago, the editing codes that Eisenstein was fond of (extreme fragmentation, discontinuity, etc.) are linked to his deep anxieties and the desire he experienced to symbolically deny his childhood (see in particular pp. 167–9).

12 'Interminable script' says one of my students (Jorge Dana), for in a film,

everything can be diegeticised.

13 *Language and Cinema* (Paris: Larousse, 1971), trans. D.J. Umiker-Sebeok (The Hague: Mouton, 1974). Cf. in particular chs. v and vi, pp. 53–90 in the French; 70–120 in the English.

14 Danielle Digne, 'L'Empire et la marque', unpublished thesis (Mémoire de troisième cycle) 1975.

15 *The Interpretation of Dreams* (vol. v) p. 499; and 'A Metapsychological Supplement to the Theory of Dreams' (vol. xiv) p. 229.

16 *Language and Cinema*, trans. Umiker-Sebeok, pp. 78–9.

17 E.g. in section 1 of 'The Unconscious'(vol. xiv) pp. 167 and 170. I use this definition of 'latent' because it is convenient here; it corresponds to the unconscious in the descriptive, not the topographical sense, and therefore does not exclude the preconscious. But it is well known that elsewhere Freud reserves the term 'latent' for the preconscious alone, thus tending to set it up in opposition to the 'unconscious'; on the topic of dreams, for example, Freud sometimes distinguishes between the 'latent content' and the 'unconscious desire', although in other passages the first of these terms covers the whole.

18 'The Unconscious' (vol. xiv) pp. 173, 191, 193–4, and *The Interpretation of Dreams* (vol. v) pp. 615, 617–8.

19 [Gilles Deleuze has written many works of philosophy, including studies of the English empiricists, Spinoza and Nietzsche. In 1973, together with Félix Guattari, he published *L'Anti-Œdipe*, a critique of Freud (also directed against Lacan) that re-emphasises Freud's notion of a libidinal economy, arguing that human beings are 'desiring machines', mechanisms channelling and rechannelling libidinal flows, that societies are no more than extensions of this channelling, and that Freud's (and Lacan's) insistence on the Œdipus complex represents a blocking of the productivity of these machines in the interests of the institution of the family and the repressive political apparatuses that institution gives rise to. Jean-François Lyotard has written studies of the visual arts from a similar (but not identical) position: cf. *Discours, figure* (Paris: Editions Klincksieck, 1971).]

20 *Le Fœtus astral* (Paris: Christian Bourgois, 1970).

21 Special number on 'Psychoanalysis and the cinema', 23 (1975) the title of the article is 'Le blocage symbolique'.

22 *Language and Cinema*, trans. Umiker-Sebeok, especially ch. vi. 3.

23 See *Language and Cinema*, trans. Umiker-Sebeok, especially ch. x. 7.

24 For example 'Le travail du film II' in *Communications*, 23 (1975).

25 See *Language and Cinema*, trans. Umiker-Sebeok, ch. x, entirely given over to this problem.

26 *Muriel* (Paris: Editions Galilée, 1975) by Claude Bailbé, Michel Marie and Marie-Claire Ropars offers a remarkable study of one of these intermediate positions.

CHAPTER 3: IDENTIFICATION, MIRROR

1 'Le temps logique et l'assertion de certitude anticipée', *Ecrits*, pp. 197–213.

2 'The Ego and the Id' (vol. xix) pp. 26 and 30 (on 'desexualised social senti-

ment'); see also (on the subject of paranoia) 'On Narcissism: an Introduction' (vol. xɪv) pp. 95–6, 101–2.
3 See p. 81 note 6.
4 [*Derrière la tête* means 'at the back of one's mind' as well as 'behind one's head'.] See André Green: 'L'Ecran bi-face, un œil derrière la tête', *Psychanalyse et cinéma*, 1 January 1970 (no further issues appeared), pp. 15–22. It will be clear that in the passage that follows my analysis coincides in places with that of André Green.
5 'The Ego and the Id' (vol. xɪx) p. 18; *The Interpretation of Dreams* (vol. v) p. 615 (= consciousness as a sense organ) and p. 574 (= consciousness as a dual recording surface, internal and external); 'The Unconscious' (vol. xɪv) p. 171 (psychical processes are in themselves unconscious, consciousness is a function that *perceives* a small proportion of them), etc.
6 'The Film and the New Psychology', lecture to the Institut des Hautes Etudes Cinématographiques (13 March 1945), translated in *Sense and Nonsense* (Evanston, Illinois: North-Western University Press, 1964) pp. 48–59.
7 See section ɪɪ of 'Current Problems of Film Theory', *Screen*, 14, 1–2 (1973) pp. 45–9.
8 On these problems see Michel Colin, 'Le Film: transformation du texte du roman', unpublished thesis (Mémoire de troisième cycle) 1974.
9 *Inhibitions, Symptoms and Anxiety* (vol. xx) pp. 87–8.

CHAPTER 4: THE PASSION FOR PERCEIVING

1 See especially *The Four Fundamental Concepts of Psycho-Analysis*, trans. A. Sheridan (London: The Hogarth Press, 1977) pp. 180 and 195–6.
2 'Repression' (vol. xɪv) pp. 146–7; 'Instincts and their Vicissitudes' (vol. xɪv) pp. 122 and 134n.; 'The Ego and the Id'(vol. xɪx) p. 30; 'On Narcissism: an Introduction' (vol. xɪv) p. 94, etc.
3 More precisely: lending themselves through their peculiar characteristics to a perversion which is not the drive itself, but the subject's position with respect to it (*The Four Fundamental Concepts of Psycho-Analysis*, trans. Sheridan, pp. 181–3). Remember that for Freud as well as for Lacan, the drive is always 'componential' (the child is polymorphously perverse, etc.).
4 'Instincts and their Vicissitudes' (vol. xɪv) pp. 129–30.
5 'Instincts and their Vicissitudes' (vol. xɪv) p. 138.
6 Lacan, *The Four Fundamental Concepts of Psycho-Analysis*, trans. Sheridan, pp. 167–8.
7 See the paragraph with this title in Jean-François Lyotard's article 'L'acinéma', *Revue d'Esthétique*, 2–3–4 (1973) pp. 357–69.
8 C. Metz, 'On the Impression of Reality in the Cinema' in *Essais sur la signification au cinéma*, vol. ɪ (Paris: Klincksieck, 1968), translated as *Film Language: a Semiotics of the Cinema*, M. Taylor (New York: O.U.P., 1974).
9 See O. Mannoni, 'L'Illusion comique ou le théâtre du point de vue de l'imaginaire' in *Clefs pour l'imaginaire ou l'autre scène* (Paris: Editions du Seuil, 1969) p. 180.

CHAPTER 5: DISAVOWAL, FETISHISM

1 'Fetishism' (vol. xxi) pp. 152–7. See also Octave Mannoni's important study, 'Je sais bien, mais quand même...' [I know very well, but all the same....] in *Clefs pour l'imaginaire ou l'autre scène.*
2 'L'Illusion comique ou le théâtre du point de vue de l'imaginaire.'
3 A startling (though only partial) resemblance with the case of 'dreams within a dream'; cf. *The Interpretation of Dreams* (vol. iv) p. 338.
4 I have studied this phenomenon at slightly greater length in 'Trucage et cinéma' in *Essais sur la signification au cinéma*, vol. ii (Paris: Klincksieck, 1972) pp. 173–92.
5 Roger Dadoun, '"King Kong": du monstre comme démonstration', *Littéra-ture*, 8 (1972) p. 109; Octave Mannoni, *Clefs pour l'imaginaire ou l'autre scène*, p. 180.
6 Reading this article in manuscript, Thierry Kuntzel has pointed out to me that in this paragraph I perhaps lean slightly too far towards fetishism and fetishism alone in discussing filmic figures that depend just as much on *cinematic perversion* in general: the hypertrophy of the perceptual component drive with its *mises-en-scène*, its progressions-retentions, its calculated post-ponements, etc. This objection seems to me (after the event) to be correct. I shall have to come back to it. Fetishism, as is well known, is closely linked to perversion (cf. pp. 69–71), although it does not exhaust it. Hence the diffi-culty. For the cinematic effects I am evoking here (playing on the framing and its displacements), the properly fetishistic element seems to me to be the '*bar*', the edge of the screen, the separation between the seen and the unseen, the 'arrestation' of the look. Once the seen or the unseen are envisaged rather than their intersection (their edge), we are dealing with scopic per-version itself, which goes beyond the strict province of the fetish.

'THEORISE', HE SAYS... (PROVISIONAL CONCLUSION)

1 Lacan, *The Four Fundamental Concepts of Psycho-Analysis*, trans. Sheridan, p. 22. [Lacan contrasts a *cause*, as an occult property, with a *law*, in which 'causes' are smoothly absorbed as variables in a function; the unconscious, however, will remain a cause in the occult sense, because its order exceeds any particular function: it is the Law rather than a law, *enunciation* rather than *statement*, '*lalangue*' rather than a *langue* – hence its privileged manifes-tation in the lapse, the mistake, the point at which discourse 'limps'.]

Part II

Story/Discourse (A Note on Two Kinds of Voyeurism)

Translated by Celia Britton and Annwyl Williams

Story/Discourse[1]
(A Note on Two Kinds of Voyeurism)

I'm at the cinema. The images of a Hollywood Film unfold in front of me. It doesn't even have to be Hollywood: the images of any film based on narration and representation – of any 'film', in fact, in the sense in which the word is most often used today – the kind of film which it is the film industry's business to produce. The film industry, and also, more generally, the *institution of cinema* in its present form. For these films do not only represent the millions that have to be invested, made to show a profit, recovered along with the profit, and then reinvested. Beyond this, they presuppose, if only to guarantee the financial feedback, that the audiences will come and buy their tickets and therefore that they will *want* to do so. The institution of cinema reaches far beyond the sector (or the aspect) which is usually thought of as directly commercial.

Is it, then, a question of 'ideology'? In other words, the audiences have the same ideology as the films that are provided for them, they fill the cinemas, and that is how the machine keeps turning. Of course. But it is also a question of desire, and hence of symbolic positioning. In Emile Benveniste's terms, the traditional film is presented as story, and not as discourse. And yet it is discourse, if we refer it back to the film-maker's intentions, the influence he wields over the general public, etc.; but the basic characteristic of this kind of discourse, and the very principle of its effectiveness as discourse, is precisely that it obliterates all traces of the enunciation, and masquerades as story. The tense of story is of course always the 'past definite';[2] similarly, the narrative plenitude and transparency of this kind of film is based on a refusal to admit that anything is lacking, or that anything has to be sought for; it shows us only the other side of the lack and the

91

search, an image of satiety and fulfilment, which is always to some extent regressive: it is a formula for granting a wish which was never formulated in the first place.

We talk about political 'regimes', economic regimes; and in French we can also say that a car, depending on how its gear-box is constructed, can have three, or four, or five 'regimes'. Desire, too, has its regimes, its short-lived or long-lasting plateaux of economic stabilisation, its positions of equilibrium in relation to defence, its gain formations (fiction is one of these, since it presents the narrated without the narrator, rather like in dreams or phantasy): adjustments which are not easy to get right, which must first go through a long process of running-in (from 1895 on, the cinema tried out a lot of different ideas before finding what is now its standard formula; adjustments which social evolution produces, and will alter as time goes by, though (as with states of political equilibrium, again) not constantly, for there are not endless possibilities to choose between, and of those that are actually functioning, each is a self-contained machine which tends to perpetuate itself and is responsible for the mechanisms of its own reproduction (the memory of every film one has enjoyed acts as a model for the next one). This is true of the kind of films which fill our 'screens' today – external screens in the cinemas, and internal screens of the *fictional*, that is, of the imaginary which is provided for us by 'diegesis', an imaginary at once shielded and openly allowed.

How should I 'set' my own position as subject, in order to describe these films? I find myself writing these lines, which are also a tribute to one of the scholars who has been most aware of all the kinds of distancing from the statement which can be created by the enunciation as a separate instance, and all the repercussions with which the statement itself can be reinvested. So, for as long as it takes me to write this, I shall take up a particular listening-post in myself (not, of course, the only one), a post which will allow my 'object', the standard-issue film, to emerge as fully as possible. In the cultural psychodrama of 'positions' I shall adopt neither the role of the person who likes that kind of film nor the role of the person who does not like them. I shall let the words on these pages come from the person who likes to see these films in quotation marks, who likes to savour them as dated allusions (like a wine whose charm lies partly in our knowing its vintage), accepting the ambivalent coexistence of this anachronistic affection with the sadism of the connoisseur who wants to break open the toy and see into the guts of the machine.

Because the film I am thinking of is a very real phenomenon (socially, analytically). It cannot be reduced to a gimmick on the part of a few film-producers out to make money, and good at it. It also exists as our product, the product of the society which consumes it, as an *orientation of consciousness*, whose roots are unconscious, and without which we would be unable to understand the overall trajectory which founds the institution and accounts for its continuing existence. It is not enough for the studios to hand over a polished little mechanism labelled 'fiction film'; the play of elements still has to be realised, or more simply it has to occur: it has to *take place*. And this place is inside each one of us, in an economic arrangement which history has shaped at the same time as it was shaping the film industry.

I'm at the cinema. I am present at the screening of the film. *I am present*. Like the midwife attending a birth who, simply by her presence, assists the woman in labour, I am present for the film in a double capacity (though they are really one and the same) as witness and as assistant: I watch, and I help. By watching the film I help it to be born, I help it to live, since only in me will it live, and since it is made for that purpose: to be watched, in other words to be brought into being by nothing other than the look. The film is exhibitionist, as was the classical nineteenth century novel with its plot and characters, which the cinema is now copying (semiologically), continuing (historically), and replacing (sociologically, since the written text has now moved in other directions).

The film is exhibitionist, and at the same time it is not. Or at least, there are several kinds of exhibitionism, and correspondingly several kinds of voyeurism, several possible ways of deploying the scopic drive, not all of which are equally reconciled to the fact of their own existence, but which attain in varying degrees to a relaxed, socially acceptable practice of the perversion. True exhibitionism contains an element of triumph, and is always bilateral, in the exchange of phantasies if not in its concrete actions:

it belongs to discourse rather than story, and is based entirely on the play of reciprocal identifications, on the conscious acceptance of the to-and-fro movement between *I* and *you*. Through the *mise-en-scène* of its contrary impulses, the perverted couple (which has its equivalents in the history of cultural productions) takes on the pressure of the voyeuristic desire – ultimately the same for both partners (as it was in its narcissistic origins, in the very young child) – in the never-ending alternation of its two sides: active/passive, subject/object, seeing/being seen. If there is an element of triumph in this kind of representation, it is because what it exhibits is not exactly the exhibited object but, via the object, the exhibition itself. The exhibited partner knows that he is being looked at, wants this to happen, and identifies with the voyeur whose object he is (but who also constitutes him as subject). This is a different economic regime, and a different tuning of desire: not that of the fiction film, but the one which classical theatre sometimes comes close to, when actor and spectator are in each other's presence, when the *playing* (of the actor, and the audience) is also a distribution of roles (of 'character parts') in a game, an active complicity which works both ways, a ceremony which is always partly civic, involving more than the private individual: a festival. The theatre still retains – even if only in the form of a caricature, of theatre as a social rendez-vous when the play is one of those insipid offerings of the *théâtre de boulevard* – something of its Greek origins, of its initial atmosphere of citizenship, of public holidays, when a whole population put itself on display for its own enjoyment. (But even then there were the slaves, who did not go to the theatre, and who collectively made it possible for a certain kind of democracy to function, a democracy from which they were excluded.)

The film is not exhibitionist. I watch it, but it doesn't watch me watching it. Nevertheless, it knows that I am watching it. But it doesn't want to know. This fundamental disavowal is what has guided the whole of classical cinema into the paths of 'story', relentlessly erasing its discursive basis, and making it (at best) a beautiful closed object which must remain unaware of the pleasure it gives us (literally, over its dead body), an object whose contours remain intact and which cannot therefore be torn open into an inside and an outside, into a subject capable of saying 'Yes!'

The film knows that it is being watched, and yet does not know. Here we must be a little more precise. Because, in fact, the one who knows and the one who doesn't know are not completely indistinguishable (all disavowals, by their very nature, are also split into two). The one who knows is the cinema, the *institution* (and its presence in every film, in the shape of the discourse which is behind the fiction); the one who doesn't want to know is the film, the *text* (in its final version): the story. During the screening of the film, the audience is present, and aware of the actor, but the actor is absent, and unaware of the audience; and during the shooting, when the actor was present, it was the audience which was absent. In this way the cinema manages to be both exhibitionist and secretive. The exchange of seeing and being-seen will be fractured in its centre, and its two disjointed halves allocated to different moments in time: another split. I never see my partner, but only his photograph. This does not make me any less of a voyeur, but it involves a different regime, that of the primal scene and the keyhole. The rectangular screen permits all kinds of fetishisms, all the nearly-but-not-quite effects, since it can decide at exactly what height to place the barrier which cuts us off, which marks the end of the visible and the beginning of the downward tilt into darkness.

For this mode of voyeurism (which by now is a stable and finely tuned economic plateau) the mechanism of satisfaction relies on my awareness that the object I am watching is unaware of being watched. 'Seeing' is no longer a matter of sending something back, but of catching something unawares. That something which is designed to be caught unawares has been gradually put in place and organised in its function, and through a kind of institutional specialisation (as in those establishments which 'cater for special tastes') it has become story, the story of the film: what we go to see when we say 'I'm going to the cinema'.

The cinema was born much later than the theatre, in a period when social life was deeply marked by the notion of the *individual* (or its more elevated version, 'personality'), when there were no longer any slaves to enable 'free men' to form a relatively homogeneous group, sharing in the experience of a few major affects and so sparing themselves the problem of 'communication', which presupposes a torn and fragmented community. The cinema is made for the private individual (like the classical novel again, which unlike the theatre also partakes of 'story'), and in the spectator's voyeurism there is no need for him to be seen (it is dark in the cinema, the visible is entirely confined to the screen), no need for a knowing object, or rather an object that wants to know, an object-subject to share in the activity of the component drive. It is enough, and it is even essential – this is another, equally well defined, path of gratification – that the actor should behave as though he were not seen (and therefore as though he did not see his voyeur), that he should go about his ordinary business and pursue his existence as foreseen by the fiction of the film, that he should carry on with his antics in a closed room, taking the utmost care not to notice that a glass rectangle has been set into one of the walls, and that he lives in a kind of aquarium, one which is simply a little less generous with its 'apertures' than real aquariums (this withholding of things being itself part of the scopic mechanism).

In any case, there are fish on the other side as well, their faces pressed to the glass, like the poor of Balbec watching the guests of the grand hotel having their meals.[3] The feast, once again, is not shared – it is a furtive feast and not a festive feast. Spectator-fish, taking in everything with their eyes, nothing with their bodies: the institution of the cinema requires a silent, motionless spectator, a *vacant* spectator, constantly in a sub-motor and hyper-perceptive state, a spectator at once alienated and happy, acrobatically hooked up to himself by the invisible thread of sight, a spectator who only catches up with himself at the last minute, by a paradoxical identification with his own self, a self filtered out into pure vision. We are not referring here to the spectator's identification with the characters of the film (which is secondary), but to his preliminary identification with the (invisible) seeing agency of the film itself as discourse, as the agency which *puts forward* the story and shows it to us. Insofar as it abolishes all traces of the subject of the enunciation, the traditional film succeeds in giving the spectator the impression that he is himself that subject, but in a state of emptiness and absence, of pure visual capacity ('content' is to be found only in what is seen): indeed, it is important that the spectacle 'caught unawares' should itself be unexpected, that it should bear (as every hallucinatory satisfaction does) the stamp of external reality.

The regime of 'story' allows all this to be reconciled, since story, in Émile Benveniste's sense of the term, is always (by definition) a story from nowhere, that nobody tells, but which, nevertheless, somebody receives (otherwise it would not exist): so, in a sense, it is the 'receiver' (or rather, the receptacle) who tells it and, at the same time, it is not told at all, since the receptacle is required only to be a place of absence, in which the purity of the disembodied utterance will resonate more clearly. As far as all these traits are concerned it is quite true that the primary identification of the spectator revolves around the camera itself, as Jean-Louis Baudry has shown.

So, is this the mirror stage (as the same author goes on to claim)? Yes, to a large extent (this is, in fact, what we have been saying). And yet, not quite. For what the child sees in the mirror, what he sees as an other who turns into *I*, is after all the image of his own body; so it is still an identification (and not merely a secondary one) with something *seen*. But in traditional cinema, the spectator is identifying only with something *seeing*: his own image does not appear on the screen; the primary identification is no longer constructed around a subject-object, but around a pure, all-seeing and invisible subject, the vanishing point of the monocular perspective which cinema has taken over from painting. And conversely, the *seen* is all thrust back on to the pure object, the paradoxical object which derives its peculiar force from this act of confinement. So we have a situation in which everything has burst apart, and in which the double denial essential to the story's existence is preserved at all costs: that which is seen does not know that it is seen (if it did, this would necessarily mean that it was already, to some extent, a subject), and its lack of awareness allows the voyeur to be himself unaware that he is a voyeur. All that remains is the brute fact of seeing: the seeing of an outlaw, of an *Id* unrelated to any *Ego*, a seeing which has no features or position, as vicarious as the narrator-God or the spectator God: it is the 'story' which exhibits itself, the story which reigns supreme.

Notes and References to Part II

1 [*Histoire/Discours* in the French text. These terms are taken from Benveniste, and are usually translated as 'Story/Discourse'.]
2 [Metz uses the term *'accompli'*, which is strictly speaking not a tense but a verbal aspect stressing the completion of an action, and which has no exact equivalent in English.]
3 [This refers to an episode in Proust's *A la Recherche du temps perdu*.]

Part III

The Fiction Film and its Spectator: a Metapsychological Study

Translated by Alfred Guzzetti

6

Film and Dream:
The Knowledge of the Subject

The dreamer does not know that he is dreaming; the film spectator knows that he is at the cinema: this is the first and principal
difference between the situations of film and dream. We sometimes speak of the illusion of reality in one or the other, but true
illusion belongs to the dream and to it alone. In the case of the
cinema it is better to limit oneself to remarking the existence of a
certain *impression* of reality.

However, the gap between the two states sometimes tends to
diminish. At the cinema affective participation, depending on the
fiction of the film and the spectator's personality, can become
very lively, and *perceptual transference* then increases by a degree
for brief instants of fleeting intensity. The subject's consciousness
of the filmic situation as such starts to become a bit murky and to
waver, although this slippage, the mere beginning of a slippage,
is never carried to its conclusion in ordinary circumstances.
    I am not thinking so much of those film shows (some still exist,
for example in the villages or small towns of countries like France
or Italy) where one can see the spectators, often young children,
sometimes adults, rise from their seats, gesticulate, shout encouragement to the hero of the story, and insult the 'bad guy': manifestations, in general, less disorderly than they seem: it is the
institution of cinema itself, in certain of its sociological variants
(i.e. the audience of children, the rural audience, the audience
with little schooling, the community audience where everybody
in the cinema knows everybody else), that provides for, sanc-
tions, and integrates them. If we want to understand them, we
must take account of the conscious game-playing and group

demands, the encouragement given to the spectacle by the play of motor activity. To this extent, the expenditure of muscular energy (voice and gesture) signifies almost the opposite of what it might first suggest to the observer fresh from the big city and its anonymous and silent cinemas. It does not necessarily indicate that the audience is a little further down the road of true illusion. Rather, we have here one of those intrinsically ambivalent behaviours in which a single action, with double roots, expresses simultaneously virtually opposite tendencies. The subject actively invading the diegesis through a motor outburst was initially aroused by a first step, however modest – however prescribed, if necessary, by the indigenous rituals of the film audience – a first step towards confusing film and reality. But the outburst itself, once it has been set in motion (an outburst, moreover, which is most often collective), works to dissipate the budding confusion by returning the subjects to their rightful activity, which is not that of the protagonists as it is evolving on the screen: the latter do not assent to the spectacle. To exaggerate things so as to see them better, we might say that what begins as *acting out* ends as *action*. (We shall thus distinguish two main types of motor outburst, those that escape reality-testing and those that remain under its control.) The spectator lets himself be carried away – perhaps deceived, for the space of a second – by the anagogic powers belonging to a diegetic film, and he begins to act; but it is precisely this action that awakens him, pulls him back from his brief lapse into a kind of sleep, where the action had its root, and ends up by restoring the distance between the film and him. It accomplishes this to the extent that it develops into a behaviour of approval: approval of the spectacle as such and not necessarily of its quality, still less of all its diegetic features; approval brought from without to an imaginary tale by a person performing real actions to this purpose.

If we consider its 'economic' preconditions (in the Freudian sense of the term[1]), the unselfconscious audience, the exuberant audience, or the audience of children, displays, in a milder form, something in common with somnambulism: it can be defined, at least in the first of its two stages, as a particular type of motor conduct characteristically released by sleep or by its fleeting, outlined homologue. This comparison can be enlightening as a contribution to a metapsychology of the filmic state, but it quickly finds its limits, since the enthusiastic audience is awakened by its actions whereas the somnambulist is not (it is therefore in their second stages that the two processes differ). Moreover, it is not certain that the somnambulist is dreaming, whereas in the case of the spectator entering into the action, the lapse into sleep is simultaneously a lapse into dreaming. Now we know that the dream, which escapes reality-testing, does not escape consciousness (it constitutes, on the contrary, one of the major modalities of the conscious); the dissociation of 'motoricity' from consciousness is therefore capable of going further in certain cases of somnambulism than in audience behaviours of the 'intervening' type.[2]

Other conditions, less spectacular than those of the shouting audience, are necessary in order for perceptual transference, the dream-like and sleepy confusion of film and reality, still very far from its total fulfilment, to become any more stable. The adult spectator, who belongs to a social group that watches films seated and silent – he, in short (that other sort of native), who is neither a child nor childlike – finds himself without defences, if the film touches him profoundly or if he is in a state of fatigue or emotional turmqil, etc., against those brief moments of mental seesawing which each of us has experienced and which bring him a step closer to true illusion. This approach to a strong (or stronger) type of belief in the diegesis is a bit like the brief and quickly passing dizziness that drivers feel towards the end of a long night journey (of which film is one). In the two situations, when the second state, the brief psychical giddiness, ends, the subject not coincidentally has the feeling of 'waking up': this is because he has furtively engaged in the state of sleeping and dreaming. The spectator thus will have dreamt a little bit of the film: not because that bit was missing and he imagined it: it actually appeared in the *bande*,[3] and this, not something else, is what the subject saw; but he saw it while dreaming.

The spectator who, as our society prescribes, is immobile and silent does not have the opportunity to 'shake off' his budding dream, as one would remove the dust from a garment, through a motor outburst. This is probably why he pushes perceptual transference a bit further than do audiences who actively invade the diegesis (there is material here for a socio-analytic typology of the different ways of *attending* a film screening). We can therefore suppose that it is the same quantum of energy that serves in one case to nourish action and in the other to hypercathect perception to the point of touching off a *paradoxical hallucination*: a hallucination because of its tendency to confuse distinct levels of reality and because of a slight temporary unsteadiness in the play of reality-testing as an ego function,[4] and paradoxical because unlike a true hallucination it is not a wholly endogenous psychical production: the subject, in this case, has hallucinated what was really there, what at the same moment he in fact perceived: the images and sounds of the film.

In the cases of which we have just spoken, and doubtless in others too, the spectator of a novelistic [*romanesque*] film no longer quite knows that he is at the cinema. It also happens, conversely, that the dreamer up to a certain point knows that he is dreaming – for instance, in the intermediary states between sleep and waking, especially at the beginning and end of the night (or when deep sleep steals away, leaving only incomplete, heavy, and fragmentary shreds), and more generally at all those times when thoughts like 'I am in the middle of a dream' or 'This is only a dream' spring to mind, thoughts which, by a single and double movement, come to be integrated in the dream of which they form a part, and in the process open a gap in the hermetic sealing-off that ordinarily defines dreaming.[5] By the specific way in which they are split open, *visées*[6] of this kind resemble the special regimes of filmic perception already discussed. It is in their gaps rather than in their more normal functioning that the filmic state and the dream state tend to converge (but the gaps themselves suggest a kinship at once less close and more permanent): in the one case, perceptual transference is ruptured and less of a piece than in the rest of the dream; in the other, it sets its limits a bit more insistently than in the rest of the film.

Freud attributed the gaps in the dream to a complex interaction between different metapsychological, and in particular topographical, agencies. In principle, the ego wants to sleep: to sleep and therefore, if necessary, to dream (to dream deeply). Indeed, when a wish rises from the unconscious, the dream presents itself as the only means of satisfying the wish without setting in motion the process of waking up. But the unconscious part of the ego, the repressing agency (the 'defence'), in accord with the super-ego which inspires it, constantly stays in a state of semi-wakefulness, since its job is to maintain the defence against the repressed (and, more generally, forbidden) elements, which themselves remain awake and active, or at least capable of activation, even during sleep. The unconscious, in its double aspect of repressed and repressing (i.e. unconscious of the id and unconscious of the ego), never really sleeps, and what we call sleep is an economic modification principally affecting the preconscious and conscious.[7] The wakefulness of one part of the ego, which permits the other part to go on sleeping, usually assumes the form of censorship (itself inseparable from 'the dream-work' and the manifest characteristics of the dream flux); this censorship, as we know, attends even the deepest dreams, those where perceptual transference is total and the impression of dreaming absent, those in short which are entirely compatible with sleep. But it can also happen that this agency of self-observation and self-surveillance[8] may be led to interrupt sleep to various degrees, the two contrary effects proceeding from the same defensive mission carried out in different circumstances.[9] Such and such a dream may create too much fear; the censorship, in its initial stage, has failed to tone down the content of the dream sufficiently, so that its second intervention will consist in stopping the dream and sleep along with it. Certain nightmares wake one up (more or less), as do certain excessively pleasurable dreams; certain insomnias are the work of the ego which, frightened by the prospect of its dreams, prefers to renounce sleep.[10] Given a lesser degree of violence in the internal conflict and therefore a lesser degree of wakefulness, this is the same process that is responsible for the various regimes of consciousness in which the subject is sufficiently asleep for his dream to continue but sufficiently awake to know that it is only a dream – thus approaching a very common filmic situation – or again when he exercises an intentional influence over the very unfolding of the dream,[11] for example, substituting for anticipated sequences another, more satisfying or less frightening, version (we have here something like a film with *alternative* versions, and cinema sometimes offers constructions of this kind).[12]

These different situations have a common feature. They stem from an active intervention of the agency which sleeps only partially, the unconscious ego; it is this that more or less energetically awakens the sleeping agency, the preconscious ego. In other cases, which in a sense end up with the same result, it is the characteristic rhythms of the latter that come directly into play: it is not yet entirely asleep, or it has already started to be so no longer, as in the 'intermediary states' of evening and morning. As for the function of *consciousness*, let us recall that it sleeps only when sleep is dreamless. Dreams, even when accompanied by deep sleep, wake it up and put it to work, for the final text of its productions is conscious. Truly deep sleep (which hardly exists) would be a psychical regime in which all the agencies slept. We can speak of 'deep sleep', in a relative and practical sense, in two circumstances: when the dream is accompanied by no consciousness of being a dream, and *a fortiori* when sleep is dreamless. These two situations taken together cover almost all the cases that ordinary language calls 'deep sleep' (or simply 'sleep', without qualification). They correspond to the maximal degree of sleep of which the psychical apparatus in its normal functioning is capable.

These metapsychological mechanisms are obviously complex, much more so than this cavalier summary indicates, but I shall retain only their implied common basis: that the *visée* of deep dreaming, the total illusion of reality, supposes deep sleep in the sense just defined. We know how much Freud insisted on this close correlation between dream and sleep (devoting a special study to it in addition to *The Interpretation of Dreams* itself), a correlation going well beyond the simple and obvious thing one might see in it, since it is not only external (i.e. 'We dream only while sleeping'), but because the internal process of the dream is predicated in its particulars on the economic conditions of sleep.[13] As a corollary, each slackening in the full exercise of perceptual transference corresponds to a weakening of sleep, to a certain manner or degree of waking. Given our perspective, all this can be summarised as follows: the degree of illusion of reality is inversely proportional to that of *wakefulness*.

This formulation will perhaps help us to understand better the filmic state by setting it in relation to the dream state as a complex mixture of similarities and differences. In contrast to the ordinary activities of life, the filmic state as induced by traditional fiction films (and in this respect it is true that these films demobilise their spectators) is marked by a general tendency to lower wakefulness, to take a step in the direction of sleep and dreaming. When one has not had enough sleep, dozing off is usually more a danger during the projection of a film than before or even afterwards. The narrative film does not incite one to action, and if it is like a mirror, this is not only, as has been said,[14] by virtue of playing the scenes Italian style or of the vanishing point of monocular perspective, which puts the spectator-subject in a position to admire himself like a god, or because it reactivates in us the conditions belonging to the mirror stage in Lacan's sense (i.e. a hyper-perceptive and sub-motor state)[15] – it is also and more directly, even if the two things are linked, because it encourages narcissistic withdrawal and the indulgence of phantasy which, when pushed further, enter into the definition of dreaming and sleep:[16] withdrawal of the libido into the ego, temporary suspension of concern for the exterior world as well as the cathexis of objects, at least in their real form. In this respect, the novelistic film, a mill of images and sounds overfeeding our zones of shadow and irresponsibility, is a machine for grinding up affectivity and inhibiting action.

In the filmic state, this diminution of wakefulness admits (at least) two distinct degrees. The first is frequently observed and consists in the very fact of the impression of reality, assuredly different from the illusion of reality, but nonetheless its far-off beginning; and all diegetic films, quite apart from their content and their degree of 'realism', characteristically play on this impression, draw their specific charm and power from it, and are made for this purpose. One step further in the lowering of wakefulness, and we have the special regimes of filmic perception of which I spoke at the outset. They intervene in a more fleeting, episodic fashion; they move a bit further towards genuine illusion (though without ever reaching it) during the brief instant of a psychical giddiness.

It remains that the spectator almost always knows that he is at the cinema, the dreamer almost never that he is dreaming. Beyond the intermediary cases, discreet indicators of a kinship at once more profound and dialectical, the diegetic film and the dream remain separated, if we consider each of them in its entirety, by an important and regular difference in the degree of perceptual transference; the impression and illusion remain distinct. The maintenance of this distinction in ordinary regimes, as well as its weakening in borderline cases, has one and the same cause, which is sleep or its absence. The filmic and dream states tend to converge when the spectator begins to doze off [*s'endormir*] (although ordinary language at this stage does not speak of 'sleep' [*sommeil*]), or when the dreamer begins to wake up. But the dominant situation is that in which film and dream are not confounded: this is because the film spectator is a man awake, whereas the dreamer is a man asleep.

7

Film and Dream:
Perception and Hallucination

The second major difference between the filmic and dream *visées* derives strictly from the first. Filmic perception *is* a real perception (is really a perception); it is not reducible to an internal psychical process. The spectator receives images and sounds offered as the representation of something other than themselves, of a diegetic universe, but remaining true images and sounds capable of reaching other spectators as well, whereas the dream flux can reach the consciousness of no one but the dreamer. The projection of the film cannot begin before the reels arrive: nothing of this sort is required for the dream to be set in motion. The film image belongs to that class of 'real images' (paintings, drawings, engravings, etc.) which psychologists oppose to mental images. The difference between the two is what separates perception from imagination in the terms of a phenomenology of consciousness. The production of the dream consists of a series of operations remaining from start to finish within the psychical apparatus. In a behaviourist system one would say that what characterises filmic perception is that it involves a stimulus, whereas dream 'perception' does not.

The *delusion coefficient* is therefore very much higher in the dream: doubly so, because the subject 'believes' more deeply, and because what he believes in is less 'true'. But in another sense (and we shall return to this), the diegetic delusion, less powerful in the absolute, is, when related to its circumstances, more singular, perhaps more formidable, because it is the delusion of a man awake. The dream delusion has been partly neutralised, ever since man dreamt, by the bromide that 'this was only a dream'.

109

This time-honoured method of trivialisation, despite such equivalents as 'it's just a film', is harder to apply to the filmic delusion, since we are not asleep at the cinema, and we know it.

With its authentic (external) images and sounds, the novelistic film helps nourish the subject's phantasy flux with supplementary material brought in from outside, and irrigates the figures of his desire; it is not to be doubted that the classical cinema is among other things a practice of affective fulfilment. (But we should not forget that it is not alone in playing this very ancient and far from contemptible role: all fiction – what Freud calls 'fancy'[1] – even in arts commonly thought nobler,[2] serves this same purpose, which an empty moralism, preoccupied with decorum, would like to distinguish from 'authentic art'.) Inasmuch as it proposes behavioural schemes and libidinal prototypes, corporal postures, types of dress, models of free behaviour or seduction, and is the initiating authority for a perpetual adolescence, the classical film has taken, relay fashion, the historical place of the grand-epoch, nineteenth-century novel (itself descended from the ancient epic); it fills the same social function, a function which the twentieth-century novel, less and less diegetic and representational, tends partly to abandon.

We observe, however, that film narratives [récits] often thwart the imagination. Given certain combinations of film and spectator, they are liable to induce reactions in which affective irritation or phantasmic allergy appear, and which are nothing other, whatever rationalisation the subject gives to them, than frustrations classically resulting in aggressivity against the frustrating agent, here the film itself. The spectator maintains with the film an object relation (good or bad object), and films, as indicated by the current and enigmatic formulas we use after seeing them, are things that we 'like' or 'don't like'. The liveliness of these reactions in certain cases, and the very existence of *filmic unpleasure*, only serve to confirm the kinship of fiction film and phantasy. Common experience shows that film very often divides the opinions of people who otherwise nearly always react in unison (but one also finds, and this is an additional confirmation, that these divergences generally manage to even themselves out when phantasy adjustment is at work right from the start and continues to operate as the film progresses: when two people see the film together, that is to say when each of them is alone without being so).

From the topographical point of view, filmic unpleasure can arise, depending on the circumstances, from two distinct sources, and sometimes from their convergent action. It can arise on the side of the id when the id is insufficiently nourished by the diegesis of the film; instinctual satisfaction is stingily dealt out, and we have then a case of frustration in the proper sense (actual frustration, in Freudian terms): hence films that seem to us 'dull' or 'boring' or 'ordinary', etc. But aggressivity against the film – whose conscious form in both cases consists in declaring that one has not liked it, that is to say, that it has been a bad object – can result equally from an intervention of the super-ego and the defences of the ego, which are frightened and counter-attack when the satisfaction of the id has, on the contrary, been too intense, as sometimes happens with films 'in bad taste' (taste then becomes an excellent alibi), or films that go too far, or are childish, or sentimental, or sado-pornographic films, etc., in a word, films against which we defend ourselves (at least when we have been touched) by smiling or laughing, by an allegation of stupidity, grotesqueness, or 'lack of verisimilitude'.

In short, if a subject is to 'like' a film, the detail of the diegesis must sufficiently please his conscious and unconscious phantasies to permit him a certain instinctual satisfaction, and this satisfaction must stay within certain limits, must not pass the point at which anxiety and rejection would be mobilised. In other words, the spectator's defences (or at least the processes of edulcoration and symbolic substitution which are sufficiently efficacious functional equivalents for them) must be integrated with the very content of the film[3] by one of those happy accidents that also preside over the relations between people and the 'encounters' of life, in such a way that the subject can avoid activating his own defences, which would inevitably be translated into antipathy for the film. In short, every time a fiction film has not been liked, it is because it has been liked too much, or not enough, or both.

Whatever the psychical paths that produce it, filmic unpleasure is a thing that exists: certain spectators do not like certain films. The fiction cinema, which in principle caters to the phantasy, can also thwart it: one person might not have imagined heroes of the particular physiognomy or stature that the screen offers to his perception and that he cannot retouch; he is secretly annoyed that the plot does not take the course he hoped for; he 'doesn't see things that way'. Those spectators whom the intellectual (unaware, all too often, of the limitations of his own species) considers naïve do not hesitate to say that they dislike a film because it ends badly or because it is too bold, too unfeeling, too sad, etc.; if they were any more ingenuous they would tell us quite clearly that the film is bad 'because the two brothers should have been able to understand each other and be reconciled' (these are only random examples, but many conversations about films are of this order, even the majority if we consider the population of spectators as a whole). The intellectual protests, this time rightly, that the characteristics of the film, as long as they are presented thus, are part of its raw content and cannot constitute criteria of evaluation. But he would be doubly naïve if he forgot, or if he concealed from himself, that something in him – which is better hidden but never entirely disappears – responds to films in the same way. These phenomena of the *phantasy being disappointed* are particularly apparent when an already known novel is brought to the screen. The reader of the novel, following the characteristic and singular paths of his desire, has already gone through a whole process of clothing the words he has read in images, and when he sees the film, he would like to find the same images (in fact to *see it again*, by virtue of that implacable force of repetition that inhabits desire, driving the child to play unceasingly with the same toy, the adolescent to listen unceasingly to the same record, before abandoning it for the next, which in its turn will fill a portion of his days). But the reader of the novel will not always find *his* film, since what he has before him in the actual film is now somebody else's phantasy, a thing rarely sympathetic (to the extent that when it becomes so, it inspires love).

We now come to the second major difference between the filmic state and the dream state. As hallucinatory wish-fulfilment, the fiction film is less *certain* than the dream; it fails more often at its ordinary mission. This is because it is not really hallucinatory. It rests on true perceptions which the subject cannot fashion to his liking, on images and sounds imposed on him from without. The dream responds to the wish with more exactitude and regularity: devoid of exterior material, it is assured of never colliding with reality (and reality includes other people's phantasy). It is like a film which has been 'shot' from beginning to end by the very subject of the wish – also the subject of fear – a singular film by virtue of its censorship and omissions as much as its expressed content, cut to the measure of its only spectator (this is another sort of *découpage*[4]), a spectator who is also the *auteur* and has every reason to be content with it, since one is never so well served as by oneself.

In Freudian theory, the dream, along with the hallucination strictly defined and the other special regimes of consciousness (Meynert's *amentia*, etc.), belongs to a particular group of economic situations, the 'hallucinatory psychoses of desire'.[5] Under this heading Freud grouped the diverse and precise conditions in which an absent object can be hallucinated if its presence is desired with enough force. This is to say that it cannot give unpleasure, at least in itself (second reactions to the hallucination can of course be painful). The diegetic film, on the other hand, which in certain respects is still of the order of phantasy, also belongs to the *order of reality*. It exhibits one of reality's major characteristics: in relation to the wish (and to the fear which is the other face of the wish), it can 'turn out' more or less well; it is not in total collusion with them; it can become so only after the fact, through an encounter or adjustment whose success is never guaranteed: it can please or displease, like the real, and because it is part of the real. Thus, compared to the dream, which is more strongly bound to the pure pleasure principle, the filmic state is based to a greater extent on the reality principle: keeping pleasure for its ultimate goal, it admits sometimes long and arduous tactical detours by way of unpleasures felt as such. This difference in psychical effect derives from an entirely material difference, the presence in the film, without equivalent in the dream, of images and sounds chemically inscribed on an external support, that is to say, the very existence of the film as 'recording' and as *bande*.

The physical reality of the film, a simple and important fact, is not without relation to the first problem considered in this study, that of sleep and waking. The hallucinatory process can establish itself, in the normal regime, only in the economic conditions of sleep.[6] In the waking situtation, and therefore in the

cinematic situation, the most common path of the psychical excitations traces out a one-way line, a directed line which is Freud's
'progressive path'. The impulses originate in the external world
(daily surroundings or filmic *bande*); they reach the psychical
apparatus via its perceptual extremity (i.e. the system of
perception-consciousness), and finally come to be inscribed in
the form of memory traces in a less peripheral psychical system,
which is sometimes the preconscious ('memories' in the ordinary
sense of the word), and sometimes the unconscious, with its own
memory, when the case involves impressions of the world that
have been repressed after reception. This itinerary goes, then,
from the external towards the internal. In sleep and in dreams,
the route is the reverse; the 'regressive path'[7] has as a point of departure the preconscious and the unconscious, as a point of
arrival the illusion of perception. The driving power of the dream
is the unconscious wish,[8] linked to repressed childhood memories; it is itself reactivated, through associations of affects and
ideas, by more recent, unrepressed, preconscious memories ('the
day's residues'); these two stimuli, once they have joined
together, constitute the preconscious dream-wish.[9] It is, therefore, a group of memories, preconscious and unconscious, that
set off the whole process, and it is these memories, remodelled
and transformed by the censorship, the 'dream-work', the imaginary adjunctions, etc. that will be deployed in the terminal
(manifest) content of what is apprehended in the dream. But in
order to arrive at this apprehension with its singular power of
illusion, the memory traces, bearers of the wish, must be hyper-
cathected to the point of hallucination, that is to say, up to the
point of vividness where they are confused with perceptions: to
the point, in sum, where they activate, if not the sense organs in
their ordinary physiological functioning, at least the system of
perception insofar as it is a psychical agency and specific *visée de
conscience*. Thus the regressive path has perception as its point of
arrival, but its particular characteristic is to cathect it from
within (this is the very definition of hallucinatory psychosis),
whereas usually perception is cathected from without, a feature
which establishes it as true perception. Freud recalls that certain
activities of waking life, such as visualising meditation or the voluntary evocation of memories,[10] also rest on the principle of
regression, but in these cases regression is arrested before its conclusion, for the memory and the mental image are here clearly

recognised by the subject, who does not take them to be perceptions. What is lacking in these *visées* is the last stage of the regressive process, the properly hallucinatory stage, that which continues until it reaches the perceptual function from within on the basis of representations that are purely psychical but highly charged with desire. Complete regression is therefore possible, as a rule, only in the state of sleep, and this is also why the film spectator, a person who is not asleep, remains incapable of true hallucination even when the fiction is of a kind to stir his desires strongly. In the waking state, the regressive flux, when it appears, runs up against a more powerful progressive counter-flux which is active almost all the time[11] and which prevents it from going to its conclusion. Sleep, however, suspends this inverse thrust by stopping the perceptions and thus frees the way for the regressive impressions, which can go to the end of their proper route. In the filmic state, which is one of the variants of the waking state, this classic analysis is fully confirmed and its formulations do not have to be modified but simply made precise: the counter-flux (which is here particularly rich, pressing, continuous) is that of the film itself, of the real images and sounds which cathect perception from without.

But if this is the case, our problem is displaced and our interrogation must take a new tack. What remains to be understood in terms of economy is that the filmic state, despite wakefulness and counter-flux, leaves room for the beginnings of regression, of which I have already spoken, and is marked by more or less consistent psychical thrusts in the direction of perceptual transference and paradoxical hallucination. More fundamentally, it is the impression of reality itself, and therefore the possibility of a certain affective satisfaction by way of the diegesis, that presupposes the beginning of regression, since this impression is nothing other than a general tendency (stillborn or more developed, depending on the case) to perceive as true and external the events and the heroes of the fiction rather than the images and sounds belonging purely to the screening process (which is, nonetheless, the only real agency): a tendency, in short, to perceive as real the represented and not the representer (the technological medium of the representation), to pass over the latter without seeing it for what it is, to press on blindly. If the film shows a galloping horse, we have the impression of seeing a galloping horse and not the moving spots of light which evoke a galloping horse. One touches here on the great and classic difficulty of interpretation that all *representation* poses. In the conditions peculiar to the cinema, it can be stated thus: how does the spectator effect the mental leap which alone can lead him from the perceptual *donnée*, consisting of moving visual and auditory impressions, to the constitution of a fictional universe, from an objectively real but denied signifier to an imaginary but psychologically real signified? It is true that an incipient regression a bit like this one is also to be found in other waking states, such as memory evocation, but this still tells us nothing (especially since conditions there are obviously extremely different) about the particular forms that this phenomenon assumes in a case like the filmic state, where it has not been studied from this point of view.

The progressive path defined by Freud also admits of a variation (a bifurcation, rather) which this text has until now left aside. In waking life, action, that is to say the ego function that consists of modifying the real in the direction of the wish, requires a whole process of perceptual monitoring preceding and permanently accompanying it. In order to grasp an object, it is necessary to have seen, and to be seeing, it. Thus all day long, impressions from without reach the psychical apparatus through the door of perception, and 'go out again' (so to speak) in the form of motor activity directed back towards the world. If the dream is predicated on sleep, this then is also because sleep suspends all action and thus results in blocking the motor outlet, an exutory that, by contrast, remains constantly available in the waking state and helps considerably in impeding regression by absorbing through muscular modification all sorts of excitations which, without it, have a greater tendency to flow back towards the perceptual outlet, which is precisely what they do in dreams.

The filmic situation brings with it certain elements of motor inhibition, and it is in this respect a kind of sleep in miniature, a waking sleep. The spectator is relatively immobile; he is plunged into a relative darkness, and, above all, he is not unaware of the spectacle-like nature of the film object and the cinema institution in their historically constituted form: he has decided in advance to conduct himself as a spectator (a function from which he takes his name), a spectator and not an actor (the actors have their assigned place, which is elsewhere: on the other side of the film); for the duration of the projection he puts off any plan of action. (Cinemas are of course also used for other purposes, but to the extent that they are, their occupants have ceased to be spectators and have voluntarily abandoned the filmic state for a sort of behaviour belonging to reality . . .) In the case of the true spectator, motor manifestations are few:[12] shifting around in the seat, more or less conscious modification of facial expression, occasional comment under the breath, laughing (if the film, intentionally or not, provokes it), pursuing intermittent verbal or gestural relations (in the case of spectators in couples or groups) with the person in the next seat, etc. The institutional situation of the spectacle inherently prevents motor conduct from following its normal course very far, even in cases where the diegesis of the film is in a position to invoke active extensions of it (i.e. erotic sequences, sequences of political mobilisation, etc.; this is where these genres contradict themselves in their pseudo-rupture of the fiction and could, in a sense, whether desirable or not, truly begin to exist as *films* only if the *cinema* as a ritual were profoundly changed, in particular with respect to the customary forms of the 'screening' ['*séance*', a word denoting 'sitting down'] itself; it is also in this regard that so-called specialised screenings or film tracts possess, in default of subtlety or charm, more coherence and honesty). In ordinary screening conditions, as everyone has had the opportunity to observe, the subject who has fallen prey to the filmic state (most of all when the grip of the fiction on his phantasy is sufficiently strong) feels he is in a kind of daze, and spectators at the exit, brutally rejected by the black belly of the cinema into the bright, unkind light of the foyer, sometimes have the bewildered expression (happy and unhappy) of people waking up. To leave the cinema is a little like getting up: not always easy (except if the film was really indifferent).

The filmic state thus embodies in a weaker form certain economic conditions of sleep. It remains a variant of the waking situation but less remote from sleep than most of the others. Here at a new turn in the road, with the partial blockage of the motor outlet, we again come across the notion of a lessened wakefulness, initially proposed in reference to the perceptual conditions of the filmic state (the two things go together, sleep inhibiting perception and action simultaneously). The psychical energy which, in other circumstances of waking life, would be dissipated in action is, by contrast, conserved, in the case of the cinema spectator, whether he likes it or not. It will follow other itineraries of discharge, by virtue of the pleasure principle, which always seeks to liquidate stases. It will turn back in the direction of the perceptual agency, to take the regressive path, to busy itself with hypercathecting perception from within. And since the film at the same moment characteristically offers rich nourishment to this perception from without, complete regression of the kind associated with dreams is obstructed in favour of a sort of semi-regression representing another type of economic equilibrium, its elements combined in different proportions, but equally marked and characteristic. What defines this equilibrium is a *double reinforcement* of the perceptual function, simultaneously from without and within: apart from the filmic state, there are few situations in which a subject receives particularly dense and organised impressions from without at the same moment that his immobility predisposes him to 'hyper-receive' ['*sur-recevoir*'] them from within. The classical film plays on this pincer action, the two branches of which it has itself set up. It is the double reinforcement which renders possible the impression of reality; it is thanks to it that the spectator, starting from the material on the screen, the only thing given him at the outset (i.e. the spots of light in movement within a rectangle, the sounds and words coming from nowhere), will become capable of a certain degree of *belief* in the reality of an imaginary world whose signs he is provided with, capable of fiction, in sum. For the fictional capacity, as we too often forget, is not exclusively (or primarily) the capacity – unequally shared and for this reason prized by aesthetes – to invent fiction; it is above all the historically constituted and much more widespread existence of a regime of socially regulated psychical functioning, and which is, rightly, called fiction. Before being an art, fiction is a fact (a fact of which certain art forms take possession).

The relation between this fictional capacity and the film of narrative representation is close and mutual. The diegetic cinema as an institution could not function – and it would not therefore have begun to exist, whereas in fact it has scarcely begun to disappear and even today accounts for the biggest share of production, good or bad – if the spectator, already 'prepared' by the older arts of representation (the novel, representational painting, etc.) and by the Aristotelian tradition of Western art in general, were not capable of systematically adopting, and renewing at will, the special regime of perception that we are trying to analyse here in Freudian terms. But inversely, the existence of a film industry which produces abundantly and has continual repercussions on the psychical effect which renders it possible and profitable (possible because profitable) works to stabilise this effect, differentiate it, frame it, enclose it, and keep it alive by offering it a continued possibility of satisfaction; thus the industry ends up by reproducing its own conditions of possibility. Moreover, although the fictional capacity was already at the root of all the mimetic arts (and although the very notion of diegesis, contrary to what certain people believe, goes back to Greek philosophy, and not to the semiology of the cinema[13]), it remains true that film, as I have tried to show elsewhere in a more phenomenological vein,[14] produces an impression of reality much more vivid than does the novel or the theatre, since the inherent effect of the cinematic signifier, with its particularly 'faithful' ['*ressemblantes*'] photographic images, with the real presence of movement and sound, etc., is to bend the fiction-phenomenon, ancient though it is, towards historically more recent and socially specific forms.

8

Film and Dream:
Degrees of Secondarisation

The set of differences between fiction film and dream, and also therefore the set of their partial resemblances, may be organised around three great facts issuing, each in its own way, from the difference between waking and sleep: first, the *unequal knowledge of the subject* with respect to what he is doing; second, the presence or absence of real perceptual material; and third, a characteristic of the textual content itself (text of the film or dream), about which we are now going to speak. The diegetic film is in general considerably more 'logical' and 'constructed' than the dream. Films of the fantastic or the supernatural, the most unrealistic films, are very often only films that obey another logic, a genre logic (like the realistic film itself), a set of ground rules which they have laid down at the outset (genres are institutions) and within which they are perfectly coherent. It rarely happens that we find in a film narrative that impression of *true absurdity* which we commonly experience when we remember our own dreams or read about others, that very specific very recognisable impression (from which intentionally absurd films, like the 'literature of the absurd' of not long ago, remain so remote) which includes both the internal obscurity of the elements and the confusion of their assemblage, the enigmatic brilliance of the zones that the wish dazzles and the dark, swarming shipwreck of the almost forgotten segments, the sensation of tension and relaxation, the suspected outcropping of a buried order and the evidence of an authentic incoherence, an incoherence which, unlike that of films that aspire to delirium, is not a laboured addition but the very core of the text.

The psychologist René Zazzo,[1] touching on the basis of a repeated remark of Freud's, rightly affirms that the manifest content of a dream, if it were strictly transposed to the screen, would make an unintelligible film. A film, I may add, truly unintelligible (an object in fact very rare), and not one of those avant-garde or experimental films which, as the enlightened audience knows, it is appropriate at once to understand and not to understand (not understanding being the better way to understand and too much effort at understanding being the height of misunderstanding, etc.). These films, whose objective social function, at least in some cases, is to satisfy a certain kind of intellectual's naïvely desperate desire not to be naïve, have integrated within their institutional regime of intelligiblity a certain dose of elegant and coded unintelligibility, in such a way that their very unintelligibility is, as a result, intelligible. What is in question here is again a genre, and one which illustrates the contrary of what it would like to show; it reveals how difficult it is for a film to achieve true absurdity, pure incomprehensibility, that very thing which our most ordinary dreams, at least in certain sequences, achieve directly and effortlessly. It is probably for the same reason that 'dream sequences' in narrative films are nearly always so unbelievable.

We encounter here the problem of the secondary revision. In his various writings, Freud gives somewhat different accounts of the exact moment that the secondary revision intervenes within the complete production process of the dream (i.e. the dream-work). Sometimes he considers that it comes into play towards the end,[2] following the condensations, displacements, and various 'figurations', and that its function is to put a hasty, last-moment logical façade over the illogical productions of the primary process. Sometimes he situates it considerably further back[3] at the level of the dream-thoughts themselves or of a choice subsequently made among them. Finally (and this is the most probable hypothesis), he sometimes refuses to assign it a segmental position within a quasi-chronology[4] and considers that the different processes resulting in the manifest dream occur in a tangle, that is to say, in a manner at once alternating, successive and simultaneous. (There is also the case where a phantasy, therefore a mental object by definition secondary, is integrated as such in the manifest dream; we shall come back to this.) But in any case, what remains is that the secondary process is only one of the forces whose combinations and compromises determine the conscious content of the dream and that its entire weight is very often less than that of the other concurrent mechanisms (condensations, displacements, figurations), all under the control of the primary process. This is surely why 'dream logic' (the logic of the dream diegesis) is truly alien, and why one object can instantly transform itself into another without provoking the dreamer's astonishment until he wakes up, why a silhouette can be *clearly* recognised as being (being, not 'representing') two persons at once, whom the dreamer, with no further ado, at the same moment considers distinct, etc. Between the logic of the most 'absurd' film and that of the dream, there will always remain a difference, because in the latter what is astonishing does not astonish and consequently nothing is absurd: whence, precisely, the astonishment and the impression of the absurd one feels on waking.

The primary process rests on the 'pure' pleasure principle, uncorrected by the reality principle, and therefore aims at the maximal and immediate discharge of psychical excitations (affects, representations, thoughts, etc.). It will thus use any of the itineraries of energy discharge, and this is the basis of condensation and displacement, which are non-bound paths; in displacement, for example, the entire psychical charge is transposed from one object to another without being bound by the constraints of reality that make the two objects substantially distinct and not susceptible to total equivalence. The secondary process, which on the other hand obeys the reality principle, always consists in fixing certain paths of thought (i.e. bound energy) and preventing the discharge of impressions by other routes; this is the very definition of the various logics of the waking state, that is, of the various logics (simply) if we take the word in its usual sense. But since the primary process belongs to the unconscious, its characteristic operations are shielded from direct observation, and we can know them, or at least have an idea of them, only thanks to privileged cases such as the symptom, the slip, and acting out, etc., in which the outcomes of these specific routes (but not the routes themselves) become conscious and manifest.

Among these privileged cases, one of the principal ones is the dream. It has a further privilege in that it is the only one that is neither neurotic, like the symptom or acting out, nor excessively minor, like slips and parapraxes. In sum, for the primary 'logic' to result in conscious productions of any importance, in a normal situation the conditions of the dream, therefore of sleep, are necessary. It is sleep, more than the dream itself, which suspends the exercise of the reality principle,[5] since the sleeping subject does not have any real task to accomplish. And when he is awake (when he is, for example, watching or making a film), the secondary process succeeds in covering over all his psychical paths, thoughts, feelings and actions, so that the primary process, which remains their permanent basis, ceases to achieve directly observable results, since everything observable, before becoming so, will have passed through the secondary logic, which is that of the conscious.

From the point of view of the cinema analyst, then, everything happens as if the secondary revision (which in the production-perception of the dream is only one force among others, and not the principal one) became in the production and perception of the film the dominant, omnipresent force, the architect of the *mental milieu* itself, the milieu and the place [*lieu*] where the film is delivered and received. When we trace the obscure kinship relations (interwoven as they are by differences) of the film and the dream, we come upon that unique and methodologically attractive object, that theoretical monster, namely, a dream in which the secondary revision does nearly everything by itself, a dream where the primary process plays only a furtive and intermittent role, a role of gap-maker, a role of *escape*: a dream, in short, like life. That is to say (we always come back to this), the dream of a man awake, a man who knows that he is dreaming, and who consequently knows that he is not dreaming, who knows that he is at the cinema, *who knows that he is not sleeping*: since if a man who is sleeping is a man who does not know that he is sleeping, a man who knows that he is not sleeping is a man who is not sleeping.

What conditions must be met in order that we may experience this specific impression of true absurdity? They are precise, and Freud often alludes to them.[6] An unconscious production, largely dominated by the primary process, must be directly presented to the conscious apperception; it is this brutal transplantation from one milieu to another, this uprooting, which provokes the conscious feeling of absurdity: as when we evoke, when awake, the memory of our dreams. In the case of film, these conditions are not met; one of them is (the presentation to the conscious agency), but the other is not, since what is presented is not a direct production of the unconscious, or at least is not any more so than are the ordinary discourses and actions of life. This is why the film, a production of a man awake presented to a man awake, cannot help being 'constructed', logical, and felt as such.

However, the filmic flux resembles the dream flux more than other products of the waking state do. It is received, as we have said, in a state of lessened wakefulness. Its signifier (images accompanied by sound and movement) inherently confers on it a certain affinity with the dream, for it coincides directly with one of the major features of the dream signifier, 'imaged' expression, the consideration of representability, to use Freud's term. It is true that the image can organise itself – and that it usually does so, in the cinema as elsewhere, caught as it is in the constraints of communication and the pressures of culture[7] – in figures as 'bound', as secondary as those of language (and which classical semiology, based on linguistics, is in a good position to grasp). But it is also true, as Jean-François Lyotard has rightly insisted,[8] that the image resists being swallowed up whole in these logical assemblages and that something within it has the tendency to escape. In every 'language', the characteristics inherent in the physical medium of the signifier [*matière du signifiant*], as I have noted at another level in *Language and Cinema*,[9] have a certain influence on the type of logic which will inform the texts (this is the problem of 'specificities' considered on the level of formal configurations). The unconscious neither thinks nor discourses; it figures itself forth in images; conversely, every image remains vulnerable to the attraction, varying in strength according to the case, of the primary process and its characteristic modalities of concatenation. Language itself, not to be confused with *langue*, often undergoes this attraction, as we see in poetry, and Freud has shown[10] that dreams or certain symptoms treat representations of words as representations of things. The image, because of its nature, because of its kinship with the unconscious, is a bit more exposed to this attraction. (What is at issue, however, is only a difference of immediacy, and we should be careful not to reinstate on this basis the psychodramatic antagonism between words and images, a great mythic theme of a certain 'audio-visual' ideology that forgets the force of social conditionings exerted uniformly on the different means of expression.)

When we consider more particularly the narrative fiction cinema, which is only one of the various possible cinemas, this kinship of film and dream – a kinship of the signifier – is doubled by a supplementary affinity involving the signified. For it is also characteristic of the dream (and of the phantasy – a point to which we shall return) that it consists of a *story*. Of course there are stories and there are stories. The film story always unfolds clearly (or the obscurity, at least, is always accidental and secondary); it is a *told* story, a story, in short, that implies an action of narration [*récit*].[11] The dream story is a 'pure' story, a story without an act of narration, emerging in turmoil or shadow, a story that no narrative agency has *formed* (deformed), a story from nowhere, which nobody tells to nobody. And nevertheless, still a story: in the dream as in the film there are not only images; there is, clearly or confusedly woven by the images themselves, a succession, whether organised or chaotic, of places, actions, moments, characters.

Thus we shall have to consider more closely – and I shall begin to do so in the fourth part of this book – the exact nature (also, the limits) of the primary operations floating on the surface of the 'secondarised' chain of filmic discourse:[12] a formidable job with research requirements that forbid taking it on here, where we would like to be content with marking its place at the heart of a vaster problem, that of the cinematic fiction in relation to waking and sleep. Nonetheless, we must say straight off that certain of the most specific, and at the same time the most common, figures of cinematic expression carry within them, even at the basic level of their 'technical'and literal definition, something not unrelated to condensation and displacement. To take a single example, whose very banality ensures that its status is neither exceptional nor uncharacteristic, the superimposition and the lap-dissolve[13] – though 'redeemed' in the punctuation codes, which weaken what is strange and disquieting in them[14] – rest on mental paths where a certain primary-order unbinding is maintained. The superimposition characteristically effects a sort of equivalence between two distinct objects: a partial equivalence, simply discursive and metaphorical (a 'bringing together', which the enunciation produces) as long as the spectator, in a process smacking of rationalisation, secondarises it at the same moment that he reads it (that he binds it). A more profound equivalence, an authentic equivalence, total, in a way, insofar as the spectator also receives it in a more immediately affective fashion. Between these two contradictory and simultaneous types of reception, whose mode of psychical coexistence I have elsewhere tried to explain,[15] the relation is one of splitting and denial. Somewhere within him the spectator takes the superimposition seriously; he sees in it something other than a familiar and neutralised artifice of filmic discourse; he *believes* in the real equivalence of the two objects superimposed on the screen (or at least in some magically transitive bond between them). He believes in this more or less: economically, the force belonging to one of the modes of reception is in a variable relation with the force of the other: certain spectators are more censored (or are more so when faced with a given superimposition); certain superimpositions are more convincing, etc. The fact of equivalence remains – equivalence that the film *figures forth* directly, without indicating 'like', 'such as', or 'at the same moment…', as language would – equivalence that thus appears a mixture of condensation and displacement. In the case of the lap-dissolve, which is a superimposition drawn further in the direction of consecutive order (in that one image ends up replacing the other), the primary equivalence of the two motifs includes a bit less condensation and a bit more displacement. But the two figures have this in common: that up to a certain point they put into play the transference of a psychical charge from one object to another (tending in the opposite direction from any daytime logic), and that in them can be read in outline (or residue) form the propensity characteristic of the primary process to abolish the very duality of objects, that is to say, to establish, outside the divisions imposed by reality, the short and magical circuits that the impatient wish requires. Thus the fiction film consoles us for things we cannot do.

The study of phenomena of this kind, whether in cinematic language itself or in the formal operations of a given film, leads us back via one of its extremities to the unconscious of the filmmaker (or of the cinema); this is the side of the 'sender'. But the other extremity (the 'receiver', that is to say, the filmic state) is equally interesting to consider. What is remarkable in this regard is that the appearance in the film of these more or less primary figures generally provokes little astonishment and confusion in the spectator. That they may be immediately subsumed in a secondary narrative logic does not explain everything; neither does historical familiarisation or acculturation to the cinema. They retain, it would seem, enough of the unfamiliar for us to have anticipated a more immediate, profound, and widespread rejection (for there are traces of it among certain spectators in relation to certain films), a rejection capable of taking diverse forms: explicit protest, laughing as a polyvalent defence and all-purpose protection, aggression perpetrated inwardly against the film (or, on the other hand, among depressives, extreme perplexity), the strong impression of illogicality. None of these reactions is unexampled but no more is any the rule, and even when they are produced, it is most often, as we said earlier, in response to the phantasy content of the film and not to what remains of the primary process in filmic expression as such, which in certain of its operations can convey more than one content. Actually it is characteristic of these operations, in the fictional regime, to be self-effacing, to work for the benefit of the diegesis, 'injecting' credibility into it and hyperactivating its hold on the emotions at the cost of diminishing themselves, in accordance with a process of *credit transfer* which struck me in connection with special effects.[16] This factor is one of those that permit us to understand why the rejection of primary configurations is not more frequent, why the film object does not surprise the spectator, why it is not an intrinsic scandal.

We now see that the filmic state combines within itself two contrary and yet convergent processes leading by inverse routes to the same result, that absence of astonishment which research should find a little more astonishing. Absence of astonishment because the film is on the whole secondary and the spectator on the whole awake, with the result that they are on an equal footing; but also, insofar as cinematic discourse is shot through with irruptions from the primary, because the spectator is a bit less awake than in other circumstances (the equal footing is maintained then, but on another foot): thus a sort of compromise is created, a middle level of wakefulness, itself institutionalised in the classical cinema, where film and spectator succeed in being regulated one by the other and both by an identical or similar degree of secondarisation. The spectator, during the projection, puts himself into a state of lessened alertness (he is at a show; nothing can happen to him); in performing the social act of 'going to the cinema', he is motivated in advance to lower his ego defences a notch and not to reject what he would reject elsewhere. He is capable, in a very limited and yet singular measure, of a certain tolerance for the conscious manifestation of the primary process. This is undoubtedly not the only instance of this state of affairs (there is also alcoholic intoxication, exaltation, etc.). But it is, precisely, one of them, with particular conditions not to be found in the others: theatrical situation, presence of a material-ised fiction, etc. Among the different regimes of waking, the filmic state is one of those least unlike sleep and dreaming, dreamful sleep.

9

Film and Phantasy

In trying to specify the relations between the filmic state and the dream state, the partial kinships and incomplete differences, we encounter at every step the problem of sleep, its absence, or its intermediate degrees. Thus we are inevitably led to introduce a new term into the analysis, the *daydream*, which, like the filmic state and unlike the dream, is a waking activity. When in French we wish more clearly to distinguish the dream [*rêve*] and the daydream [*rêverie*], we call the latter, in a fixed syntagm which is in fact redundant, the 'waking daydream'['*rêverie éveillée*']. This is Freud's 'Tagtraum', the daytime dream [*rêve de jour*], in short the *conscious phantasy*. (We know that the phantasy, conscious or unconscious, can also be integrated within a dream whose manifest content it comprises or completes; but in this case, it loses certain characteristics of phantasy and takes on certain characteristics of dream; it is therefore the phantasy occurring outside the dream that is now in question.)

Chapters 6, 7 and 8 of this study have already indicated, albeit negatively and so to speak by omission, some of the features linking the diegetic film to the daydream, for they are often the same ones that separate it from the dream. We shall content ourselves with approaching them from the other direction (necessarily displacing them) and filling them out where necessary.

It is noteworthy, first of all, that the degree and manner of logical coherence of the novelistic film are rather like those of the '*petit roman*' or 'story', which are Freud's terms for the conscious phantasy,[1] that is to say, that the relation of forces between the secondary revision and the various primary operations is pretty much the same in both cases. A likeness which does not depend, as we might first suppose, on the fact that the film and the day-

129

dream are both conscious productions, since the dream is so too and yet is much less logical. It is not, therefore, the specific co-efficient of coming-to-consciousness (consciousness in its descriptive, not topographical, sense) which intervenes here; coming-to-consciousness, or its absence, is an exponent affecting the final product of a psychical process, whereas the relative resemblance of the film and the daydream can be understood only at the level of the modes of production. Not that these modes are identical in the two cases. But we shall see that through their very difference they succeed in reconverging, at least with respect to the final degree of secondary coherence.

If film is a logical construction, it is because it is the product of men awake, film-makers as well as spectators, whose mental operations are those of the conscious and preconscious. These operations therefore constitute the psychical agency which we can consider as directly producing the film. Although the driving force of the psychical processes in general, among them the making and viewing of films, is always of an unconscious order, there still exists an important difference between such cases as the symptom or the dream, where the primary mechanisms work in a relatively open way, and those where they are by contrast more completely hidden. In the second group appear most of the waking activities, provided they are not too neurotic. To define them (and film along with them) as *preconscious productions* has therefore a sense that is not absolute and requires specification: we mean by this that between the unconscious forces where they take root and the manifest process in which they result (discourse, action, etc.), the interposed transformational relay, that is to say the preconscious and conscious operations, in the end constitutes the agency that does the greatest share of the work so that the visible result is rather different – rather *distanced* (keeping the word's force as passive participle) – from the original source and from the type of logic belonging to it: thus it is in the ordinary processes of life in society and in the greater part of the productions of culture.

The conscious phantasy – or rather, simply the phantasy in its different conscious and unconscious versions, inseparable from each other and grouped in 'families' – is rooted in the unconscious in a fashion that is more direct and that follows a shorter circuit. It belongs more to the unconscious system (the unconscious in its topographical sense), even when its manifestations, or some of them, enter into consciousness, for it is thematically close to the ideational representative of the instinct and energetically close to the instinct's affective representative;[2] whence its disturbing seductive power when aroused by a film or anything else. This kinship with the instinctual sources enters into the very definition of the phantasy flux, with the result that we could see it (in the relative sense stated above) as a production of the unconscious. It assuredly is that, but is nonetheless distinguished from other productions of the unconscious, the dream, the symptom, etc. – and this is the second element of the definition – by its internal logic, wherein there appears the inherent mark of the preconscious and of the secondary process: the phantasy is directly organised as a relatively coherent story (or scene) whose actions, characters, places, and sometimes moments are connected and would not be disowned by the logic of the narrative or representational arts (we know that 'logical dreams'[3] are often those whose manifest content, in whole or in part, coincides with a whole phantasy or a whole segment of a phantasy). Thus, although phantasy is always near the unconscious by virtue of its content, and although the conscious phantasy is only a slightly more distant version, a budding prolongation (a 'derivative', as we say) of the unconscious phantasy, nonetheless phantasy (even in its submerged parts) always carries the more or less clear imprint of the preconscious in its modes of 'composition' and formal layout; this is why Freud saw it as a sort of hybrid.[4]

This internal duality characterises the conscious as well as the unconscious manifestations of a phantasy thrust which stems from one and the same root-stock, but the degree of secondariness obviously tends to increase when one of the shoots crosses the threshold of consciousness and thus becomes accessible to the daydream. When the daydream takes hold of it, we can even establish in certain cases a kind of intentional intervention by the subject, which is like the first stage in drafting a film scenario; the daydream is born of a conscious phantasy, already coherent in its own way but often brief, instantaneous and fleeting in its recognisable and unwished (recognisable because unwished, because always a bit compulsive) intensity; the act of daydreaming as such often tends to consist in artificially prolonging the emergence of the phantasy for a few additional moments, thanks to a rhetorical and narrative amplification which for its part is fully wished and has already the character of diegetic composition.

(We see that the daydream and the conscious phantasy are not merged together completely; but the former is the direct prolongation of the latter.)

The filmic flux is more explicit than that of the daydream, *a fortiori* than that of the conscious phantasy. It cannot be otherwise since film supposes a material fabrication that obliges one to choose each element in all the detail of its perceptible appearance, whereas the daydream, a purely mental fabrication, can tolerate more vague and 'blank' spaces. But this is a difference of precision, a difference in the degree of realisation, one might say, and not in the degree of secondariness, or in any case much less so than in the difference between the film and the dream. The 'little stories' that we tell ourselves somewhat resemble, by virtue of their coherence of the directly diegetic sort, the big stories that story films tell us (whence the enduring success of the latter). It is rare that the narrative line as a whole in a fiction film actually puts one in mind of a dream; it is frequent, even the rule, that it broadly conforms to the *novelistic formula [formule romanesque]* characteristic of the daydream, of the 'fancy' in Freud's sense (Freud defined the term precisely by reference to artistic works of representation).[5]

This typological kinship is often doubled by a real filiation of a genetic order, although this more directly causal connection is not indispensable to the resemblance and is less often in evidence. Certain fiction films have more than 'the air' of a daydream; they derive directly from the daydreams of their author (here again we meet Freud's 'fancy'): films that we call 'autobiographical', works of narcissistic film-makers or young creators particularly bound up with themselves, showing little resistance to the desire to 'put everything' into their film; but this is also true in a more distanced and less adolescent form of many narrative films whose explicit *donnée* has nothing autobiographical about it, and, at the limit, of all fiction films, and even others, since no one would produce anything without his phantasies. Nevertheless, when the relation of the work to the phantasy is not established at too manifest a level, it is not any closer or more characteristic than in any other action of life; this is notably the case when the phantasy that has inspired the film is unconscious, so that its trace in the film undergoes considerable transposition (but the transposition can also be effected by a calculated distancing, when the phantasy is conscious). We can say therefore that there are indeed films that in this sense do not proceed from their author's phantasies or daydreams.

The degree of secondarisation and its essentially diegetic manner are not the only features linking the classical film and the daydream. The filmic state and the conscious phantasy also suppose a rather similar degree of wakefulness. They are both established at an intermediary point between minimal wakefulness (sleep and dream) and maximal wakefulness, prevailing in the execution of practical tasks actively directed towards a real goal. An intermediary but not median degree, since it is on balance closer to waking and moreover forms part of it (this is because we conventionally designate as a waking state the whole higher part of the scale of wakefulness together with the totality of its internal degrees). The median degree would be situated lower than that of the daydream or film; it would correspond to certain states which precede or immediately follow sleep in the strict sense of the word.

In the filmic state as in the daydream, perceptual transference stops before its conclusion, true illusion is wanting, the imaginary remains felt as such; just as the spectator knows that he is watching a film, the daydream knows that it is a daydream. Regression is exhausted in both cases before reaching the perceptual agency; the subject does not confuse the images with perceptions, but clearly maintains their status as images: mental representations in the daydream,[6] and in the film representation of a fictional world through real perceptions (not to speak of the true daydreams, mental images recognised as such, accompanying the viewing of the film and embroidered around it; they are never taken for real; on the other hand, the subject sometimes has trouble distinguishing them from the diegesis, but this is precisely because both belong to a rather closely related mode of the imaginary). In all of this, the filmic state and the conscious phantasy clearly belong to waking.

To waking but not to its most characteristic manifestations. It suffices to compare them to other states of waking and notably to those summarised by the word *activity* in its ordinary sense, with its connotation of doing things and moving about. Film viewing, like daydreaming, is rooted in contemplation and not in action. Both suppose a temporary, largely voluntary, change in economy by which the subject suspends his object cathexes or at least renounces opening a real outlet for them, and withdraws for a time to a more narcissistic base (more introverted, to the extent that the phantasies remain concerned with objects),[7] as sleeping and dreaming cause him to do to a greater degree. Both have a certain power to relax, the attenuated metapsychological equivalent of the refreshing power that belongs to sleep and defines its function. Both are performed in a certain solitude (correlative of the re-narcissification), pleasurable or painful according to the circumstances; we know that active participation in a collective task does not encourage daydreaming and that immersion in the filmic fiction (in the 'projection', so well named) has the effect, stronger in proportion as the film is pleasing, of separating groups or couples who entered the cinema together and sometimes have a certain difficulty re-achieving that togetherness when they leave. (People with good personal rapport find it necessary to agree to have a moment of silence here so that the first words they exchange are not jarring: although these words may comment on the film, they mark its end, for they bring with them activity, waking, companionship. This is because in a certain sense one is always alone at the cinema, again a little as in sleep.)

Thanks to this relative lowering of wakefulness, the filmic state and the daydream allow the primary process to emerge up to a certain point, which is rather similar in the two cases. We have said earlier what certain cinematic figures owe to a limited step in the direction of regression. The primary power of the superimposition, for example, has something very deadened, very exhausted about it when compared to that of condensation or displacement, its equivalents in actual dreaming. But if we consider these same operations in the daydream, the degree of belief that they meet with on the subject's part perceptibly diminishes, and thus is brought nearer to that which a film superimposition can arouse. The conscious phantasy superimposes two faces for the fun of it, without believing in their substantial fusion (which is no cause for doubt in the dream), and nevertheless believing in it a little, since the daydream is a step in the direction of dreaming. This divided regime, naïve and crafty at the same time, wherein a bit of the wish is reconciled with a bit of reality thanks to a bit of magic, is ultimately rather close to that on which the subject's psychical attention is modelled when he is confronted with a cinematic superimposition like the traditional one of the faces of lover and beloved.

If the film is akin to the daydream with respect to secondarisation and wakefulness, it is separated from it by an irreducible third trait, the materialisation, lacking in the daydream and in phantasy generally, of the images and sounds. In this respect the daydream, wherein the representation remains mental, is on the same side as the dream, and the two are jointly opposed to the filmic state. This opposition, already noted in connection with the dream, takes on another sense when it is the daydream with which the film is compared.

The dreaming subject believes that he is perceiving. Passing from the dream to the filmic state, he can only be a loser, and even doubly so: the images are not his; they can therefore displease him; and he believes in them less strongly, despite their objective reality, than he believed in those of his dream, since the power of the latter attained the point of actual illusion. In terms of wish-fulfilment, the film is twice inferior to the dream: it is alien, it is felt as 'less true'.

In relation to the daydream, the balance is shifted. There remains the disadvantage of an external imposition (an imposition, in short), and the subject is in general less satisfied with films that he sees than with daydreams he manufactures. (The case of the film-maker here differs from that of the spectator; or rather, he is the only spectator for whom the film is not another person's phantasy but an externalised prolongation of his own.) On the other hand, we do not give more credence to our phantasies than to the fiction of the film, since true illusion is not to be had in either case; so as far as this is concerned the emotional pay-off provided by the film is no less than in the daydream. It is a question in both cases of a pseudo-belief, a consented-to simulation. Thus the material existence of the filmic images (along with all that issues from it: stronger impression of reality, superiority of perceptual precision and therefore of the power of *incarnation*, etc.) helps recover some advantages that compensate more or less completely for the images' immediately alien origin: their profound conformity to one's own phantasy is never guaranteed, but when chance permits this to a sufficient degree, the satisfaction – the feeling of a little miracle, as in the state of shared amorous passion – derives from a sort of *effect*, rare by nature, which can be defined as the temporary rupture of a quite ordinary solitude. This is the specific joy of receiving from the external world images that are usually internal, images that are familiar or not very far from familiar, of seeing them inscribed in a physical location (the screen), of discovering in this way something almost realisable in them, which was not expected, of feeling for a moment that they are perhaps not inseparable from the tonality which most often attends them, from that common and accepted yet slightly despairing impression of the impossible.

In the social life of our age, the fiction film enters into functional competition with the daydream, a competition in which it is sometimes victorious by virtue of the trump cards of which we have just spoken. This is one of the sources of 'cinephilia' in its ardent forms, the *love of the cinema*, a phenomenon requiring explanation, especially when we recognise the intensity it can attain among certain people. By contrast, the competition between film and dream as techniques of affective satisfaction is less lively, less sharp: it still exists, since both play this role, but they play it at more widely differing moments and according to less similar regimes of illusion: the dream responds more to the pure wish in its original madness; the film is a more reasonable and measured satisfaction wherein enters a larger share of compromise. Filmic pleasure itself, in order to establish itself as pleasure, requires many prior assumptions: that this is only the cinema, that other people exist, etc. (This is not the case with the dream.) Thus the neurotic in a crisis often abandons cinemas when previously he frequented them: what he sees there is already too remote from him, fatiguing, tiresome. (This occasional cinephobia, not to be confused with calm and permanent abstentions, is a degree more neurotic than the badly controlled cinephilia of which it is the reversal; in cinephilia, the incipient hypertrophy of introversion and narcissism would remain hospitable to external contributions, which the crisis renders suddenly unbearable.)

If the film and the daydream are in more direct competition than the film and the dream, if they ceaselessly encroach upon each other, it is because they occur at a point of adaptation to reality – or at a point of regression, to look at it from the other direction – which is nearly the same; it is because they occur at the same *moment* (same moment in ontogeny, same moment in the diurnal cycle): the dream belongs to childhood and the night; the film and the daydream are more adult and belong to the day, but not midday – to the evening, rather.

10

The Filmic *Visée*

The filmic state which I have tried to describe is not the only possible one; it does not include all of the rather diverse *visées de conscience* that a person can adopt before a film. Thus the proposed analysis would badly suit the frames of mind of a film critic or a semiologist actively researching, in the course of a professional viewing (shot-by-shot study, etc.), certain well specified features of the film, putting himself by this means into a regime of maximal wakefulness, a work regime; it is clear that perceptual transference, regression, and degree of belief in his case will be much weaker, and that he will perhaps retain something of this mind-set when he goes to the cinema for fun. What is in question in this case is no longer the filmic state which cinema as an institution in its ordinary functioning plays upon, counts on, foresees and favours. The film analyst by his very activity places himself in this respect outside the institution.

Moreover, the preceding description concerns only certain geographical forms of the institution itself, those that are valid in Western countries. The cinema as a whole, insofar as it is a social fact, and therefore also the psychological state of the ordinary spectator, can take on appearances very different from those to which we are accustomed. We have only attempted *one* ethnography of the filmic state, among others remaining to be done (for which Freudian notions would be perhaps less helpful and certainly less directly useful, since they were established, despite their pretension to universality, in an observational field with cultural limits). There are societies where the cinema scarcely exists, as in certain regions of black Africa outside the cities; there are also civilisations which like ours are great producers and consumers of fiction films (e.g. Egypt, India, Japan, etc.) but where the social context is sufficiently remote from ours to preclude, in the absence of a specialised study, any extrapolated proposition with respect to the significance that the very act of *going to the cinema* can assume there.

A third limitation, often recalled along the way: the only films in question were narrative (or fictional, or diegetic, or novelistic, or representational, or traditional, or classical, etc. – terms which we purposely used as provisional synonyms but which from other points of view must be distinguished). Most films shot today, good or bad, original or not, 'commercial' or not, have as a common characteristic that they tell a story; in this measure they all belong to one and the same *genre*, which is, rather, a sort of 'super-genre' ['*sur-genre*'], since certain of its internal divisions (not all: some narrative films are unclassifiable) themselves constitute genres: the Western, the gangster film, etc. The real meaning of these films, especially the most complex of them, is not reducible to the story-line, and one of the most interesting modes of assessment is precisely that which, when faced with a story film, bases itself on everything that outruns the story. However, a narrative kernel remains present in nearly all films – in those where it constitutes the main point as in many others where the main point, even if located elsewhere, hinges on it in various fashions: on it, under it, around it, in its gaps, sometimes in opposition to it – and this fact itself must also be understood, this very broad historical and social collusion of cinema and narrative.[1] It serves no purpose constantly to repeat that the 'only interesting cinema', the only cinema that one likes, is precisely that which does not tell a story: an attitude common in certain groups and not without its idealist aestheticism, precipitate revolution-ism, or desire for originality at any price. Can we imagine a historian with republican sympathies who for this reason would judge the study of absolute monarchy useless?

Here again we encounter the need for a *criticism* of the diegetic cinema. 'Criticism' in a sense neither necessarily nor uniformly polemical, since this cinema, like every cultural formation, is composed of important works side by side with mass-produced goods. Critical analysis of the traditional film consists above all in refusing to see it as the natural outcome of some universal and timeless essence or vocation of the cinema, and in thus showing it to be one kind of cinema among other possible ones, in unmasking the objective conditions of possibility of its functioning, which are masked by its very functioning, *for* its very functioning.

This machinery has economic and financial gears, directly sociological gears, and also psychical gears. At the centre of the latter, we always encounter afresh the impression of reality, the classical problem of filmological research. In an article (already cited on page 119 which owed its title to this,[2] I attacked the problem, in 1965, with the tools of phenomenology and experimental psychology. This is because the impression of reality results partly from the physical (perceptual) nature of the cinematic signifier: images obtained by photographic means and therefore particularly 'faithful' in their function as effigies, presence of sound and movement that are already a bit more than effigies since their 'reproduction' on the screen is as rich in sensory features as their production outside a film, etc. The impression of reality is founded, then, on certain objective resemblances between what is perceived in the film and what is perceived in daily life, resemblances still imperfect but less so than they are in most of the other arts. However, I remarked also that the similarity of the stimuli does not explain everything, since what characterises, and even defines, the impression of reality is that it works to the benefit of the imaginary and not of the material which represents it (that is, precisely, the stimulus): in theatre this material is even more 'similar' ['*ressemblant*'] than in films, but this is surely why the theatrical fiction has a less powerful psychological reality than the film diegesis. Consequently, the impression of reality cannot be studied simply by comparing it with perception but we must also relate it to the various kinds of fictional perceptions, the chief of which, apart from the representational arts, are the dream and the phantasy. If cinematic fabulations are endowed with this sort of credibility, which has struck every author and compels observation, this is at once, and contradictorily, because the psychical situation in which they are received involves certain features of reality and because it involves certain features of the daydream and the dream, which also belong to the pseudo-real. The theoretical contribution of psychology (study of perception, study of the conscious), with its extensions into classical filmology, ought therefore to be complemented by that of metapsychology, which can play a part, like linguistics (which it does not supplant), in renovating the study of film.

To the extent that the impression of reality is linked to the perceptual features of the signifier, it characterises all films, diegetic or not, but insofar as it partakes of the *fiction-effect*, it belongs to narrative films and to them alone. It is before such films that the spectator adopts a very particular *visée de conscience* which is confounded neither with that of the dream, nor with that of the daydream, nor with that of real perception, but which retains a little of all three, and is installed, so to speak, at the centre of the triangle that they mark out: a type of look whose status is at once hybrid and precise and which establishes itself as the strict correlative of a certain kind of looked-at object (the psychoanalytic problem thus hinges on a historical problem). Faced with this cultural object, which is the fiction film, the impression of reality, the impression of dream, and the impression of daydream cease to be contradictory and mutually exclusive, as they are ordinarily, in order to enter into new relations wherein their usual distinctness, while not exactly annulled, admits an unprecedented configuration leaving room at once for overlapping, alternating balance, partial coincidence, staggering, and ongoing circulation among the three: authorising, in sum, a sort of central and moving zone of intersection where all three can 'meet' each other on a singular territory, a confused territory which is common to them and yet does not abolish their distinctness. A meeting which is possible only around a pseudo-real (a diegesis): around a *place* consisting of actions, objects, persons, a time and a space (a place similar in this respect to the real), but which presents itself of its own accord as a vast simulation, a non-real real; a 'milieu' with all the structures of the real and lacking (in a permanent, explicit fashion) only the specific exponent of real being. The film fiction thus possesses the strange power of momentarily reconciling three very different regimes of consciousness, for the very characteristics that define the fiction have the effect of driving it, hammering it like a wedge into the narrowest and most central of their interstices: the diegesis has something of the real since it imitates it, something of the daydream and the dream since they imitate the real. The *novelistic* as a whole, with its cinematic extensions, enriched and complicated by auditory and visual perception (absent in the novel), is nothing other than the systematic exploitation of this area of encounters and multiple criss-crossings.

If films which are not *at all* narrative (there are in fact rather few of these) should one day become more numerous and more highly developed, the first effect of this evolution would be to dismiss, at a single stroke, the threefold play of reality, dream, and phantasy, and therefore the unique mixture of these three mirrors through which the filmic state is now defined, a state that history will sweep up in its transformations as it does all social forms.

Notes and References to Part III

CHAPTER 6: FILM AND DREAM: THE KNOWLEDGE OF THE SUBJECT

1 [Economic conditions are those relating to the quantifiable instinctual energy in the psychical processes. Freud's metapsychology also includes the topographical, consisting either of the unconscious, conscious and preconscious, or id ego, and super-ego; and the dynamic, consisting of conflicts and interactions of forces. For more complete definitions of these and other Freudian terms from a French perspective, see J. Laplanche and J.-B. Pontalis, *The Language of Psychoanalysis*, trans. D. Nicholson-Smith (London: The Hogarth Press. 1973).]

2 Freud, 'A Metapsychological Supplement to the Theory of Dreams' (vol. XIV) pp. 226–7.

3 [In Metz's terminology, film is described materially as the combination of a *bande sonore* ('sound track') and *bande-images* ('image track').]

4 'Institution of the Ego', in 'A Metapsychological Supplement to the Theory of Dreams' (vol. XIV) pp. 233–4.

5 Freud, *The Interpretation of Dreams* (vol. V) pp. 488–9.

6 [*Visée* or *visée de conscience* (roughly, 'orientation of consciousness'), a term borrowed from Sartre, is that which is by definition opposed to the content of consciousness. As Metz explains, 'If I see an apple in front of me and if I imagine an apple, the content of consciousness is the same in the two cases, but there are two different *visées*: in the first case, I '*vise*' the apple as present (this is what we call perception), in the second as absent (this is what we call imagination, hope, regret, desire, etc.). I can also '*vise*' it as past (this is memory). The principal *visées* of consciousness (for the same content) are: present-real (to perceive), past-real (to remember), past-unreal (to regret), present-unreal (to imagine), future-real (to decide), future-unreal (to hope), etc.']

7 *The Interpretation of Dreams* (vol. V) pp. 571–2; 'A Metapsychological Supplement to the Theory of Dreams' (vol. XIV) pp. 224–5.

8 'On Narcissism: an Introduction' (vol. XIV) pp. 95–7.

9 *The Interpretation of Dreams* (vol. V) pp. 579–80.

10 Freud, 'Mourning and Melancholia' (vol. XIV) pp. 252–3; 'A Metapsychological Supplement to the theory of Dreams' (vol. XIV) p. 225.

11 *The Interpretation of Dreams* (vol. v) p. 572.

12 In *Film Language*, trans. Taylor, pp. 217–18, I tried to analyse, under the heading 'potential sequence', one of these constructions, which appears in Jean-Luc Godard's film, *Pierrot le Fou*.

13 'A Metapsychological Supplement to the Theory of Dreams', in its entirety and especially (vol. xiv) pp. 234–5.

14 Jean-Louis Baudry, 'Ideological Effects of the Basic Cinematographic Apparatus', *Film Quarterly*, 28, No. 2 (Winter 1974–5) pp. 39–47.

15 Jacques Lacan, 'The Mirror Stage' in *Ecrits*, trans. Sheridan, pp. 1–7.

16 'On Narcissism: an Introduction', (vol. xiv) pp. 82–3; 'A Metapsychological Supplement to the Theory of Dreams' (vol. xiv) pp. 222–3.

CHAPTER 7: FILM AND DREAM: PERCEPTION AND HALLUCINATION

1 Freud, *Introductory Lectures on Psycho-Analysis* (vol. xvi) pp. 375–7.

2 As Malraux says: 'Theatre isn't serious but bull-fighting is . . . novels aren't serious but mythomania is'. (Translated from *La Condition humaine*, Editions Gallimard, 1946 (Le Livre de Poche) p. 212.)

3 This idea has already been expressed by an American researcher, Christian Koch, in a curious and rather interesting Ph.D. thesis (as yet unpublished, unfortunately), 'Understanding Film as a Process of Change', University of Iowa, Iowa City, 1970, 272 pages typescript.

4 [*Coup* being the word for a 'cut', *découpage*, a word with no English equivalent, refers to the division of the action into shots.]

5 'A Metapsychological Supplement to the Theory of Dreams' (vol. xiv) pp. 329–30.

6 *The Interpretation of Dreams* (vol. v) pp. 543–4.

7 Ibid., pp. 533–49; 'A Metapsychological Supplement to the Theory of Dreams' (vol. xiv) pp. 226–8.

8 *The Interpretation of Dreams*, especially (vol. v) p. 561.

9 'A Metapsychological Supplement to the Theory of Dreams' (vol. xiv) p. 226.

10 *The Interpretation of Dreams* (vol. v) p. 543; 'A Metapsychological Supplement to the Theory of Dreams' (vol. xiv) pp. 230–1; 'The Ego and the Id' (vol. xix) pp. 19–20.

11 *The Interpretation of Dreams* (vol. v) pp. 543–4.

12 According to the psychologist Henri Wallon, the sum of a spectator's impressions during the projection of a film is divided into two clearly separated and unequally weighted series, which he calls respectively 'visual series' ('diegetic series' would be a better term) and 'proprioceptive series' (the sense, persisting in a weakened form, of one's own body and therefore of the real world). Cf. 'L'acte perceptif et le cinéma', *Revue internationale de filmologie*, 13 (April–June 1953).

13 On reading this sentence, Gérard Genette commented that the people who took 'diegesis' to be a completely new concept were unknowingly right to a certain extent. Film theory borrowed the general idea, and the term, from

Aristotle and Plato. But the borrowing involved some distortion. For the Greeks, *diegesis* (like its correlate, *mimesis*) was a modality of *lexis*, that is, one of a number of ways of presenting the fiction, a certain technique of relating a story (and at the same time the act of relating); it is a formal (or, more exactly, modal) concept. In current studies, 'diegesis' tends to denote rather that which is related, the fiction itself as material content, with its connotations of the pseudo-real and the referential universe ('mondité', as we would have said at the time of the Liberation).

To this extent, then, 'diegesis' as the term is used today can be seen in its strict sense as an innovation which theorists of the cinema have introduced into general aesthetics – theorists of the cinema, and more specifically (let me take this opportunity to recall) the filmologists working ten to fifteen years before the semiological movement. *Diegesis* is one of the (very few) basic technical terms which Etienne Souriau considered indispensable to film analyses; cf. his *Préface* (pp. 5–10) to *L'Univers filmique*, a collection of articles by different writers (Flammarion, 1953); or (better still) his article entitled 'La structure de l'univers filmique et le vocabulaire de la filmologie' (*Revue internationale de filmologie*, 7–8, pp. 231–40).

14 ['On the Impression of Reality in the Cinema', *Film Language*, trans. Taylor, pp. 3–15.]

CHAPTER 8: FILM AND DREAM: DEGREES OF SECONDARISATION

1 'Une expérience sur la compréhension du film', *Revue internationale de filmologie*, 6, p. 160.
2 'A Metapsychological Supplement to the Theory of Dreams' (vol. XIV) p. 229; *The Interpretation of Dreams* (vol. V) p. 575.
3 *The Interpretation of Dreams* (vol. V) pp. 592–5, 489–90.
4 Ibid., pp. 498–9, 575–6.
5 'A Metapsychological Supplement to the Theory of Dreams' (vol. XIV) pp. 233–4.
6 In particular in *The Interpretation of Dreams* (vol. V) pp. 431–3, 528–9 (concerning psychotic discourses), 530–1, 595–6 (concerning condensation), etc.
7 On this point see Text 7 ('Au-delà de l'analogue, l'image') of my *Essais sur la signification au cinéma*, vol. II.
8 *Discours, figure* (Klincksieck, 1971).
9 *Language and Cinema*, trans. Umiker-Sebeok, pp. 161–83, especially pp. 170–3.
10 Freud, 'The Unconscious' (vol. XIV) pp. 197–9; 'A Metapsychological Supplement to the Theory of Dreams', (vol. XIV) p. 229; *The Interpretation of Dreams* (vol. IV) pp. 295–304.
11 See *Film Language*, trans. Taylor, pp. 20–1.
12 Research in this direction has already begun; cf. especially Thierry Kuntzel, 'Le travail du film', *Communications*, 19 (1972) 25–39.
13 [A superimposition looks like a double exposure, although strictly speaking a double exposure is made at the time of shooting and a superimposition at

the time of printing. Good examples of superimposition occur towards the end of Pasolini's *Medea*. A lap-dissolve (or simply, a dissolve) consists of the fade-out of one shot superimposed on the fade-in of a new shot.]

14 See 'Ponctuations et démarcations dans le film de diégèse' (rpt. in *Essais sur la signification au cinéma*, vol. II, pp. 111–37).

15 In 'Trucage et cinéma', *Essais sur la signification au cinéma*, vol. II, pp. 173–92.

16 Ibid.

CHAPTER 9: FILM AND PHANTASY

1 Freud also employs others: the English word 'daydream', '*rêve*' in the French sense of a daytime dream, that is to say, precisely a '*rêverie*' (*The Interpretation of Dreams* (vol. V) pp. 491–2 and p. 491, note 2). [Freud glosses the German *Tagtraum* with the French '*petits romans*' and the English 'stories'.]

2 ['Ideational representative' and 'affective representative' are Freud's terms for the delegates of the instinct in the respective spheres of ideas and affect.]

3 *The Interpretation of Dreams* (vol. V) pp. 490–2.

4 Or 'half breed' ('The Unconscious' (vol. XIV) pp. 190–1). In the same passage Freud insists on the fact that the phantasy stock remains always unconscious, even if certain of the formations extending it have access to consciousness. In *The Interpretation of Dreams* (vol. V) pp. 491–2 the author stresses that the conscious phantasy and the unconscious phantasy strongly resemble each other in their internal characteristics and structures; their difference is one of content only; the unconscious phantasies are those in which the wish is expressed in a clearer or more urgent fashion and which have undergone repression of this fact.

5 *Introductory Lectures on Psycho-Analysis* (vol. XVI) p. 376; the artist draws his inspiration from his 'day-dreams'; 'he understands, too, how to tone them down so that they do not easily betray their origin from proscribed sources. Furthermore, he possesses the mysterious power of *shaping some particular material* until it has become a faithful image of his phantasy...' (my italics).

6 'The Ego and the Id' (vol. XIX) p. 20; 'A Metapsychological Supplement to the Theory of Dreams' (vol. XIV) pp. 230–1; *The Interpretation of Dreams* (vol. V) pp. 542–3.

7 'On Narcissism: an Introduction' (vol. XIV) p. 74; Freud reproaches Jung for using the notion of introversion in too vague and general a sense; it should be reserved for cases where the libido has abandoned the real object for the phantasy object but has remained directed towards an object [rather than towards the ego]. When the libido flows back from the object into the ego and no longer into the imaginary object, we can speak of (secondary) narcissism. Along the path of disengagement from the object, narcissism represents a step beyond introversion.

CHAPTER 10: THE FILMIC *VISÉE*

1 Cf. *Film Language*, trans. Taylor, pp. 44–5 and 185–227 ('The Modern

Cinema and Narrativity').

2 'On the Impression of Reality in the Cinema', *Film Language*, trans. Taylor, pp. 3–15.

Part IV

Metaphor/Metonymy, or the Imaginary Referent

Translated by Celia Britton and Annwyl Williams

Metaphor/Metonymy,
or the Imaginary Referent

Throughout this book, I have been concerned with the question of the *psychoanalytic constitution of the cinematic signifier*. In using this formula I am attempting to describe the as yet partially unknown set of trajectories through which the 'practice' of the cinema (the social practice of a particular signifier) is rooted in the large-scale anthropological figures which Freudian theory has done much to elucidate: what is the relationship between the cinematic situation and the mirror stage, or the infinity of desire, or the voyeuristic position, or the contrary currents of disavowal etc.?

This enormous question – ultimately that of the 'deep-structural' grounding of the cinema as a social institution – involves many other aspects, including no doubt some I am completely unaware of: because he who writes (= 'I') derives his existence solely from such limitations; and also because the question itself, as far as the cinema is concerned, has never really been set out in these terms (at the point where a semiotics, an unconscious and a history converge), so that groping one's way like children in the dark is in this case one of the least blinkered modes of progress. (Those more absolute spirits who have all the answers are groping too, the only difference being that they don't know it.)

I have now (autumn 1975) reached a point where I can see another facet of my problem: namely, metaphorical and metonymic operations in the film sequence – *operations*, I should stress, rather than localised metaphors or metonymies that could be isolated – and, more generally, the 'means of representation' (as the term is used in Freud's *The Interpretation of Dreams*), and the exact place they occupy, in particular films, between the primary and secondary processes (= study of the degrees of secondarisation).

This also involves the ways in which condensations and displacements intervene in the textual generation of film: it is easy to point to their existence, and to offer a few examples, less easy to map out, even roughly, a kind of epistemological space within which this or that way of talking about them could find its validity. On the basis of what 'theoretical minimum' (since at the moment a minimum is all we can hope for) can we proceed to construct a coherent discourse on the element of *primary rhetoric* in the textual weave of film?

This question is different from those I have considered up to now (i.e. spectator identification, the screen as scopic space, modalities of belief-disbelief, etc.) in that it directly concerns the filmic text. It therefore also touches on the cinema as institution, the system as a whole, since the text is a part of this. But it is not quite on the same level as studies of the mirror relationship, the scopic regime, disavowal, etc., all of which were squarely lodged in a space – or rather a 'moment' – which was not exactly that of the film, or exactly that of the spectator, or even that of the code (and the list could be extended): I had placed myself as it were beyond these distinctions, on a sort of common ground which included them all at once, and which was none other than the cinema-machine itself, envisaged in its conditions of possibility. With the figures of the image- or sound-sequence, we are indeed still 'within' the machine; but our point of entry is now more clearly indicated as being that of filmic textuality.

Before coming on to the cinematic aspect of the question, I feel that some preliminary work is needed, an effort at conceptual clarification, which makes its own demands – demands which, in this instance, are considerable, since the attempt at orientation will meet along its path (and as the very condition of its reality) several distinct and pre-existing fields of knowledge, which do not automatically 'match up'; the work of research consists precisely in seeking, within a cinematic perspective, the possible patterns of their articulation. In the most advanced of the current reflections on film, you get the feeling that different ideas are tending to converge on a textual problematic that is always *fundamentally* (in principle) the same – take for example the notions of displacement, metonymy, syntagm and montage, to name just one 'series'. But as soon as you try to take it a bit further, you come up against the fact that in their respective areas of origin each of these notions has a fairly complex past of its own; and so, getting to grips with anything more than insubstantial clichés or fashionable catch-phrases – since a concept always goes back to the place of its elaboration in the history of knowledge even, and especially, if it is to be carried over to another field – requires some degree of willingness to work back through the problems, not to remain trapped in a position which knows nothing of its antecedents.

In this rather complicated and very interesting area (interesting perhaps just because it is complicated), we find on the one hand rhetoric, the old classical rhetoric with its theory of figures and tropes, including metaphor and metonymy. On the other hand there is post-Saussurean structural linguistics, a far more recent phenomenon (rhetoric maintained its dominance for some twenty-four centuries), with its major dichotomy between the syntagmatic and the paradigmatic, and its tendency to remodel the rhetorical heritage along similar lines of division (Jakobson). There is also psychoanalysis, which introduced the ideas of displacement and condensation (Freud), and then in its Lacanian orientation 'projected' them on to the metaphor/metonymy couple. I am therefore committed to a course whose specifically cinematic phases will be cut across by other lines of investigation which will seem to turn their back on film: but only in order to return to it more effectively.

11

'Primary' Figure, 'Secondary' Figure

Metaphor, metonymy. A random sampling of the different occurrences of these figures shows that their degree of involvement in
the primary process – or the secondary process, if you start from
the other end – varies quite considerably from one case to the
next.

I need to start (it will gradually become clear why) with an
example of unquestionable banality. I shall choose the French
word '*Bordeaux*'.[1] This is first of all the name of a town (= a
'toponym'). Then it begins to denote the wine produced there: a
classic development, a text-book example of metonymy: the place
of production instead of the product, one of the types of meaning-
shift based on contiguity (geographical contiguity, in this case).
But it is clear that the primary force and unconscious resonance
of this association (which, prosaic as it is, must nevertheless at
some point have forced its way into the language) are by now
very much weakened in many cases when the word is pronounced or heard. Many, not all: how do we know? (I will come
back to this.) Faced with this kind of metonymy, Freud could say
that the 'psychical energy' (the meaning), before 'binding', and
in order to become bound, went through 'freer' modes of circulation: the famous wine could have been given other names, the
provisional termini of other symbolic routes; the name of the
town could have been transferred to another of its products or attributes (like the political term '*Girondin*' during the Revolution).
The code (the French language) has retained just one of these
semantic trajectories: this is not to say that it is illogical, for it is
quite 'intelligible' (in retrospect), but it was chosen – and here
already, behind the metonymy, the metonymic *act* appears –
from a number of possible associations (some of which were

154

perhaps embarked upon and then dropped, with the result that they are known only to scholars), and these too would have been more or less logical. One has only to leaf through any work on etymology to learn that *'guillotine'* is so called on account of its inventor's name (Guillotin), that *'style'* derives from the Latin *'stilus'* (a pointed instrument used for writing), etc. It's the same each time: you think 'Oh yes!', but you would never have been able to guess. Diachronic semantics states that this word 'comes' from that one, or that this has 'given' that; in this way it identifies trajectories which are rarely *inevitable*; each one has ruled out others which would also have made sense; the act of choosing is never, in itself, really 'logical'.

Conversely, symbolisation as 'bound energy', once it has become fixed in the now lexicalised metonymy (*Bordeaux*) is still a circuit, still circulates – from a place-name to the name of a drink, in my example. 'Bound' but not immobile: on the contrary, the word implies that it is the very mobility (the displacement) which is henceforth coded, as a *mapped-out* route. It should not be forgotten that throughout his work[2] Freud always gave as the most typical example of bound energy what he called the 'thought process' (so-called normal thought, not dream thought), a process which he believed required two preconditions: a permanently high degree of cathexis of the psychical apparatus, corresponding roughly to the phenomenon of attention, and the displacement of small quantities of energy, controlled in transit from one representation to the next (otherwise, we would be dealing with a disruptive association, and in extreme cases hallucination which, as we know, seeks 'perceptual identity' rather than *'thought* identity'[3] – my emphasis). So, even if he mostly studied its primary versions (or if it is these that have most often been retained), displacement for Freud denotes psychological mobility in general: it is the energy hypothesis itself,[4] the economic model of psychoanalysis. This transit, in the instance of *Bordeaux* wine, is of the order of the metonymic, and is so to speak posthumous: sedimented in the language, so that the subjects (if by that is meant the individuals, since the code is also a 'subject') do not need to follow it through themselves in its more or less primary entanglements. In the case of the metonymy whose end-result is the naming of *'Roquefort'*, which has a very similar mechanism, it is of course possible for some French speakers to know the cheese whilst remaining ignorant of the very existence of the place ('*Bordeaux*' continues to be known as a toponym because the town is bigger): but, even with '*Roquefort*', it is possible for them not to know about it only because the language does. Here, in any case, we are dealing with very considerably secondarised metonymies.

ON 'WORN' FIGURES

Obviously one might hope, at least for a while, that these problems could be solved by stating that '*Bordeaux*', or '*guillotine*' (along with the innumerable other examples of the same kind), is not a metonymy but the present result, in itself not metonymic, of an earlier metonymy. Linguists often make such distinctions (without necessarily exaggerating their importance): for instance they talk of 'worn metaphors', or of figures which were once figurative and are no longer so, etc. A rhetorician like Fontanier, whose importance at the beginning of the nineteenth century is well known, was working along similar lines when he excluded *catachresis* from his list of true figures and put it in with the 'non-figurative tropes': since catachresis (the 'arm' of a chair, the 'leaves' of a book) is a mode of reference which, even if there is something obviously figurative about it, has become the ordinary name of the object referred to, and in fact, its only real 'name'. (We might note, however, that this argument can be turned back against one of the most enduring ideas of the rhetorical tradition, namely the mythical status of primacy accorded to the 'literal meaning': since the most literal term for invoking certain referents is a figurative one...)

To restrict the definition of figures to those which are still perceived as such, and to exclude those which are not, is merely a terminological convention (which for my part I shall not conform to). True, it possesses the advantage of reminding us how important it is to locate historically that fairly precise moment when figurations which have now become routine made an active impact, and of not confusing this with whatever happened subsequently. But after duly distinguising between the two cases, we are still left confronting what seems to me the core of the problem; and here the distinction is no longer of much use to us, especially if it is interpreted as permissson to establish a watertight partition between figures which are active and those which are defunct. Because what we still have to grasp, beyond the gesture towards categorisation (which retains its value as just that), is precisely the most difficult point: namely, that every sig-nifying matrix (such as metonymy) remains the same in its specific outline – in what *defines* it in opposition to the others – whether it is 'alive' or 'dead'; that it is able, by its very nature, to appear in both forms. To put it another way: if, once 'dead', it were really no longer a figure at all, how would we know that it is a metonymy rather than a metaphor? And to make the question even more radical: how can coded configurations *signify* at all, if they have nothing in common with those innovating pressures still pushing their way through, where signification can be appre-hended in the very process of its construction?

This is what I shall call the paradox of the code (its defining paradox): in the final analysis the code must owe its features, and indeed its existence, to a set of symbolic operations – the code is a social *activity* – and yet it exists as a code only to the extent that it collects and organises the 'inert' results of these operations. To make the instance of the code itself 'dynamic', in some form or other, as generative linguistics does, does not get rid of the problem: it is true that for the latter the language system consists above all in rules of modification (= 're-writing'), and not in a list of morphemes or even of sentence-types; but these rules are themselves (ideally, assuming them to be perfectly known) fixed in their operation and in their number, and one of the properties of a language is that it conforms to them. This is the notion of grammaticality – yet another case, and an even clearer one, of the strange and common phenomenon of immobilised mobility, arrested transference. Arrested, but still carrying meaning: a coded operation is always, in some way or another, an act which each occurrence reproduces, even if henceforth it is programmed in advance and more or less immutable. And conversely, if I may be permitted to 'jump' without warning to the other end of my problem, we should remember that the most primary trajectories of the unconscious, in a given subject, are programmed by his structure and by the events of his childhood, that they manifest an irresistible tendency to 'reproduce' themselves (the term belongs to psychoanalytic terminology as well), and to be dis-charged along more or less fixed routes of association: this is *rep-*

etition, a central concept in Freudian thought. The opposition of 'bound' and 'free', as apart from the terms conventionally used to express it, should not mislead us: the free exists behind the bound, since every process begins in the unconscious, and the bound in the free, since the unconscious is a specific organisation of affects and representations.

FIGURAL, LINGUISTIC: THE FIGURE EMBEDDED IN THE 'LITERAL MEANING'

Specialists in the history of languages have indicated how certain lexical changes illustrate very clearly this surprising coefficient of homogeneity between new semantic paths and their trite repetitions at a later stage. If words are constantly changing their meaning (or picking up new meanings), if meanings, too, 'change their words' very easily, this is largely through the play of figurative uses which are subsequently lost as such; they become literal meanings, and thus perpetuate the unwinding of the diachronic process by a double rebound effect: supplanting the old literal meaning, and stimulating the growth of new figurative meanings (so that everything is ready, once again, for a new cycle of the spiral).

In Vulgar Latin the word '*testa*' meant 'a fragment of earthenware or glass', or a 'phial', and its signifier, following the laws of phonetic change, became '*tête*'; it began to be used with increasing consistency to designate the part of the body which now bears that name [i.e. 'head'] and changing from a slang metaphor to an ordinary term, it gradually ousted '*caput*', which has lost this meaning (but cf. '*couvrechef*' [= some form of headgear], '*hocher le chef*' [to shake one's head], etc.). The signified (the part of the body) has changed its signifier; the signifier (*testa-tête*) has changed its signified, since nobody nowadays sees a reference to 'an earthenware fragment' in it; the other signifier (*caput-chef*), pushed to one side by the first one, has followed suit: through another demetaphorised metaphor, it now denotes a man in command (a figure which is still alive in the expression 'to be at the head of': death certificates, it would seem, are not that easy to sign in some cases; there are partial deaths). This little shake-up, whose active principle turns out to be comparison (contracted into metaphor), is not necessarily over: today's slang has new figures for '*tête*' [head], since the latter is no longer figurative: '*citron*' [lemon], for instance (or '*fiole*' [phial], which strangely enough revives '*testa*'), and these will perhaps one day gain enough ground to drive out '*tête*': the signified will have acquired a new 'literal' designation.

These entanglements of the figurative and the non-figurative, these pressures (displacements in the widest sense) whereby coded and emerging meanings are in a continual process of transmutation, are among the driving forces of lexical evolution. One is reminded of that 'dizzy intricacy' of rhetoric which Gérard Genette has described so well, 'the whirligig of figurative defined as what is not literal and literal defined as what is not figurative'.[5] A complex and self-perpetuating entanglement: also an *intimate* one, suggesting some bond of kinship (hard to understand) between the two opposites. Languages, across the centuries, are never static, and changes in the code are as inevitable as the code itself. This is due, among other factors, to natural languages' permanent capacity for constantly reabsorbing fresh associative connections: for fixing them and so making them last and, simultaneously, defusing them of their subversive potential; for connecting them while rejecting them, and for rejecting them while ratifying them (as in the eternal disavowals of our own lives). Every code is a collection of reworkings, of double repercussions: the primary is recuperated by the secondary, the secondary is anchored in the primary. And this set of reworkings is itself, over time, constantly reworked, like a monument – *monumentum*: memory, trace, relic – a monument which is being restored but which must have been in the process of restoration in every phase of its history, and which can have known no other 'condition'; similar in this respect to the history of civilisation and to everyone's biography.

The 'figurative' . . .? The *figural*, rather: is not one of its principal effects to modify the status of the non-figurative? Insofar as this is true it must also be the case that figurative meanings existed before literal meanings. Figures are not 'ornaments' of discourse (*colores rhetorici*), embellishments added on afterwards for our pleasure. They do not essentially pertain to 'style' (*elocutio*). They are the driving forces that shape language. If we go back, even mythically, to the origins of speech, we are obliged to admit that the *first acts of naming*, the most 'literal' meanings of all, could have been based only on some symbolic association which was later stabilised, on some 'wild' variety of metaphor or metonymy, since up until then the object had no name at all. One way or another, the precise, referential, purely denotative term must also have been *invented*. An onomatopoeia, or a change of key (metaphor), an animal referred to by its cry (metonymy; cf. the Latin '*pipio*', which has given the French '*pigeon*'), etc. The first literal meanings were of necessity figurative, as when children say a 'quack-quack' to mean a duck.

Confusion between the actual working-through of meanings and their subsequent settling down is basically not a great danger; the difficulty, in fact, lies rather in understanding how it comes about that the symbolic function operates entirely through the continual movement back and forth between the two states, as though the code existed only in order to be transgressed, and as though the advance of signification in turn needed the code behind it (to lean on) and would inevitably end up in a new, but never definitive, coding. Cultural evolution has, in this respect, a lot in common with the happenings of everyday life: faced with a clear manifestation of the primary process – like the typical acting out of your best friend having a row with you – or conversely of the secondary process – for instance a calm deliberation hinged on real circumstances (if such a thing exists) – everyone knows where they stand. In the same way, we are not in danger of forgetting the difference between Hugo's '*pâtre-promontoire*' [shepherd-promontory] and the word for 'head' in ordinary French. The 'mystery', in these two pairs of examples and in all the others, is much more that we are forced to suppose that, somewhere way back, these two diverging evolutions had a common origin.

I have said that the association of ideas which resulted in the name of '*Roquefort*' is today no longer alive. But if I know this little town, if I went there once on holiday (it was during the Occupation, I remember; I was a small boy, with my parents, and we used to go to the Aveyron every summer, in search of a few provisions) then the word will evoke a whole landscape for me, Millau and Saint-Affrique, and the stony bend in a little street, old and steep: then I am actively retracing the path of the metonymy (not just that of my childhood), and the language, in its time, did exactly the same thing, since the manuals of semantics tell us that there is a link between the product and the place where it is manufactured. A disturbing resemblance. And one which is equally relevant in the case of metaphor: you cannot just reiterate the fact that a considerable part of the lexicon is made up of 'worn metaphors' of the *testa* type (an assertion that Antoine Meillet already considered to be traditional and not very significant, albeit correct):[6] however worn they may be, why is it that they are, precisely, metaphors, that is to say, figures which along with others are at the source of the purest and most striking poetry? Why, in other words, is one led to the conclusion that, far from poetic language being a 'deviation' and ordinary language a norm, ordinary language, as Julia Kristeva has so often emphasised, is a temporarily depoeticised and limited subset of more basic symbolisations which resemble those of poetic language? (Charles Bally, a direct disciple of Saussure, has analysed at length the 'expressiveness' of the most everyday language,[7] and he demonstrates that it does not differ essentially from poetic figurations.) A problem, then, which is both old and new (like all real problems). And which, in the case of the cinema, is raised in a more acute form; one might say: is *closer* to us, in the sense that the layer of code between it and us is thinner (the questions 'reach us' more quickly). The *moment of the code* appears in a less stable and substantial form than is the case with natural languages; it does nevertheless exist, and the difference has to do with its degree of relative autonomy. (Far be it from us to invoke that mythical opposition between 'originality' and 'the rules'.)

ON EMERGENT FIGURES

I am afraid that the reader is beginning to get tired of hearing about earthenware fragments and '*Bordeaux*'. Perhaps we should move on to a different kind of metonymy, more immediately primary, or more obviously so. In which case I shall have to talk more about myself, since any example taken from a language or a cinematic code would be vitiated by the simple fact of its prior existence. So – for several days now, roughly since the time I began work on this article, a pneumatic drill in a neighbouring street has been constantly getting on my nerves, and continues to do so as I am writing this. I have got into the habit, when 'talking' to myself, of calling this text, whose title is not yet finally decided, the *pneumatic drill article*. It's a ridiculous name. I could have found other, more logical solutions – if only 'my latest article' or, more colloquially, 'my thing on metaphor/metonymy' (in accordance with its approximate subject). 'Pneumatic drill' is a primary association,[8] and I can guess more or less (in retrospect, of course, and only partially) the path it has taken through my unconscious. If I concentrate on my work I no longer 'hear' this persecutory din; but in another sense, I do hear it and it upsets me: the word 'persecutory' flows spontaneously from my pen. I write in spite of this noise, and also against it. A struggle for existence, no less, is going on between it and me: if I hear it too clearly, I can no longer write, and if I write, I can no longer hear it, or hardly. In my phantasy it represents (this time by condensation) all the various obstacles – to which I am by nature cruelly sensitive – which make 'research' into something perpetually impossible, because of the freedom from distraction which it requires and which is almost never to be found: an act whose every realisation is a victory over the extreme improbability that characterises it initially, and which has no place within everyday life but only against it: a small schizophrenia. Calling my present work 'pneumatic drill' gives me an outlet for my hatred of all sources of distraction, but I also express, in a sort of reaction-formation, another feeling (just as infantile as the first, or as any affect): a modest triumph: because despite the pneumatic drill, my article looks as though it's going to get written: I therefore confer on it, as though on some victorious general, the name of the vanquished enemy. A nickname, a sign of omnipotence...

I could follow this little fragment of self-analysis through into more murky areas. It so happens that this summer I have been more than usually hindered from working, partly through the (unintentional) 'fault' of people close to me or in my family. I realise that the pneumatic drill, in my phantasy, is simply taking over their role (so my conscious metonymy is *also* an unconscious metaphor). The people you care about disturb you more than anyone else, and this is not even paradoxical (basically, it corresponds to the fact of ambivalence). The 'naming' of my article takes me back, step by step, to a configuration of an Oedipal nature. Here, then, is a substantially 'primary' metonymy, whose relations with an unconscious are specifiable, and which is therefore original, not to be found in any code or any text-book.

And yet, I have only to explain to someone a small part of what I have just said here, I have only to inform him of the mere fact that the drill was there while I was writing, for the name to become immediately intelligible to him and for him to be able to use it himself. Here we sense the beginnings of a secondarising tendency (= 'deprimarisation'). My listener will not have to go back along the whole chain. But this is because the first association (the physical proximity of the noise) itself constitutes a chain: the very principle of metonymy can be seen at work in it, and if a stranger understands me, it is because he too can draw on this principle of symbolisation (so he is not in fact a stranger): he is, as Freud would say, capable of displacing energy from one representation to another contiguous one (the contiguity here is both spatial and temporal). My metonymy – which in principle is anecdotal and private, idiolectal, born of the moment and not meant to outlive it – could easily become secondarised to a considerable degree, given a kind of 'collapse' into its most obvious single link: the overdetermination would be lost, and with it the metaphor which lay beneath the metonymy. This socialisation is a matter of pure chance (like the lexical changes in natural languages): thus, within the circle of my closest friends (which already forms a possible *sociolect,* tiny though it may be), 'pneumatic drill article' could become informally the 'real' name of my article, the one normally used to refer to it: its vernacular name, as a linguist would say. And after all, don't we talk about Sainte-Beuve's *'Mondays',* simply because these chronicles appeared in the press every Monday? A rather similar metonymy. The only difference is that its use is far more widespread. But then Sainte-Beuve is a classic.

THE METALINGUISTIC ILLUSION

So whenever the terms 'metaphor' or 'metonymy' appear in the pages that follow, they will refer, unless otherwise stated, to specific paths and their mutual differences: neither will be associated with any idea of originality or banality, of logicality or illogicality, with the primary or the secondary, or with any particular degree of codification.[9] I do not think it is possible to judge in advance the exact point which each figure occupies on these different bipolar axes, in a study where it is precisely this that is in question, and which is geared (however indirectly) towards the cinematic text, where the particular overlapping of primary and secondary is, in the present state of research, far from clear.

If, indeed, I return from my little autobiographical example to the metonymy of '*Bordeaux*' (chosen for its anonymity) with the aim of throwing light on it retrospectively, I realise that short of a special analysis nothing can really establish the true nature, the number and exact 'depth' of the symbolic paths which have linked the representation of a wine to that of a town. Because in 'pneumatic drill' as well, a superficial link, severed from everything else, was sufficient to guarantee the minimal meaning. When I am told that in '*Bordeaux*' *the* metonymic link *is* geographical contiguity, I do not have to believe it, because clearly the function and purpose of the semantic treatise is to inform me of the simplest, the most conscious and most widespread of the associations which may exist or be created between the place and the drink, without worrying about the others. There is no reason why I should assume that '*Bordeaux*' is less overdetermined than 'pneumatic drill' (or less overdeterminable than '*Roquefort*', whose backward trail I began to follow up a few pages ago).

In short, the grammatical and rhetorical tradition reduces what is really, in '*Bordeaux*' or any other example, just a provisionally established nodal point in the infinity of associations, to a single one of the numerous strands in the 'skein' that it potentially unwinds. Potentially, but also in reality, because this skein must certainly have had an effect, one way or another (more or less consciously), at the time when the figure appeared, and *in order to* make it appear: if we restricted ourselves to the one official link in the chain, without these extra determinations, how could we explain the fact that some associations get through and others don't, that some 'take' and others don't, when the others also contain a link which is plausible and easy to justify (*some* link can always be found) — a possible pretext for a certain degree of socialisation?

Depending on periods, individuals, and social practices, one can sense or invent many evocative itineraries between the idea of '*style*' in its multiple resonances and the idea of a pointed instrument held in the hand (*stilus*) other than that connecting the tool with the action (= traditional sub-category of metonymy), and it is difficult to identify those which have had the most influence on the stabilisation of the final circuit. Linguists know that a lexical formation or a phrase catches on by virtue of its 'expressiveness' rather than its logic (for example: 'raining cats and dogs'), and the notion of expressiveness takes us straight into those kinds of harmonics which, if one only follows them up far enough, lead to the unconscious.

The link which gets established is usually the one which is deemed to be more 'immediate' than the others, more accessible to common sense, more innocent, too (that's why it's visible); in short, more consistently likely to become conscious. It is the part of the skein which has come into view, the end which is least liable to be censored. And it is also (but the one phenomenon results directly from the other) the only one that is promoted to *metalinguistic status*: laid out clearly in the manuals of rhetoric or semantics, wrenched from the interlocking tissue of associations, to be exhibited on the stage of language as code, to become part of the language's consciousness, of its native grammar which is like its *ego,* and hence heavily infiltrated by the super-ego and the imaginary.

All this breeds the constant danger of what amounts to an optical illusion, which we must try not to fall for. We are often tempted to attribute the figure as a whole, especially if it is very common, to the secondary process. But in so doing we forget that the secondary section of its circuit is by definition the easiest to perceive, and that it is, furthermore, reinforced by a sort of conscious over-cathexis (rather like *attention,* in the Freudian sense) deriving from the power of the metalinguistic operation which, in books that 'deal with' language by superimposing a second codification on it, consistently bases the whole superstructure of its explicit definitions on this one segment, and on it alone.

There are no secondary figures. Even the most banal can develop, through the flow of 'free association', at all the levels of primarisation that one could wish for, like a flower opening out, petal by petal. There are only figures which are secondarised in varying degrees: by the way in which they are used, by the particular level of themselves at which they have been folded away, closed like a book that could have told us more and which we have not read through to the end.

There are no primary figures. That was the point of my 'pneumatic drill' example – a metonymy connected with my desire, but which anyone could use without knowing the first thing about it, so long as they were informed of the circumstantial anecdote. There are only figures which have escaped secondarisation in varying degrees, through not being 'taken up' socially on a sufficiently large scale; or else, at another level of non-generalisation, because they may be known, but only to those who read poetry, and so have not entered the widest circle of the code, namely ordinary, language, 'Clothed in candid honesty' is certainly famous, but only if you have read Hugo. Here the primary resonance is still quite alive. But it is already much less so in an expression like 'covered in shame', which is nevertheless very similar in its semiotic mechanism, but has *fallen* (as we say, so appropriately) into common usage.

The difficulties raised here are partly due to historical factors in the constitution of fields of knowledge. At the time when the notions of metaphor, metonymy, and more generally the various lists of figures were being worked out, primary processes and psychoanalysis obviously didn't come into it. The rhetoricians, in their *rabies taxinomica* (if I may be forgiven this hybrid mixture of Latin and Greek), made strenuous efforts to classify a very large number of types of associative paths. But they remained firmly – all the more firmly since they were unaware of it, and since the question, even, did not exist historically – within the sphere of more or less conscious associations of ideas. The body of work we have inherited from them belongs, therefore, within a framework which for them was the only possible one, and which for us, looked at retrospectively, coincides to a very considerable extent with the secondary process. There can be no doubt that this is one of the reasons for the difficulty we have in mentally dissociating notions such as metaphor and metonymy from a vague but persistent connotation of secondariness ('It's just rhetoric, it's a catalogue of set expressions, etc.'); the only marginally significant exception we will ordinarily allow is in the case of 'poetic figures' (which are thus mysteriously divorced from the others, not without prejudice to an overall understanding of the symbolic).

When we think along these lines we are ourselves victims of another rhetorical figure, which Charles Bally called '*évocation par le milieu*',[10] and which belongs fundamentally (as we shall see) to metonymy in the wider sense. Words are coloured by qualities which pertain to their original users, or those who have used them most frequently (a transfer from the speaker to the statement); *'combinat'* suggests the Soviet Union (although this has nothing to do with the denotative signified of the word, i.e. a set of more or less interdependent industries) because the word was first used, at least in France, in connection with the USSR's five-year plans, and so is perceived as a translation or semantic calque from the Russian (perhaps it really is? I have no idea). In the same way the notions of rhetoric seem very secondary to us (as one might say of something that it seems 'very English'), because the writers who produced them, when seen from our twentieth century, look a bit as if they belong to the secondary. As a result, we may well forget that the possibilities of their conceptual equipment may, as often happens, considerably exceed what they themselves saw in it or said about it.

12

'Small-scale' Figures, 'Large-scale' Figures

We know that Lacan sees the principle of metaphor in condensation, and the principle of metonymy in displacement. In Freudian terms, we would say that condensation and displacement
are the 'prototypes' of metaphor and metonymy, the latter being
the chief 'figurations' of the symbolic order: of language, where
Jakobson has demonstrated their importance, and also of the
unconscious.

It is noticeable that, right from the start, Lacan places metaphor and metonymy in a position which does not 'lean' in the
direction of either the primary or the secondary process. It is as
though metaphor and metonymy were introduced 'alongside'
this dichotomy, which itself, as we might expect, occupies a far
less central place in Lacan's texts than it does in Freud's. The
metaphor-metonymy pair as presented by Lacan cannot be
straightforwardly assigned to either one or the other of the Freudian 'processes'. This is because it is assigned elsewhere: to the
Symbolic. The two terms of the pair profoundly affect language
and discourse, in other words fairly secondary instances, as well
as dreaming which is distinctly more primary.

If we are going to measure, from a semiological point of view, the
scope of this move by Lacan, there is an initial circumstance
which must, I think, be kept in mind. 'Metaphor' and
'metonymy' as concepts (as *words*) are obviously associated with
rhetoric rather than with modern linguistics. And it is true that
linguistics intervened only very late on in the history of the two
notions. But Lacan, as he says himself[1] (and as can easily be seen
from reading his work anyway), uses both terms in the extended

and heavily bipolarised sense given them by Jakobson, which is much influenced by the parallel opposition of paradigm and syntagm in structural linguistics. I think that this distinction is of greater consequence than it might seem, and I shall examine it in more detail later (Chapter 13). But we should note here and now that in the rhetorical tradition metaphor and metonymy were two quite circumscribed and particular figures – two items always somewhat buried (to varying degrees, depending on which one of the numerous classifications was proposed) in the midst of a long and scrupulously detailed catalogue which included many other figures (antiphrasis, euphemism, hypallage, hyperbole, etc.). Clearly such specialised stylistic subdivisions – which, in any logical generative system, would come rather late on, quite close to the 'pheno-text' – cannot be seen as relatable to condensation and displacement, two major types of psychical paths which operate on an enormous scale, with multiple variants: it would be like taking two different botanical classifications and trying to draw up a list of correspondences between the 'sub-kingdoms' of the one and the 'species' or 'varieties' of the other.

Metaphor and metonymy as Lacan thinks of them are 'objects' whose level of generality – their powers of organisation within a taxonomic framework, or of 'dominance' in a generative perspective, if one was to *derive* figures from them – is of the same order as that of condensation and displacement; and that is why the idea of a homology can legitimately be entertained. In the Jakobsonian 'reworking' of the rhetorical heritage, metaphor and metonymy are kinds of super-figures, headings under which other things can be grouped together: on one side the figures of similarity, on the other those of contiguity. If a rhetorician had drawn up his two columns in this way, he would have had several distinct items to enter under each of the headings.

Earlier on I quoted a well known line of Victor Hugo's (from *Booz endormi*): '*vêtu de probité candide et de lin blanc*' [clothed in candid honesty and white linen]. The rhetorical vulgate would probably call this a *zeugma*: the same term ('*vêtu*') governs two others ('*probité*' and '*lin*') which are syntactically parallel (nominal complements of the adjectival participle), but incompatible on another axis (here, abstract versus concrete), so that only one of them ('*lin*') is strictly appropriate to what it relates to; outside the specific figuration which is precisely what has to be defined, a person can be clothed in linen, but not in honesty. This is just one example of the *small-scale* encoding of figures, in line with the rhetorical habit of mind, which multiplied the divisions.

This same fragment of text can be classified very differently if we relate it to the metaphor-metonymy system, which is characterised by having only two compartments. These two ways of describing the (actually occurring) terminal segments are in no way contradictory, because they are not even on the same level of analysis (contradiction can occur only within a common procedure). We can legitimately claim that the Hugo line, while remaining an example of zeugma, contains a metaphorical impulse (honesty is like a garment), and also a metonymic one: Booz, whose honesty has been established, was (also) clothed in linen: these two attributes, the 'abstract' and the 'concrete', tend to merge, in their common whiteness (= a further metaphorical intervention: 'candid/white'), into a sort of transcendental garment, simultaneously ideal and literal, since both belong to Booz and are thus 'contiguous'.

This off-the-cuff analysis is only meant to show that the figures of rhetoric, numerous and intricate as they are, could be reorganised in terms of the more recent binary division of linguistics: a retroactive modelling that would make each of the original 'small' figures into a sub-category of metaphor, or metonymy, or both at once. But whether or not you undertake a project of this kind, you must clearly distinguish the two parameters that it would be working between, and not attempt to raise questions that can lead nowhere, like 'Is this figure a zeugma *or* a metonymy?'. The problem is often posed in terms of this kind, but the questioning itself unknowingly contains several assumptions, none of which corresponds to the historical reality: (i) that zeugma and metonymy are mutually exclusive; (ii) that there is only one definition of zeugma and only one of metonymy; and (iii) that a segment of text can 'be' (intrinsically, in the nature of things) a zeugma or a metonymy, whereas in fact only in relation to *systems*, some of them better than others, can they be classified one way or the other.

STATUS AND LIST

If I have placed so much emphasis on these taxonomic problems, it is mainly because I am thinking ahead to the problems that we shall have to face when we get to the cinematic text. Whenever you come across possible *correspondences between series* (here for instance the psychoanalytic 'series', the linguistic series, the rhetorical series, the filmic series), the first temptation – because it seems more 'concrete', makes you feel you're 'getting somewhere' faster, coming up with 'results', and because concrete results are mythical entities strongly promoted by our ideology – the first temptation is to plunge immediately into 'extensive' work, to aspire to an exhaustive inventory – a list. For example: what, in the last analysis, are the main figurative devices specific to the cinema? Which of them are primary and which secondary? What is the filmic equivalent of metaphor, or condensation? We are not always sufficiently aware of the need for a preliminary, more 'intensive' consideration, inevitably rather epistemological in nature, of the principle itself and the validity of any eventual correspondence. At the stage I have now reached in the writing of this text I have as yet no idea (I mean this literally, in all honesty) of the 'table' of cinematic figures I shall end up with, even assuming that I'm heading towards a table – which I am rather beginning to doubt.

There is here a problem which I have often come across in my research, and which I would like to *name*: let me call it the problem of the status and the list. A question like 'What is a cinematic code?' can receive two kinds of answer: a status-answer ('A cinematic code is a system constructed by the analyst, which is not explicitly present in the film but is presupposed by the fact that the film can be understood'), or a list-answer: 'A cinematic code, well, it's things like the so-called punctuation system, or the standard conventions of editing, or the way you organise the movements in and out of frame, etc.'.

Let us take the film close-up, and the question of its *position* (as a surface structure) in some classificatory schema constructed on the basis of the two 'entry points' Metaphor and Metonymy. In this example, the preliminaries (i.e. the problems of status) which must be dealt with before we can begin to assign it a place in the schema are six in number (at a minimum estimate):

1. Why have we decided to use 'metaphor' and 'metonymy' in their linguistic (i.e. bipolar) sense rather than in the narrowly particularising sense they have in rhetoric?

2. Since the close-up obviously contains an element of synecdoche, are we going to say that metonymy (even in the broad, more Jakobsonian sense) covers synecdoche, or that the latter is a separate case? We should remember that this intermediate position is not without its precedents: Fontanier for instance proposed grouping all the tropes together into three main types – metonymy, synecdoche and metaphor.

3. Assuming that we limit ourselves to metaphor and metonymy, is there necessarily any advantage in thinking of them as mutually exclusive, and couldn't the close-up involve a combination of both principles?

4. How do we know that the close-up itself, from a purely cinematic point of view, is a single entity, and that its *realisation* in a film does not require several distinct underlying operations, some of which could be metaphorical and others metonymic?

5. How far is the actual definition of metaphor and metonymy, in terms of rhetoric or linguistics, separable from verbal language and from the specific entity of the *word*? That is, will it even be possible to find completely isolable metaphors and metonymies in the cinema? Should we not rather try to identify the textual traces of the metaphorical process and the metonymic process? (This question sends us back to strictly linguistic objects: the powerful social existence of the word is surely the tree for which we cannot see the wood? The metaphor is easy to pick out, and so makes us overlook the metaphorical: the same goes for metonymy and the metonymic.)

6. On the psychoanalytic level, doesn't condensation by its very action imply a set of displacements, so that these two types of movement, while they remain distinct, would appear to be so to speak 'inside' one another?

These are the sorts of problems I shall be concerned with; producing an immediate list of the principal cinematic figures is not part of my aim. Each of the questions, depending on the answer it receives, will profoundly influence all the surface distributions that can be tried out at a later stage. This 'answer', each of the answers, amounts in fact to a type of *'management'* of the discourse

on film; it is a choice involving one's conception of the requirements that a theory has to satisfy, and not a natural property of
close-ups in films which one could discover simply by observing
them carefully enough.

13

Rhetoric and Linguistics: Jakobson's Contribution

When you come to deal with the current version of the metaphor-metonymy opposition (which has existed for the last twenty years) the most immediate danger is the confusion that tends to 'collapse' paradigm into metaphor, and syntagm into metonymy, thereby reducing the two pairs to a single one in which linguistics ends up dissolved in rhetoric. The frequency with which this phenomenon of neutralisation occurs is easily observed, and in no way accidental: in the first place because there is a very real homology between the two binary divisions (which I shall come back to); secondly because the writer who has most clearly formulated what it is that keeps them apart, Roman Jakobson, has himself occasionally ignored the distinction in other, more elliptical, passages which can mislead the unwary, or those who read too hastily; and finally, because the Metaphor/Metonymy double-act has an amazing reputation and, given the chance, could easily threaten to 'swallow up' its less fortunate rival, Paradigm/Syntagm.[1]

So we have a four-term homology, in which metaphor and paradigm share the basic feature of 'similarity', metonymy and syntagm that of 'contiguity'. The two words I have put in inverted commas are Jakobson's, those which for him assume the crucial role of bridging-concepts between the two parallel pairs. It is thanks to them, thanks to their focussing power, that the four older terms, already familiar in themselves, came together in a configuration which was new as such: in this way Jakobson marked out the site of a problematic which ever since has had its own history and undergone numerous reworkings. The text entitled 'Two Aspects of Language and Two Types of Aphasic Disturbances'[2] appeared in 1956; this date could be noted, if we

174

wished to be precise, as marking the opening of the dossier, or in any case its opening to a reasonably large audience.[3]

One aspect of Jakobson's intervention was its 'pulling together' in a particularly positive way of a whole linguistic tradition which had previously been represented in a more diffuse fashion, but which was already fairly evident. In the 1956 article, Jakobson does not use the words 'paradigm' and 'syntagm'. But he bases his whole construction on the idea of the two great axes of language: selection and combination, substitution and contextuality, alternation and juxtaposition, choice and ordering. This idea figures prominently in the work of many structurally orientated linguists, even though they disagree over other points. Retracing the path of its development would take us through several different stages, including Ferdinand de Saussure's *Cours* with its opposition between 'associative' and 'syntagmatic', Hjelmslev's glossematics which distinguishes throughout between relations *in absentia* (of the 'either-or' type) and relations *in praesentia* (of the 'both-and' type), the work of the Prague school, especially in phonology, that of André Martinet which introduced the 'paradigm/syntagm' terminology (which has become standard), the earlier works of Jakobson himself, etc. The separation in question already corresponded more or less exactly to the traditional division between morphology and syntax in pre-structural grammars: two regions which are of course separated by the boundary of the word, but which can also be differentiated (and the two frontiers coincide to some extent) through the predominance of paradigmatic considerations in morphology, and syntagmatic ones in syntax.

Jakobson's intervention thus finds its place within, and in a way sums up, a very solid linguistic ancestry. But it has a double significance. It can also be read as part of another history, or in relation to it: the history of rhetoric. Or rather, it is the 'projection' (almost in the geometrical sense of the word) of a linguistic division on to the territory of rhetoric that best defines Jakobson's contribution to this debate which has been going on for so long and is at the same time so recent. For here we have two figures out of so many others, metaphor and metonymy, apparently being the only ones to survive, and hence assuming the appearance of Generic Figures, corresponding to two great 'families'. Why these two, if not because (as I shall try to show) they are felt to exemplify more clearly than the others the 'pure' principles of similarity and contiguity respectively – that is, precisely those involved in the paradigm/syntagm distinction? In this way, the rhetorical legacy undergoes a remodelling in linguistic terms, it is put through a kind of re-cycling process which the author does not try to conceal (since he himself posits the homology of the two principal pairs), but which he nevertheless fails to make thoroughly explicit, with the result that some readers might think that the metaphor-metonymy division belongs entirely to rhetoric, or that theories of figures have always, for twenty-five centuries, recognised it in this form.

It is perfectly true that the rhetorical tradition, while not presenting them in such a strongly polarised way, had identified a set of figures which operated more on the basis of similarity, as opposed to others which were grounded rather in some form or other of contiguity. For example catachresis (the 'foot' of a table), which I have already mentioned, undoubtedly relies on a resemblance, or at least on the fact that one similarity among other possible ones gets taken up: a table touches the ground at four points, like certain animals with their four feet, or like man on his two feet. But in catachresis, the figurative term (foot) has no 'literal' term to supplant;[4] it is itself, or it has become, the literal term. The simile, too, is in some respects akin to metaphor: in both cases there is a felt resemblance, which the simile lays out in all the explicitness of its extension ('That child is as sharp as a monkey'), and which the metaphor simply asserts without explaining it, 'skipping' the intermediate stages: 'That little monkey guessed it all'. But here again it is metaphor which is more striking than its rival, and which throws more light on the active principle of similarity – by its elliptical concentration, which is lacking in the simile, and also because it has driven the word 'child' right out of the sentence, thus clearly demonstrating the active supplanting of one word by another, which was only potential in the simile.

We find a somewhat similar situation in the other hemisphere, which is organised around the relation of contiguity in its various forms; that is, around co-occurrences which can actually be observed and not, as before, around similarities which are perceived or merely sensed. For instance *hypallage*, which (in rhetoric) consists of a sliding in the grammatical relation of government: a term (often an adjective) which is grammatically governed by one word in the sentence belongs by virtue of its meaning (its 'literal' meaning) to another. Thus in Virgil (*Aeneid* vi, 268) we find the famous *'Ibant obscuri sola sub nocte per umbram'*: 'They advanced, dark, in the night' etc. (instead of 'They advanced in the dark night...'). The sensation of darkness shifts along a chain of contiguous referents, it moves away from the setting (the night, the dark sky) and attaches itself to the characters, to the 'dark' group they form, to their nocturnal progress. (Here we observe, in this coming apart of the impression and the object, something very close to one of the forms of Freudian 'displacement', which *The Interpretation of Dreams* calls displacement of affect,[5] with the famous dream of the 'breakfast ship'.[6]) We can see that the metonymic element in hypallage necessarily mobilises a whole group of words, since it bears on relations of government: it is therefore lexicalised to a much lesser extent (even if it provides a starting point for a possible semantic evolution of the word 'dark') than metonymy proper, which in this respect better illustrates the force of contiguity, and extends to putting one word in the place of another on the grounds that the two referents are in some way adjacent or near each other: it will connect an activity and its result (e.g. the 'works' of a writer), a recognised symbol and what it symbolises (e.g. 'The Crescent' in the sense of 'The Turkish Empire'), a container and what it contains (e.g. 'to drink the bottle'), a material object and the specific action which corresponds to it (e.g. an 'order' as the word is used in restaurants to refer to food ordered), etc.: these represent, along with their standard definitions, some of the permanent sub-categories of metonymy in rhetoric.

There is also the whole problem of synecdoche, classically defined as 'the part for the whole or the whole for the part' (the second half of the formula is generally forgotten). For instance the seventeenth century use of *'voile'* [sail] in the sense of *'navire'* [boat] (a text-book example, also used by Lacan[7]), or 'a hundred francs per head' instead of 'a hundred francs per person'. The dominant tendency today is to consider synecdoche as a variant of metonymy, a development sanctioned by Jakobson[8] (followed by Lacan), but which is also to be found in other authors: Stephen Ullmann, for example, fully endorses it;[9] it is often taught in schools, as well. Gérard Genette has shown, with remarkable precision,[10] that this linking of synecdoche to metonymy – which is neither right nor wrong, since it depends on the conventional definitions you adopt – owes the better part of its prestige to an impression, however rough, of spatial contiguity: behind the relation of the part to the whole, we can sense another, more strictly metonymic relation (hence the subordination of the one figure to the other) between the part and other parts of the same whole. It is true (I am summarising Genette's argument) that one can't really see how the sail is 'contiguous' to the boat; but the sail is in fact next to the mast or the ropes within the overall area of the boat. When the word 'crown' (another of Genette's examples) comes to mean 'monarch', this can be read as a synecdoche since the crown is one of the elements which pertain to the monarch (the part for the whole), but equally as a metonymy exploiting the privileged relation between the attribute of a function and the man invested with that function: an ideal 'contiguity' (in an abstract space), which cannot but bring to mind one of the most traditional and least questioned forms of true metonymy, the symbol in place of the symbolised (cf. 'Crescent', mentioned above). It is therefore via an enlarged concept of spatiality which may if necessary be metaphorical (!) – but also with the more valid justification of a real, even if not spatial, contiguity – that synecdoche has gradually been 'reduced' to metonymy; where, however, we should realise that it remains a special case, to some extent separate; it is still quite commonly known by its own name, and has survived the collective shipwreck of terms like 'paronomasia', 'hypotyposis' and their very many elegant or not so elegant friends.

Rhetoric, then, has above all given us long lists of 'small-scale', closely defined figures, but this does not mean that they cannot subsequently be regrouped into larger figural regions. This constitutes as it were a *second stage* of the rhetorical method (which can, in Jakobson, look very much as if it is the first or the only one). And it is perfectly true that some of the rhetoricians were interested in working towards a metaclassification of the figures. Dumarsais suggests the possibility of a 'subordination of tropes' according to 'their due ranking in relation to each other'; he proposes three main families, based respectively on the principles of 'connection' (metonymy–synecdoche), 'resemblance' (metaphor), and 'contrast' (irony). Fontanier takes this line further, anticipating Jakobson: for him there are now only three true tropes (rather than three families), metonymy, synecdoche and metaphor. (Comparing him with Dumarsais, we see that, in what will become the hemisphere of contiguity, metonymy and synecdoche both recover their autonomy but that conversely, in the future hemisphere of similarity, resemblance and contrast have joined forces.) Vossius, for his part, distinguished four main 'genres', each containing a figure especially characteristic of the generic principle, the four 'eidetic' figures being metonymy, synecdoche, metaphor and irony. (Here, each of the two hemispheres remains split in two.) This quadruple division in fact occurs quite frequently in the rhetorical tradition, and particularly in Vico's work (We should not forget that irony, or *antiphrasis*, is originally a specific figure, a formal object, and not, as it is nowadays, a tone or an affect: it consists in saying one thing instead of its opposite, or at least instead of a very different signified: 'Thank you very much' instead of 'You've played a dirty trick on me'.)

So the metaphor-metonymy dichotomy is as it were prefigured, albeit rather uncertainly, in zigzags and dotted lines, successive and contradictory additions and deletions, the merging and splitting up of categories forever in process of redefinition – persistently prefigured, nevertheless, by a whole body of rhetorical work which while it wantonly multiplied the number of figures also aimed, conversely, to amalgamate some of them with others, yielding to the charms of the generic after the dizzy delights of the specific. Prefigured, also, in that metaphor and metonymy are usually mentioned near the top of the principal lists of 'super-figures', even if they are not yet the only ones there.

It is precisely this final stage in which the figural field as a whole contracts at the very moment that it splits into two, this central and exclusive dominance of a binary division – a distribution which the rhetorical tradition may suggest but which it does not directly authorise –that will take over with Jakobson, under the pressure exerted by another field, the homological influence of another dichotomy, namely paradigm/syntagm.

Metaphor as Jakobson defines it is tailored to the paradigm, and metonymy to the syntagm. Not only does he say so, and even 'introduce' the two pairs simultaneously; the consequences of this 'imposition' (this superimposition) can also be traced right through to the details of the theory. I shall mention only a few of these, which seem to me characteristic.

For instance, the famous 'contiguity' principle, which has guaranteed the rule of metonymy over half the whole empire: Gerard Genette, as I was saying a moment ago, has noted the slightly vague nature of the concept, which plays a kind of double game, implying physical proximity and yet being used for very diverse types of connection, not all of which are spatial: in what sense, for instance, is one to understand the 'contiguity' of the inventor and the invention in 'guillotine', already quoted? The fact is that the *impression of contiguity* owes its current success to an outside force, which comes from the existence of the syntagm, so striking and so central a phenomenon in linguistics, consisting (far more clearly) of a set of spatio-temporal contiguities between the various elements that make up an actual instance of discourse. The sense of contiguity derived from this has surreptitiously infiltrated the definition of metonymy, and distorted it somewhat: you tend to visualise some vaguely spatial proximity whenever you come across an empirically observed (non-metaphorical) connection.

The same thing happens, it seems to me, when Jakobson presents the principle of contrast (which in rhetoric was often kept separate) as merely one of the forms of similarity: this is again the influence of structural linguistics, with its concept of the paradigm and the resonances which belong to it. The paradigms of language can contain 'members' distributed around a single semantic pole at varying distances (as in 'Warm/Hot/Boiling', or the general phenomenon of parasynonymy) and, equally well, terms grouped together because they are opposites ('Hot/Cold', and all antonyms); in either case, the language presents us with a delimited field within which we have to choose – this being the definition of the paradigm. Strictly speaking it is linked neither to resemblance nor to contrast, but to the existence of a *series of interchangeable items*, covering both configurations, which from this point of view are simply two sub-categories. In phonology, contrast even tends to predominate over resemblance as the principle of association between terms (the principle which *opens* the paradigm): vowel/consonant, oral/nasal, voiced/unvoiced, etc. (Here we touch on the familiar Saussurean idea of difference as the ultimate basis of language.) Moreover it is no accident that the term *opposition*, suggesting contrariety rather than similarity, is the one most often used by structural linguists of all persuasions to denote the connection between interchangeable terms, even when they 'resemble' each other (for instance, they will refer to the 'opposition' between *bad* and *wicked*): this is because they actually have something else in mind: they are thinking in terms of choice, and hence of exclusion. In any case the relation of opposition can, as we know, only arise on the basis of an underlying 'resemblance'; it presupposes that the two terms may be compared with respect to something: temperature in 'Cold/Hot', voicing (present or absent) in 'Voiceless/Voiced', etc. This is the principle of Greimas' 'semantic axes',[11] or of the phonological theory of 'features' (it is also a psychoanalytical principle, that of ambivalence).

Since every paradigm sets up several units in competition for a particular place in the syntagmatic chain, these must obviously resemble each other in some respect as well as being incompatible on another level. The reason modern French can offer me a choice between singular and plural is that they are different, yet similar in that they are both to do with 'number'. In an article which has become famous among linguists,[12] Jean Cantineau shows that the language system is a complex tissue of relations in which distinctive oppositions occur against a background of features that are constant for that opposition, but which themselves become distinctive in the next paradigm (so that 'resemblance' and 'contrast' continually presuppose one another): /p/ contrasts with /t/ (= labial versus apico-dental) on the common basis of their plosive character, but the feature 'plosive' is not always a constant; it becomes a relevant variable when /p/ or /t/ is contrasted with any of the fricatives, and so on.

In short, all the experience of linguistics has led in the direction of bringing resemblance and contrast together under a single principle, basically that of *comparability* (commutation, equivalence, choice, substitution). One can see why, in introducing the notion of 'similarity' as the factor common to the metaphor of rhetoric and the paradigm of linguistics, Jakobson immediately proceeds to divide it into two principal forms:[13] direct similarity which he exemplifies with synonyms (which is thus equivalence through resemblance), and a less direct similarity which, the author tells us, appears in pairs of opposites and presupposes a 'common nucleus' (in other words, equivalence through contrast). Although Jakobson, in choosing the term 'similarity', subordinates contrast to resemblance, unlike linguistics which tends rather to operate the reduction the other way round, this reduction itself bears the stamp of a projection of the concept of the paradigm back on to the theory of figures: showing how the machinery of linguistics has come to plough the field of rhetoric.

14

Referential, Discursive

Despite this act of 'alignment', Jakobson has never claimed that either metaphor and paradigm or metonymy and syntagm are identical. The oppositions are parallel, but they remain distinct. This is the point that has been most often forgotten. The homology has led people to collapse the two pairs, and it is not uncommon nowadays to hear the name 'metaphor' applied to a muddled combination of metaphor and paradigm, and 'metonymy' to some hypothetical mixture of metonymy and syntagm. (In both cases, as we see, the dominant usage prefers the rhetorical term to the linguistic one.)

A recurring theme of semiological discussions is the belief that film editing is a typically metonymic procedure. In fact, however, while some types of editing, depending on the content of the edited images, are indeed metonymic (like those sequences which align several shots of different parts of the same landscape, the same apartment, etc.), the basic principle of editing (all editing) resides in an operation which is wholly syntagmatic, and not metonymic, since it consists in juxtaposing and combining elements *in discourse* – in the filmic chain – without these motifs necessarily having any metonymic connections as referents, that is to say in 'reality', or in that imaginary reality which constitutes the diegesis. Some kinds of editing are effective precisely because they lack any such pre-existing relation; in general terms, these would be unexpected transitions of whatever kind, moments when the film suddenly puts together two shots which you wouldn't normally think of connecting.

We need to go back to the text of Jakobson's article. There[1] we read that the principle of 'similarity' and the principle of 'contiguity' can each operate on two different axes: the *positional* axis, which is that of the discursive chain, of syntax, and the *semantic* axis, involving the signifieds or referents, the 'topic' of the discourse.

So there is not (really) any confusion. Positional contiguity corresponds to syntagmatic relations as such, i.e. the coexistence of a number of constituent elements which characterises every statement in every 'language': temporal contiguity as in the speech chain, spatial contiguity as in paintings, or both together as in the cinema. We must give up that sort of 'amalgamation' whereby we hastily summon up metonymy whenever a text juxtaposes two elements: because 'whenever', in this case, means 'always', and the concept then becomes so inflated that any relevance it might have had is lost in the effect it creates of an all-embracing synonymy. Like any other sequence, the filmic chain *is* contiguity (before any possibility of metonymy even exists); it is nothing more than a long series of contiguities: this is the 'montage-effect', in its widest sense, whether it is created by collage, camera movements or the changing positions of the objects being filmed; whether it operates consecutively (from shot to shot, from sequence to sequence) or simultaneously, between the elements of a single shot, and so on. These juxtapositions taken together (the 'positional contiguities') *create the film* on the most literal level of its content, its textual material: every film (every discourse) is a vast expanse of syntagmatic relations.

Positional similarity, likewise, is what constitutes paradigmatic relations: each realised unit (word, image, sound, etc.) acquires its meaning through a comparison with the others which could have appeared in the same place (the same place in the discourse: that is why it is 'positional'). This permanent principle is in itself nothing to do with metaphor: when I say that a house is 'pretty' (and not that it is 'beautiful') I have chosen my word from a dual paradigm, but one in which the meaning of both terms (and hence my final statement), in the current state of the language, is fairly literal, not really metaphorical. The same applies when a film-maker decides, for instance, to use a fair rather than a dark-haired actor (another paradigm), because he corresponds better to his conception of the role.

Metaphor and metonymy, on the other hand, operate by definition on similarities or contiguities which are perceived or felt to exist between the *referents* of the two units involved in the figure (or between their signifieds: the distinction is not relevant at this level): 'semantic' similarities and contiguities. The metaphor 'eagle' (applied to a great genius) can of course end up replacing the words 'great genius' in a given sentence, and thus enter into a paradigmatic relation with them; but it can also not do so, as in the sentence: 'This great genius, like an eagle...'. What comes first in both cases, and what makes it possible to have the two different versions, is the similarity felt to exist between the eagle and the genius as 'things', not as words; on the basis of this, the degree to which the corresponding words are made to substitute for each other can vary according to the particular sentences involved. Referential similarity can result in discursive similarity, but the two are distinct. In film as well, metaphor is not paradigm, even if it occasionally creates it. The traditional image of breaking waves or leaping flames (to suggest an outburst of passion), as it appears at a particular point in a particular film, must like any image have been chosen from a number of other possibilities: this is a *paradigmatic* act. But over and above this, and in contrast with a good many film shots, its meaning relies on an association of a different order: between desire and fire as phenomena, not as film 'shots'; and this is a *metaphorical* act.

As far as 'contiguity', i.e. metonymy and syntagm, is concerned, you find similar possibilities of interconnection between the order of the 'positional' and that of the 'semantic'. They encourage the confusions that I am trying to sort out, but do not excuse them, since interaction is not the same as identity: in fact it's the opposite, since it assumes that both instances are maintained. I have already said that ordinary descriptive editing (just as one example) is both syntagmatic and metonymic: several partial views of one space are placed end to end; this end-to-end is positional or discursive (= a syntagm), since it actually constitutes the sequence; and the subdivisions of space which are represented are assumed to be 'semantically' adjacent (in the referent and in the diegesis; or in actual reality, if the film is a faithful documentary). This 'real' contiguity is (here) the basis of the succession of images on the screen; of a metonymic act. You can also see the interaction of the positional and the semantic as working in the reverse direction: it is then the filmic contiguity which, retroactively, creates the impression that there was already some contiguity existing between the referents: this being the notorious *referential illusion*, the foundation of all fiction and all 'impressions of reality': the spectator thinks that the different images have all been taken out of a single huge block of reality endowed with some kind of prior existence (and called 'the action', or 'the setting', etc.) whereas in fact this feeling derives solely from the juxtapositions operated by the filmic signifier.[2] In short, the syntagm inevitably assumes the appearance of metonymy (it creates metonymy). The phenomenon is especially obvious in cases where it becomes impossible to claim any plausible 'pre-existing connection' between the referents of the images that the editing puts together (something that Béla Balázs was very much aware of[3]). Thus even the referential illusion itself, if we wish to demonstrate its mechanisms and its efficacy, leads us to maintain a (conceptual) separation between the positional contiguity of the syntagm and the semantic contiguity of metonymy.

INTERSECTIONS OF THE REFERENTIAL AND THE DISCURSIVE

The constant danger of confusion between discursive and refer-ential concepts (paradigm/syntagm and metaphor/metonymy) is to a large extent due to another, equally permanent, phenom-enon, which is characteristic of every enunciation in every code, and is so banal that people do not usually bother to analyse it.

Associations between referents, whether they proceed via simi-larity or contiguity, can always be *stated*, and once they are, they in turn become the principle and the driving force behind various discursive sequences which may be codified to varying degrees. Conversely, every 'similar' or 'contiguous' association which appears in discourse more or less suggests the idea of a parallel association between the corresponding referents.

One can postulate, in short, that there are two sorts of simil-arities and two sorts of contiguities running through discourse: there are those which pertain specifically to discourse and consti-tute it as a formal object (paradigms and syntagms), and those (metaphor and metonymy) which insert themselves between this object and its *other*, if only its asymptotic other (its ideal limit of exteriority), whether they are first perceived in the referent and then inscribed in the discourse, or whether the force of the discourse itself leads us to recognise or imagine them in the referent. Clearly, these two opposite processes combine in every case, and the relation of forces, the economic factor, is as usual the only real variable.

Let us take a very brief, very ordinary statement: 'That man is an ass'. It brings into play different discursive laws (linguistic laws, in this example), some of which are paradigmatic (like the existence in French of the categories 'subject noun' or 'predicate nominal', each consisting of a class of items which are inter-changeable on the basis of similarity) and others syntagmatic, such as the necessity, for the sentence type I have used, of lining up a subject, a copula ('is'), and an attribute. So my sentence is shaped by a set of positional similarities and contiguities: ulti-mately, the set which makes up the code of 'the French language'. But it also registers a similarity of a different order, one which, nevertheless, still takes us back to discourse: the metaphor that makes me refer to someone stupid, a fool, as an 'ass'. I have per-ceived or felt a resemblance between an animal and a certain type of man. This resemblance applies to the actual phenomena and not the language, but it has nevertheless modified my sentence, because I have said 'ass' and not 'fool'. And conversely, if I was aware of the resemblance in the first place, this was partly because the language, with its figurative sense of the word 'ass', helped me to see it. But (in our minds) the resemblance, even if it is forged by language, applies to the objects. And that is precisely why it tends to find its way back into the discourse, into other discourses. And so it goes on: the circle of discourse and refer-ence, each being the *imaginary* of the other: the other of the other.

This circle starts off as a square (the anteriority implied by 'starts' is conceptual, not real). Before they begin to interact, to move to and fro, the order of discourse and that of the referent each displays, in a very clear-cut way, its similarities and its con-tiguities. There is no possibility of confusion. The 'schema' is as follows:

	Similarity	Contiguity
In the discourse	Paradigm	Syntagm
In the referent	Metaphor	Metonymy

Let us stop for a moment to consider the terminology. The reader will perhaps have noticed that I prefer to call 'referential' the axis that Jakobson defines as semantic. The latter term seems to me too general; it covers every aspect of meaning, and could be applied to paradigms and syntagms insofar as they too produce meaning.

For the same reasons, 'discursive' seems to me clearer than 'positional': there are what could be called positions in the referential dimension, and they are not confined to the statement. What distinguishes paradigm-syntagm from metaphor-metonymy is the opposition between the internal laws of discourse and its real or imaginary effect of reference to something outside discourse, rather than between the order of positions and that of meaning.

'Contiguity' can be retained without any major disadvantage. But it should be remembered that the concept, whether in the syntagm (see p. 184) or in metonymy (pp. 176–80), involves far more than spatial proximity.

'Similarity', on the other hand, is not very good. The members of a paradigm are interchangeable rather than similar (cf. pp. 180–2): from one point of view they exclude each other, which the term 'similar' is far from suggesting; from another point of view they present a common nucleus, which is not quite the same as a similarity. As for metaphor, we have seen that it can function on the basis of contrast as well as similarity. The disadvantage of 'similarity' is always that it suggests resemblance far too strongly, when this is merely incidental. One might think of using 'equivalence' instead, but the word suggests an idea of substitutability (of random selection) which is not appropriate for either metaphor or paradigm.

Moreover, the principle of contiguity also gives rise to phenomena of equivalence, as when two words become interchangeable through metonymy (e.g. 'steel' and 'sword'). The equivalence/contiguity pair would therefore seem to be rather shaky. If we wished to replace 'similarity', I would propose (I can find no better solution) the term *comparability*, which is in clear contrast with 'contiguity'. Its only disadvantage – in my view a minor one – is obviously the possible confusion with 'comparison' in the rhetorical sense (comparison, or simile, as opposed to metaphor). In other respects, 'comparability' is as suitable, on the referential side, for similarity as for contrast, and on the discursive side (paradigm) for the common nucleus as for the differential element.

The foregoing distinctions enable us to set up four main types of textual concatenation, with reference to the cinema. They are only ideal types, but they help to situate the real occurrences:

1. *Referential comparability and discursive contiguity*, that is, a metaphor presented syntagmatically. Two filmic elements – two images, two motifs in the same image, two whole sequences, or an image and a sound, a background noise and a word, etc. – two elements which are both present in the chain are associated by resemblance or by contrast (or else they create this resemblance or contrast by their association). For example: the famous 'opening' of Charlie Chaplin's *Modern Times*, which juxtaposes the image of a flock of sheep and that of a crowd pushing and shoving at the entrance to a subway station.

   These kinds of links (which I shall call 'type 1') were, of course, all discussed at length in the classic editing schemes of the theorists of silent film, under various names (montage by 'similarity' by 'contrast', etc.); similarity and contrast, as in rhetoric, were sometimes held to be two different principles of editing, and sometimes two variants of the same principle.

2. *Referential comparability and discursive comparability*. This is the metaphor presented paradigmatically. The filmic elements are associated in the same way as in 1, but they are presented as the terms of an alternative; in the film sequence, one replaces the other, while simultaneously evoking it. Only one of the two is present; the vehicle no longer accompanies the tenor,[4] it drives it out (thereby 'representing' it all the more). For example: the stereotype quoted earlier which puts images of flames in the place of a love scene (as in seventeenth century French, 'my flame' for 'my love').

   It can of course happen that the film presents the beginning of the amorous play directly, and substitutes the pyrotechnic cliché for its subsequent, and presumably more embarrassing, developments (as in a sequence from Autant-Lara's *Le Diable au corps*). We are then dealing with one of the possible combinations of type 1 and type 2. The difference between the signifying matrices (i.e. the 'deep' level) does not coincide with the terminal inventory of 'surface' occurrences; the production and the product could never be isomorphic. Is it necessary to recall (as Freud has already done[5]) that when you analyse a dream which has actually been dreamt, you find 'passages' where condensation and displacement operate at the same time, and yet remain distinct in terms of their definition as typical trajectories?

3. *Referential contiguity and discursive comparability*, or metonymy presented paradigmatically. One element drives another out of the film, as in type 2, but they are associated on the basis of a 'real' or diegetic contiguity rather than resemblance or contrast; or else the paradigmatic act itself creates or reinforces this impression of contiguity. For example: the famous image from Fritz Lang's *M* which, after 'M' has raped and murdered the little girl, shows the victim's abandoned balloon held captive in the telegraph wires (I am thinking here, obviously, of the shot showing just the balloon). The toy replaces (evokes) the corpse, the child. But we know from the preceding sequences that the balloon belongs to the child.

   However, it does not only belong to her. It looks like her as well: there is something poignant and pathetic about it, as there is about her. So, the image in question overdetermines type 3 by type 2 (metaphor presented paradigmatically). But the two types remain, if only because some metaphors function without any metonymic underpinning (or pretext): this is the definition of what is sometimes called non-diegetic metaphor.

4. *Referential contiguity and discursive contiguity*, or metonymy presented syntagmatically. The elements are associated in the same way as in type 3, but both are present, and are combined, in the film; or at least in the segment of it under consideration. For example: again from *M*, the earlier images in which we see the little girl with her balloon, which thus accompanies her in the diegesis (it is her toy) and also on the screen (they appear together).

I have just, deliberately, used the 'same' balloon and child example twice – for 3 and 4. The point is that it is not in fact the same. Many difficulties traditionally encountered in this kind of analysis stem from the desire to assign a 'symbolic element' (here, the balloon) dominating a whole, and sometimes quite long, filmic episode, to one particular category. The semiotic mechanism of the symbolising operation can, however, change several times en route, while the symbolic element remains identical. The same applies to dreams: a theme can be *insistent*, it can recur more than once, substantially unchanged, and yet appear in different concatenations each time: the content of the dream is not the same as the dream-work. To the extent that thematic analysis, above all concerned with 'content', predominates in the discussion of film, the theme of the balloon in *M* will be considered as unitary and more or less indivisible (it will be said, for instance, that it 'runs through', or 'dominates', or 'punctuates', a whole section of the film); but anyone more interested in the cinema itself and its textual operations will be struck by the diversity of the changing configurations in which the (*recurrent*, rather than constant) image of the balloon is 'caught up' as much as by their persistence: this is the problem of *repetition*, which is always a mixture of the invariable and the variable.

FIGURE AND THEME

The nature of a figure cannot be defined at the level of the film as a whole. This is from the outset an impossible enterprise (unless the figural element only appears once in the film), since we are faced with *several* figurations which do not necessarily involve the same principle, a fact which tends to be forgotten when the motif, in its materiality, is common to all of them. 'A single theme' is not synonymous with 'a single figure'. Or (depending on the terminological conventions) 'a single figure' is not synonymous with 'a single figuration'.

This problem, along with others like it, has been raised in a way which I find most convincing by Marie-Claire Ropars in her excellent analysis of the figurations of *October*, the Eisenstein film.[6]

For example, the film contains the famous and much-discussed images of harps and balalaikas – a figure for the soothing speeches of the Mensheviks at Smolny. These shots are traditionally defined as non-diegetic metaphors: the tenor (the Mensheviks) belongs to the action, but the vehicle (the harps) remains outside it; it intervenes in the film solely because of its symbolic properties. (This is basically how non-diegetic metaphor is defined in film criticism – I am simply being a little more explicit.) But Marie-Claire Ropars makes the very pertinent observation[7] that in an earlier passage of the film a character runs his hand across a representation of a harp on a glass door: it is therefore, equally, a diegetic metaphor, the vehicle and tenor both having a 'realistic' correlate.

I had the impression, reading the article as a whole, that for the author this distinction between two kinds of metaphor is of secondary importance compared to the textual activity of writing, the aim and result of which is actually to intertwine these two modes, and often to shift the figures from one to the other in a double movement out of the diegesis and back into it again. But this movement, which the article certainly demonstrates, does not lessen the theoretical importance of the notion of diegesis as an analytical tool; on the contrary, it presupposes it.

It is impossible to decide whether the *theme* of the harps, on the level of the film as a whole, is diegetic or not. But the decision can be made for each one of its textual appearances: this is basically what the author does, and it is certainly worth doing. When a character in the action brushes against a representation of a harp, the motif is of course diegetic: it is the metonymic underpinning of the future metaphor, as Marie-Claire Ropars demonstrates.[8] In the sequence at Smolny, where the harps form a counterpoint with the Mensheviks, the theme (the same one) is transformed into a non-diegetic metaphor: there are no harps in the action at this point, even if there were before; a metaphor, moreover, in the Jakobsonian, rather than the rhetorical, sense (but it is Jakobson's definition which is relevant to this study, as to the article I am discussing). The metaphor is *presented syntagmatically* (which would be a simile for a rhetorician) since, taking the whole sequence, the harps and the Mensheviks are both present on the screen. So, in this case, it is the play of the editing that establishes the metaphor: a connection which my 'type 1' tries to account for, and which Marie-Claire Ropars, for her part, brings to light with the example of the harps and a number of others, showing the determining role of repetition, alternation and the interweaving of elements. I feel however that she does not attach sufficient importance to the distinction between two very real phenomena which are closely linked, but different: the 'return of the metonymic into the metaphor',[9] that is, metaphors which later become metonymised in some way or other,[10] and, on the other hand, the *syntagmatic operation* (not in itself metonymic), the editing, which is an indispensable factor in the generating of metaphor, as it is in any subsequent metonymic reworking. Let us once again modify the *frame of reference*, which alone can justify the attribution of items to one category or another. Each harp image (at Smolny) *taken in isolation* is a metaphor-paradigm (type 2): the vehicle has temporarily driven out the tenor and is, for the moment, the only trace of it in the signifier. *Just before* and *just afterwards* this ceases to be so, since the image of the Mensheviks reappears; but these shifts are what the work of the film consists in. Finally, bearing in mind the global structure of the film (fourth point of view), it is interesting to note, following Marie-Claire Ropars,[11] that the theme of the harps, taken initially from the action (and having therefore a metonymic pretext, despite the author's reservations), is progressively turned into a metaphor through the play of textual (I would add: syntagmatic) interconnections, and thus becomes gradually detached from the diegesis, until in a third phase it ends up as a sort of ideal metonymy, returning to the diegesis on a symbolic level, which the author analyses in detail.

In other words, the textual *movement* of a film – *what* precisely, at each moment, is in the process of changing or of being generated? – refers dialectically to, as it were, states or positions through which the movement passes and which plot its course. Their status is that of ideal reference points, and at the same time (this is no contradiction) they are fully realised in short pieces of the text.

EDITING, THE SUPERIMPOSITION AND THE CLOSE-UP

Jakobson's 1956 article, which has done so much to implant the metaphor-metonymy conception, contains a short passage[12] referring to the cinema. The author mentions the synecdochic basis of the close-up (this idea was already present in his 1933 article in Czech on film[13]), 'metonymic editing in general' (a theme which is taken up again in the 1967 Italian interview[14]), and 'superimposed dissolves' as similes (= the metaphorical principle).

The expression 'superimposed dissolves' which the author (or the translator?) himself puts in inverted commas, seems to denote the superimposition and the lap-dissolve both at once. Personally I think they are both syntagmatic: the syntagm being simultaneous in the case of the superimposition, consecutive (although with a 'moment' of simultaneity) in the lap-dissolve. This is as far as the discursive axis is concerned. As for their metaphorical or metonymic character (sometimes their *double* character, which does not mean hybrid or indiscernible) it depends on the relation between the two images in question in each case, and I doubt whether it can be attributed to the superimposition or the lap-dissolve as such. The relation is metaphorical if one of the two images is extra-diegetic, metonymic if they are both aspects of the same action (or the same space, etc.), and double if one of these aspects resembles the other, or is compared to it, or connotes it in some sense, etc.; the 'superimposed dissolves' cannot be attributed en bloc to the metaphorical principle; they are not all comparative. This brings us back, in a different way, to the problem of *classifications which cut across each other*, one which is central to this study: just as each occurrence of a figure does not necessarily derive from the same generative principle, so one can no more expect that whole categories (such as the 'superimposition' on the one hand and 'metaphor' on the other) are going to match up on a one-to-one basis, for they have been set up in different areas of experience (and, what is more, in historically separate fields of knowledge). The important thing is not to wish they would coincide, but to work on the ways in which they intersect.

Jakobson's position on 'metonymic editing' varies from one text to another. Editing, in itself, is neither metaphorical nor metonymic: it is syntagmatic. This is more or less what Jakobson says in his 1933 Czech article: the basic characteristic of the cinema is that it 'transforms the object into a sign'; the film mobilises 'fragments of the world' but turns them into the elements of a discourse in the very act of 'ordering' them (= editing), and this ordering can operate in accordance with two main associative principles, metaphor or metonymy; the author adds that metaphorical editing (by similarity or contrast) is less common, and that in ordinary ('linear') films editing is likely to be metonymic, content simply to endorse referential contiguities in time or space. His position is the same in the 1967 Italian interview: metonymic editing predominates in American and Soviet films, and in documentaries; it corresponds roughly to a 'realistic' treatment (although the author is doubtful whether it is ever possible for an art to be truly realistic). But the Italian text states in another passage that editing is inherently metonymic; here the author shifts surreptitiously from the discursive to the referential axis, after having himself differentiated between them. In the 1956 article, the allusion is so brief (= 'metonymic editing in general', and nothing more) that one cannot tell which of the two interpretations would apply. Quite apart from Jakobson's own work, this very common theme of metaphorical poeticity as opposed to metonymic prosaicism is in my view dangerous given its remarkable power to combine a high degree of imprecision with a strong attraction for hasty or voluntaristic theorisers.

As for the synecdochic basis of the close-up – the third comment relating to cinema in the 1956 article – it returns to an idea expressed in 1933, an idea which applies not only to the close-up but also more generally: namely that one of the main ways in which the object is transformed into a sign, in the cinema, is by selectively representing one part of the object ('*pars pro toto*', remarks the author), thereby choosing the meaning one wants to give it over and above this representation (but through it); the silent cinema permitted synecdoche on one axis only, that of the image (= the selection of the visible on the screen); sound and talking films offer several synecdochic axes for each individual element: it can be seen but not heard, or vice versa, and so on. 'Synecdoche' is obviously being used here in a very broad sense; ultimately, it is the actual choice of textual materials. In 1956, the reference to the close-up brings us nearer to true synecdoche. The close-up is indeed a 'part', or at least more clearly so than ·distant shots. But not every 'part', in the cinema or elsewhere, involves the process of synecdoche: it must also, up to a point, stand for the whole ('sail' [*voile*] even in the seventeenth century, can also mean 'sail', quite apart from all the intermediate cases). The different close-ups analysed in films would seem to be spaced out along an axis which includes even more intermediate cases, as a result of the absence of the *word* – a problem which I shall come back to. At one of the poles, there are detail shots which have a purely descriptive value, and nothing beyond that: here the force of synecdoche is hardly apparent, or not at all (this would be the ideal limit). At the other extreme – an example of this would be the famous image from *The Battleship Potemkin* where the mutinying sailors have thrown the Tsarist doctor overboard and we see his pince-nez dangling in the ropes – the discursive realisation of the 'part' is meaningful only insofar as it evokes the 'whole', and we are then dealing with a figurative device which, in the visual order, has something in common with (verbal) synecdoche; we can give it the conventional name of 'cinematic synecdoche'.

15

Metaphor/Metonymy: a Dissymmetrical Symmetry

The reader will perhaps have suspected, from the preceding pages, the possibility of a dissymmetry in the respective status of metaphor and metonymy which, if confirmed, would be liable to jeopardise the parallel itself. Pure metaphor, with no metonymic complications, occurs only with extra-diegetic images or sounds (and in 'non-diegetic' films, with genuinely *alien* images or sounds): it is a highly marked operation, actually quite rare even in avant-garde productions. Pure metonymy links together, in the film, images or sounds which are already linked in some way – in time, in space, etc.: it is the phenomenon of contiguity in the diegesis, if the film has one, or more generally in the social experience which pre-exists the film. This mode of discursive association, based on 'natural' proximities, is very frequent, even in films which manage more or less to escape the narrative-representational regime (but not the shooting process or, therefore, contiguities in the field of view, or many others). So how can an opposition which contrasts an 'exceptional' configuration with a general principle of articulation retain any meaning? Is the pair perhaps beginning to get out of step?

This impression derives, as do a number of other difficulties, from the latent confusion which has gradually developed between metonymy and syntagm. In the above paragraph, I have deliberately reproduced it in an attempt to show how it occurs: the 'metonymy' it refers to, a common type of concatenation, is not a metonymy, although it provides the basis on which one could always arise. It simply expresses a syntagmatic principle, and an exceedingly basic one: the units which combine in discourse are bound to correspond to ideas or representations which combine in mental experience. This double contiguity, in the enunciation and in the mind, the ever-possible starting point for some metonymic construction, does not itself produce such a construction. The elements can coexist without the fact of their proximity being organised into a particular configuration, as in filmic sequences which simply present, in succession, successive stages of some process or other. Metonymy presupposes contiguity, but not all contiguities are metonymic. The word '*Bordeaux*' is a metonymy when it refers to the wine: not because the wine is produced near the town – if this were so, the whole world would be a series of metonymies – but because this proximity has (in the case of '*Bordeaux*', not anywhere and everywhere) given rise to a specific operation, namely a transfer of the signifier. Metonymy is a *figure* of contiguity. A figure, just like metaphor: it does not happen automatically, any more than metaphor does: it, too, must be put into operation. Contiguity in its raw, non-figurative state is simply the general linking up of ideas and objects; in the order of discourse, it corresponds to syntagmatic relations.

It follows that metonymies are not to be found at every point of every film. The average ratio of metaphorical to metonymic acts varies according to the film, the genre, the director, and so on, but what both metaphor and metonymy have in common goes beyond the level of localised figures (they end up as these, but are never reducible to them), and consists in their status as identifiable semantic movements, with a definite position which sets them apart from the overall expanse of the text. In Fritz Lang's *M*, the rows of knives in the shop window come to 'designate' the character of the killer, or at least that part of him which cannot help killing. It is a metonymic type of trajectory, but the presence together in the diegesis of a silhouette and a knife-merchant's window is not in itself sufficient to establish the link: the film contains plenty of other referential juxtapositions (visible on the screen), most of which never develop into figures. In the case of the knives, it took a particular emphasis in the way the scenes were shot – for instance, when M stares for a long time into the window, with the reflection of his face framed by the shining blades – it also took the establishment of a stronger association between the weapon and the idea of murder than might or might not arise from the juxtapositions of the plot, it took the powers of textual repetition, etc. And yet this is not an 'extreme' case of metonymy: it has no rigid, well-defined outlines. The suggested link runs right through a considerable part of the film, and the metonymic process never actually 'solidifies'; the image of the knives does not at any point become a real equivalent of the character, it is merely a privileged association. But it is, precisely, privileged: it does not dissolve into the generalised contiguity of the film, and it *is*, in a way, localisable: if not in a single shot (and in the whole of the shot), at least in certain structural features which recur over several shots. (Not all localisations are immediately obvious, or occur only once in the film, or coincide with a global unit such as the shot.)

FROM METONYMY TO METAPHOR

Many filmic metaphors are based more or less directly on an underlying metonymy or synecdoche. This is well demonstrated by Marie-Claire Ropars with reference to Eisenstein's *October*, in the article I have already discussed (pp. 191–3. Through the play of editing and composition, one element of the film becomes to a certain extent the symbol of another element (metonymy), or of a larger filmic entity (synecdoche); and these elements all belong to the referential dimension of the film, i.e. to its diegesis or, if it does not have one, to some 'peripheral' area of experience. In the George Raft gangster films, familiar to *cinémathèque* audiences, the coin that the hero tosses in his hand becomes a kind of emblem of the character: his equivalent, in some degree. It suggests his casualness, his relationship to money, etc., so it resembles him (metaphor), but we also see him handling it (metonymy), and this little game forms part of his behaviour in general (synecdoche). Many filmic symbols, as we know, correspond roughly to this mechanism: the work of the signifier emphasises a particular element of the visual or sound sequence, and this then gathers further connotations which are so many *allusions* to other motifs in the film.[1]

This is something which Jean Mitry, following other writers, has rightly stressed. He comes to the conclusion that many so-called metaphors in film are really metonymies.[2] A healthy reaction, insofar as there is a tendency to baptise any symbolic operation a 'metaphor' (and not just in film criticism[3]), whereas the symbolic is to be found at the intersection of the metaphorical and the metonymic (in their oscillation, as Rosolato puts it[4]), and metonymy is at least as symbolic as metaphor.[5] But one should not fall into the opposite 'reduction' either, and define these false metaphors as pure metonymies. The latter do exist (I shall come back to this), but most of the time we are dealing with figurations which are both metaphorical and metonymic, in varying proportions: one term suggests another because they *evoke* each other by virtue of their proximity, and also because they *resemble* each other in some respect. Significantly, the two words are almost synonymous.

In *The Battleship Potemkin* the Tsarist doctor's pince-nez – momentarily immobilised and, so to speak, kept from falling into the sea by the insistent gaze of the close-up (as well as the ropes in which it is entangled), 'caught' by the camera when its owner has just dropped it (there is here a hint of a negative metaphor, a 'contrast') – the pince-nez conjures up in the spectator the representation of the doctor himself (that is why it is there): synecdoche. But in the preceding images we saw the doctor wearing the pince-nez: metonymy. The pince-nez connotes the aristocracy: metaphor. But it can do so only because the nobility – outside the diegesis, in the society of the time: another level of the 'referent' – liked to wear pince-nez: metonymy again. And so it goes on. It becomes clear that a filmic occurrence, in the particularity of its configuration, is more often distinguished by the exact form of the skein into which the metaphorical and metonymic strands are twisted, than by the presence or absence of either element.

Every figural operation in a text corresponds to mental paths that can be laid down in the minds of creator or spectator. Each figure is only the terminus of a route, or of more than one route. The fact that there is – provisionally – a single terminus tells us nothing about the number or nature of the itineraries which meet in it. With these latter we can already glimpse, 'behind' metaphor and metonymy, the problem of condensation and displacement, which I shall be discussing at length, and without which, I am sure, no theory of the figural in art can be sustained. But even at this preliminary stage, we can hardly fail to notice that the impression of resemblance and the impression of contiguity – taking these terms in the widest possible sense – are always the major pretexts for psychical transfer from one representation to another. The idea, in this rather too general form, was around long before the analyses of Lacan. It is commonly found in works of semantics or rhetoric, even in those which do not take it as the basis for their classifications. It is also in Freud, in at least two passages[6] (there are bound to be others that I have forgotten): associations of ideas are based on two principles, 'direct contact' (metonymy), and 'contact in the figurative sense' which corresponds to similarity (metaphor).

Nor is there anything surprising in the fact that either one of these principles, once activated, may well ricochet and set the other off. The orchestration of a contiguity can only make it easier to perceive a resemblance or a contrast, even if it does not guarantee it: this corresponds to metaphor based on metonymy, which I have been talking about.

FROM METAPHOR TO METONYMY?

What is more surprising is the absence of the opposite phenomenon, metonymy based on metaphor, or in other words metaphor which gives rise to metonymy. It does of course happen, especially (but not only) in more or less non-representational contexts (this is partly what defines them), that metaphorical juxtapositions – 'ideas', sparks, incongruous encounters of the sort the Surrealists liked – invade the surface fabric of the text and are responsible for a large proportion of the final contiguities, which is to say most of the work as such. But in these cases metaphor is creating not metonymy but the syntagm. It does not serve to fabricate or underline relations of proximity in the world, or in the diegesis (which is in fact progressively abandoned by movements like Surrealism, as they become established), but to activate relations between elements coexisting in the discourse, and ultimately (although this limit is never reached) to exclude any juxtapositions coming from elsewhere.[7]

We have seen how, on the contrary, the play of metonymy helps metaphors to emerge. A metonymic denotation such as *Roquefort* (for the cheese) can allow me to perceive affinities which would otherwise not have 'struck' me: the rough taste of the food, its uneven texture (knobbly in places, sometimes coarse, or crumbling into small fragments) give me a sense of something sturdy and harsh which belongs to the environment, at once mountainous and southern, in which it is produced. These affinities are perhaps illusory. Perhaps the metonymy has not brought them to light, but actually created them from scratch? Of course ... I wouldn't want to decide either way, and it makes no difference: apart from the fact that a resemblance or a contrast are never either true or false, since they must in any case be experienced and are nothing more than this experience, the similarities which arise here are established (in my mind) between a small town and a cheese, and not between two words: they are 'referential', hence metaphorical, similarities.

This brings us back, from a different angle, to a very real element of dissymmetry between metaphorical and metonymic operations, or more precisely between their respective conditions of possibility – similarity and contiguity; a dissymmetry which is not inherent in cinematic language (assumed to be predominantly metonymic in that it puts together in a particular order images and sounds taken from the real world), or in the diegetic film (or representational art in general), assumed to be totally metonymic because they rely on imaginary reference. It is a mistake to invoke these two themes, which express (badly) a certain truth, at any and every opportunity. *The privilege of metonymy*, some of whose partial consequences we have come across here, has its origins much further back than any film (or book, or picture), in the characteristics which define the metaphorical and the metonymic acts at their inception – which distinguish them, account for there being two of them.

The metonymic act is inherently more *probable*, and almost certainly more frequent, than the metaphorical act. The latter part of this study will, not accidentally, focus on a similar dissymmetry – the same one, in fact – between condensation and displacement in the psychoanalytical field. It is of course Lacan's view that displacement and metonymy strike a better bargain with the censorship of the unconscious;[8] that alone would be enough to account for their greater *ease* of action (the word can be taken in as many senses as you wish).

Freud commented in *The Interpretation of Dreams*[9] that the associations between memory-traces do not all establish themselves with equal facility. Some of them (and the present-day reader will recognise in these a permanent opening for metonymy) are to a certain extent prefabricated; they have their source in impressions which arrive together – but 'together', of course, in varying degrees – at the perceptual 'entrance' to the psychical apparatus (the system Pcs.). Others however, and especially, according to Freud, the various associations by resemblance, are not given in advance to the same extent; they require the creation of more new paths, and greater involvement on the part of the unconscious. This last point (as I have said) is taken up by Lacan.

Nothing is in fact 'written into' the perceptual data. But it is clear that contiguities are more dependent on them. One *can* discuss the degrees of proximity (hence certain rather futile debates as to where the referential universe of a text ends), but any discussion of the greater or lesser force of resemblances, or even the resemblances themselves, is bound to go on interminably since they are far more dependent on individual reactions.

In this sense, contiguity is a 'real' connection (felt to be real), and resemblance a 'felt' connection (felt to be felt). Which no doubt explains all those fashionable generalisations about metaphorical creativity and metonymic prosaicism.

Psychoanalysis may be needed to understand this dissymmetry properly, but not to observe its existence, which semantics and rhetoric have already done. Thus Stephen Ullmann, expressing the idea in his own way,[10] can state that connections based on contiguity, possible sources for metonymy, are 'given' or 'external'; those based on resemblance are never more than 'latent' in things, they always have to be partly 'invented'. Metaphor, he goes on to say, has something more 'inspired' about it than metonymy (but he does not take this term in any melodramatic sense).

ON THE 'DISTRIBUTION' OF METAPHOR AND METONYMY

The dissymmetry of the figures probably allows us to account rather better, especially in the case of the cinema, for the apparent *distributional irregularities* which mark the various combinations of the metaphorical and metonymic processes on the level of the single figure. The most frequent case, as we have seen,

is that of the 'double' figure, infinitely variable in its exact proportions. But what about figures which are not double, i.e. those
produced by just one of the two figurations? Or again (the
problem is simply where to draw the line) those where one of the
pair definitely outweighs the other, taking upon itself the most
active role in the symbolic work?

Metaphor without metonymy is rare; strictly speaking it
would require a motif completely alien to the rest of the film, or to
the contiguities 'given' in any social field of perception which
could be related to the film. Many cinematic metaphors contain
metonymies within them. Association on the basis of contiguity is
somehow 'easier', and hence also makes it easier for other developments to arise: metaphor takes advantage of it. The 'pure'
metaphor spurns any such support; in this case an element forces
its way into the fabric of the text, without the pretext of any
'natural' linking, the only justification for the invasion being its
resemblance to another element – a more disruptive operation.
(In my schema on pp. 189–90 this is type 1 with no admixture of 4,
or 2 with no infiltration from 3.) This is not only valid for the
cinema. Gérard Genette has shown[11] that Proust's metaphors
and similes almost always operate between two elements given in
the narrative; the resemblance, in other words, grows out of the
fact of proximity, which then serves to reinforce it. This is logical,
especially in a totally diegetic work like this, where there is a good
chance of finding the vehicle within the universe of the work
itself, instead of having to bring in something from outside.

Metonymy without metaphor (a motif symbolising another
without there being *any* similarity or difference between them,
that is, type 3 without anything of 2, or 4 without anything of 1) is
also quite rare. Once a contiguity has been put to work by the
film – and unless this is the case it remains a simple contiguity
and not a metonymy – in preference, inevitably, to other coexisting referents shown on the screen, it is hard not to perceive some
'similarity' between the terms whose proximity is, in every sense
of the word, *represented* in this way, with a kind of insistence (as in
the example of George Raft and his coin, mentioned earlier). So
the dissymmetry is paradoxical: the peculiar capacity of contiguity to appear self-evident makes it probable *both* that metaphors will have a metonymic basis (i.e. pure metaphors rarely
occur) *and* that metonymies will develop into metaphors (i.e.
pure metonymies rarely occur). 'Purity' is as hard to find at the

top end of the scale (metaphor) as it is at the bottom end (metonymy).

Two rarities, then. But they are not equally rare. And this is a further element in the paradox: the empirical nature of contiguities, whether this is real or just a myth, is also a factor – and the two opposite results stem from the same cause – in the relative frequency of metonymy in its more or less pure forms, which is higher (other things being equal) than that of metaphor. One element of the film can symbolise another without resembling it particularly, or without any such possible resemblance predominating in the process of symbolisation. The emphasis placed on their coexistence is enough, or almost enough, to make one of them act as an *index* of the other. It becomes a kind of *emblem*, as in the logos (I'm thinking of things like Citroën's double V sign) which evoke an institution through constantly being associated with it in people's minds, without there being any obvious connection between them: the contiguity works on its own (by which I mean: there is no resemblance involved; or else the resemblance has been lost over time).

This kind of transfer has its equivalent in film, and is in fact quite common. Thus whenever a character is endowed with some peculiarity, a little detail of behaviour, appearance, etc. which we notice (here we touch on the problem of *typage*) which regularly accompanies his presence on the screen or the sound-track, sometimes to the point of actually representing, more or less *replacing* him, this corresponds to the metonymy presented first ·syntagmatically (type 4 above), and then paradigmatically (type 3); a metonymy which is all the more pure in that the chosen feature lacks any intrinsic affinity with the hero, and becomes 'characteristic' simply by virtue of being his constant escort (there is of course a whole range of intermediate cases). There is the character who always whistles the same tune (and who can eventually be evoked by the sound-track alone, without appearing on the screen), the man who smokes an enormous cigar (which, placed in an ash-tray, will alert us to his presence, close by but out of frame), the club-footed gang-leader (hence close-ups of shoes: metonymy-synecdoche), and so on. *Places* in films can be treated in the same way: think of the role played by the signs with a gigantic capital K in Orson Welles' *Citizen Kane*. So can shadows, which are metonymic by definition (although this is an 'impure' example, slightly paradoxical in that there is a whole tradition of considering them as metaphors); for instance Arthur Robison's warning *Shadows*,[12] expressionist cinema in general, horror films, etc.

16

Figure and Substitution

Yet another difficulty in this knot of problems now arises, this time in connection with the idea of *substitution* (one element driving another out, replacing it, etc.). A common line of argument assimilates it to metaphor,[1] and assumes that metonymy, conceived of as an order of co-presences, is its opposite – a further instance of confusion between the discursive axis (paradigm/syntagm) where the proposition holds good, and the referential axis, where the division does not work in the same way. Certain formulations in Jakobson's 1956 article (especially if it is read too quickly) have possibly contributed to this isomorphic 'forcing', this temptation to generalise the alignment of terms; particularly because the text contains two antithetical series of terms, both quite long, and there is an inherent risk in this arrangement that the reader will take all the terms of each series to be quasi-synonymous. On one side Jakobson places 'selection', 'substitution', 'similarity', and 'alternation', and on the other 'combination', 'contextuality', 'contiguity', and 'juxtaposition': the idea of replacement comes across strongly in the first group, and the opposite suggestion of accumulation in the second. Since the same text presents the metaphor-metonymy pair, the tendency is to model it willy-nilly on the same semantic opposition (choice *versus* co-actualisation), forgetting the passage[2] which distinguishes the semantic (referential) level from the discursive level.

As for this latter, it is true that *replacement* is coextensive with the paradigm and that these two notions coincide completely. The paradigm is defined from the outset as a commutational class of which only one member, temporarily 'replacing' the others, can appear at a given point in the textual sequence. If you use the imperfect tense, that means you give up the possibility of using the future in the same place. If you decide on alternating editing you cannot also use linear editing for the same sequence. Syntagmatic activity on the other hand never involves substituting one thing for another; it is based entirely on the opposite procedure, and is exclusively concerned with *arranging* (disposing) elements which are all present in the discourse – there is no question of choosing between them. In order to construct an attributive sentence, we must 'string together' a subject, a copula and a predicate; if we looked upon these three units as being in competition, and wondered which of them should replace the others, we would be moving out of the framework of the attributive syntagm, which would cease to exist as such. Similarly, alternating editing (another type of syntagm) would also cease to exist if we were to try to choose between the two series of images which constitute it, that is to say, if a relation of selection were established between them.

It is not the same for the metaphorical and the metonymic; it *cannot* be the same since they are not defined directly in terms of the discursive chain but in terms of a real or imaginary referential dimension. A resemblance between two 'objects' is the starting point for a (possible) metaphorical operation: but we have no way of knowing whether the corresponding signifiers will both figure in the statement, or whether one of them will take the place of the other. The same applies to the metonymic process, when two objects, without being in any way similar, are frequently linked together in experience. It is all too often forgotten that the idea of substitution (or its complementary opposite, juxtaposition) is alien to the notions of metaphor and metonymy; and irremediably so, since their very definition precludes it.

At this point a brief revisiting of classical rhetoric might well be useful, less for its historical value (I have anyway no special competence in the field) than for the powers of demonstration which rhetoric still possesses. The rhetoricians usually used the term 'simile' for that variant of metaphor, in the modern sense, which is defined (contrary to present-day expectations) precisely by the co-presence in the sentence of both terms of the comparison; that is to say, by its non-substitutive structure ('as pretty as a picture'); it is rather like type 1 of my cinematic classification ('metaphor-syntagm'). Of course (and this certainly accounts for some of the confusion) rhetoric usually reserved the actual term 'metaphor' for a different form of the metaphorical process which, unlike simile, was based on the substitution of the vehicle for the tenor (metaphor-paradigm, in effect my type 2) : 'Those lions fought to the finish', for 'Those valiant soldiers fought to the finish'. But the fact that these two possibilities exist within the area of the 'metaphorical' as Jakobson defines it should serve to remind us that this area does not fully coincide with the order of substitution, i.e. the paradigmatic.

There is a very similar dislocation between the metonymic and the order of juxtaposition (the syntagmatic). Metonymy as defined by the rhetoricians included both figures of co-presence ('My sword, avenging steel, will wipe out this insult') and figures of substitution ('My avenging steel will wipe out this insult', where 'steel' has driven 'sword' out of the sentence); there were metonymy-syntagms and metonymy-paradigms, and we find an equivalent distinction in the cinema, in the opposition of types 4 and 3. (I should emphasise that it is a question of a formal iso-morphism: you do not find the same figures in film, but rather the same distinctions; to look for the same figures, in such a different language, would be a hopeless task as well as a completely arti-ficial attempt to apply the rules of one system to another; but the underlying principles remain, since *their* scope is by definition general, and it is these which will eventually enable us to find our way around filmic figurations.)

For a rhetorician, the work of metonymy would have been more 'complete' in type 3 (paradigm) than in type 4 (syntagm): just the opposite of what you expect if you assimilate metonymy to juxtaposition. The reason is that in the substitutive metonymy, as opposed to the other type, the metonymic vehicle ('steel') has absorbed the meaning of the tenor ('sword') sufficiently well to be able to replace it in the discourse. In the same way, the work of metaphor is carried further in metaphor proper (substitutive metaphor) than in the ordinary simile. Rhetoric, in short, consid-ered the *paradigmatic criterion*, the possibility of discursive substi-tution, to be the final stage or apotheosis, so to speak, of all symbolic thrusts, whether metaphorical or metonymic, and not a privilege reserved for figures of similarity. The commutability of two terms implies that the semantic transfer from one to the other, whatever its nature, is sufficiently well established to render the terms more or less equivalent: as long as they are both present in the statement, we cannot be sure that the symbolising term has fully taken on the meaning of the symbolised one, and can therefore do without it. (There is here, latent in rhetorical theory, almost a kind of father-son relationship.) Hence the very special and ever-increasing importance which the rhetorical tradition accorded to *tropes* in the context of the larger set of figures. I shall be discussing this further in connection with the problem of the word, an entity which does not exist in the cinema. The rhetorical trope is generally defined as a figure possessing two characteristics: it bears on a clearly delimited unit (usually a word), rather than the construction of the whole sentence; and it modifies the actual meaning of this word (or gives it a new additional interpretation) instead of simply affecting its contextual resonances. To clarify this, one might say that *antithesis* is the most typical example of the 'non-trope figures', since it lacks both the defining features of the trope. Rhetoric held the trope (whether metaphorical or metonymic) to be the perfect figure, or even the only 'true' figure (Dumarsais, Fontanier). And the trope is by definition substitutive: the whole of the signified has migrated from signifier 1 (the symbolised) to signifier 2 (the symbolising), so that signifier 2 has 'changed its meaning' (it has acquired a 'figurative meaning' in the place of or in addition to its literal meaning), and can replace signifier 1 in the discourse: for instance 'steel' in the absence of 'sword', or 'flame' without 'love' – the ultimate triumph of the metonymic, and of the metaphorical.

For links based on resemblance and links based on contiguity have in common the fact that right from the start they contain the possibility of a future substitution (not always realised), a sort of transitive psychical movement which 'passes' from one term to the other, a force which tends towards substitution: in metaphor as in metonymy, the signifying chain reduplicates itself, a space of language opens up, one signifier is held suspended 'behind' another (Lacan[3]). This is in fact the definition of all *figures* for some rhetoricians: the hollowing out of a gap between the literal and the figurative (Genette[4]). And in psychoanalysis, it is a common feature of condensation and displacement, both of which hollow out a gap between the manifest and the latent. It is simply that this substitutive thrust, viewed in its effects in explicit discourse (the written sentence, the filmic sequence, etc.) will sometimes be taken to its conclusion, in which case it spills over into the paradigmatic (metaphorical or metonymic), whereas in other cases the two terms, still virtually equivalent, remain in juxtaposition in the text and so form a syntagm. Dreams operate in the same way: a certain character represents my father and so enables me to expel him from the dream flux. But in another dream, I will see him alongside my father. Yet the figuration (either displacement or condensation) is the same in both dreams: Mr X = my father. But the vehicle can either replace the tenor, or exist alongside it. This is the distinction between the paradigm and the syntagm, and it does not coincide with either metaphor/metonymy or condensation/displacement.

17

The Problem of the Word

In comparing film language with verbal language from the point of view of their symbolic functioning (and therefore, especially, of their position in relation to any figure or figuration), one is inevitably, and constantly, faced with the problem of the word (or the lexeme: from the perspective adopted here, they are one and the same; the word consists either of a single lexeme or of several permanently 'welded' together). Natural language is made up of words (and lexemes) ; whereas film language has no semiotic 'level' that would correspond to these: it is a language without a lexicon (without a vocabulary), insofar as this implies a finite list of fixed elements. This does not, however, mean that filmic expression lacks any kind of predetermined *units* (the two things are frequently confused). But such units, where they do exist, are patterns of construction rather than pre-existing elements of the sort provided by the dictionary. The difference should not of course be interpreted in terms of metaphysical 'essences', or used to sanction the pervasive myths which set up 'the word' and 'the image' in opposition to each other: a pattern of construction is itself a fixed unit (only on a higher level), and the word, conversely, is nothing other than a construction (but one stage further down: a construction of phonemes, or graphemes in the case of the written word). Nevertheless, on the more technical level of a comparative typology of semiological mechanisms, the difference is extremely important.

Many of the typical characteristics of natural language are clearly shown by the formalisations of transformational generative grammar to derive from the fact that such a language can be 'described' (in the logical sense) only by means of a model containing two basic lists rather than one: a list of permitted combina-

212

tions of elements (what generative linguistics calls the 'grammar' in the strict sense, or the set of 'rules'), and a list of permitted elements which, in the same terminology, constitute a 'lexicon' or 'vocabulary' (the latter term is closer to ordinary usage): adopting this system we could say that the peculiar characteristic of film language is that it can be described in terms of a single list – that it possesses a grammar, up to a point, but no vocabulary.

The question of whether or not a particular code contains words entails quite a lot of structural consequences, the full extent of which, in the present state of semiological research, has probably not yet been measured. It may even be the case that they can only be properly 'evaluated' one at a time, like many complex and many-sided phenomena whose underlying unity, or common root, only comes to light at a later stage, in a more advanced state of knowledge, after an initial survey of their diverse and provisionally separate manifestations. Be this as it may, I would now like to take advantage of the opportunity which this study offers me (or forces on me) to look at just one such manifestation, one which concerns metaphor and metonymy fairly directly.

FIGURE/TROPE

The image which present-day scholarship has of metaphor and metonymy, even if it is not always conscious of the fact, remains obstinately bound up with the representation of the word as a specific unit; hence the (familiar) difficulty we often have in applying them to a 'language without words' like the cinema. Why is the problem constantly 'haunted' by the word, as a visible or invisible presence which distorts so many discussions?

I have already argued that the reorganisation of all figures into a single, all-embracing pair – metaphor and metonymy – was at least as much the work of structural linguistics as of rhetoric. But the figures which are reorganised in this way, and indeed the concept of the figure, come to us from the rhetorical tradition. The convergence of these two points of origin results, for different reasons, in a blurring of the distinction – which is actually quite clear – between the problem of figurations and the problem of the word.

The pressure exerted by the linguistic field is easy to understand since the specific object of this discipline is, precisely, a 'verbal language' in which the word (or the lexeme) is a unit of prime importance. The influence brought to bear in the same direction by the rhetorical background is less immediately explicable, in that the rhetoricians never said, or thought, that the various figures which they identified operated exclusively at the level of the single word. On the contrary, they usually devoted a considerable part of their work to figures extending over several words or coinciding with a complete clause, and in so doing they prepared the way (or so one might hope) for those who would later be dealing with cinematic textuality. *Periphrasis* by definition mobilises a sequence of several words, and *suspension* a whole sentence (it consists in delaying the end of the sentence by accumulating interpolations); *alliteration* (the repetition of phonemes, especially consonants) presupposes that different words are brought together on account of their pronunciation ('The moan of doves in immemorial elms/And murmuring of innumerable bees'); *ellipsis* (eliminating some syntactic elements and leaving only the minimum necessary for comprehension) is always a sentence-based figure; so are *reticence*, or *aposiopesis* (when a sentence is broken off, and left in suspense, indicating a sudden burst of emotion), and also *anacoluthon* (a break in the construction, two incompatible syntactic patterns coexisting in the same sentence: 'That friend of yours, I'll tell him...'). A specialist could easily supply more examples.

The idea that not all figures operate with the word as their unit is to be found quite plainly expressed in works of rhetoric down the centuries. What we now call 'figures', using the term generically to cover all the eventual subdivisions, were usually defined by treatises on rhetoric as 'ornaments', or 'colours' (*colores rhetorici*); within the 'ornaments' category, a subdivision which recurs constantly (though the terminology has often varied, and though the dividing line has been drawn in different places) is the one which differentiates between the 'colours' pertaining to a strictly localised unit of discourse (almost always the word), and those whose very nature presupposes a wider syntagmatic frame of reference (a phrase, a clause, a sentence): a subdivision which was usually formulated by means of the distinction between *Tropes* and *Figures*, with 'figure', far from implying a connection with the word, being actually defined in opposition to it; sometimes, however, 'figure' is the generic term (as it is today) and the tropes form a subset of the figures; but the principle of classification remains more or less the same (the criterion is that of the word). It would seem, then, as though the rhetorical tradition should have 'prepared' us to think of figurations as kinds of turning movements, with a fifty-fifty chance, so to speak, of surmounting the barrier of the word; should have taught us to *dissociate the figural from the lexical*.

On the whole, it did nothing of the sort. I think there are three main reasons for this. Firstly, the rhetoricians' 'non-trope' figures include some which although they operate across more than one word remain by definition (or else in practice, in the vast majority of their recorded occurrences) attached to the word-unit. For example, *antithesis*, a semantic contrast coinciding with a syntactic parallelism ('The guilty do this..., the innocent do that...', where 'guilty' and 'innocent' are both in the position of grammatical subject). There is obviously nothing to prevent antithesis applying to entire clauses (that at least is the principle); but we all know, if only from our memories of rhetoric lessons at school, that it is commented on most frequently when it involves two words (and if the example is an 'extended' one, it tends to get divided up into several antitheses, one for each pair of words). In any case, to say that it requires *two* words is ambiguous, showing that it needs the sentence as its framework, but also that it operates essentially on the word-unit. This ambiguity, this hovering between the frame of the sentence and that of the word, is more clearly apparent in other non-trope figures, including two which I have already discussed. *Zeugma* ('clothed in candid honesty and white linen') incorporates the sentence-word oscillation in its very definition: the same term ('clothed') governs two others ('honesty' and 'linen') which are syntactically parallel (noun complements of the adjectival participle) but are incompatible on another axis (here, abstract versus concrete): so that the play of the figure is *in* the sentence, but *on* the word (cf. p. 169. The same applies to *hypallage* (p. 177): a term (often an adjective) which is governed grammatically by one word in the sentence belongs by virtue of its 'literal' meaning to another. And so on.

Secondly, it is not irrelevant that the two modern 'super-figures', defined to coincide with the linguistic dichotomy of paradigm and syntagm, have been given the *name* of metaphor and metonymy rather than that of the other rhetorical figures now subsumed under these two headings. Even once we have chosen to adopt Jakobson's definition of the concepts, it is difficult to avoid being influenced to some extent, and via a kind of condensation (or *contaminatio,* in Latin terms[1]), by the classical meaning of the corresponding words. This inevitably affects the real scope of the concepts, and the way in which we put them into practice: when 'metaphor' and 'metonymy' are used in the modern, binary, sense, they often nevertheless retain – although this may not be deliberate – some residual allusion to classical metaphor and classical metonymy. These, unlike some other classical figures which have retroactively become variants of metaphor and metonymy in the current sense, were tropes; and so the *privilege of the word* tends to persist unnoticed, infiltrating even the broad definition of the metaphorical trajectory and the metonymic trajectory, where it is singularly out of place: we talk about figures in general, but we are often thinking of the word-based figure in particular. We should not forget that the rhetoricians used 'metonymy' to denote, not the whole set of symbolic figurations based on referential contiguity, but only those of them that resulted in a change in the meaning of a word (this is the tropological criterion); otherwise, hypallage, for example (see above), would have come very close to metonymy since it consists of a sliding along the chain of referents; but the rhetorical tradition keeps it separate. Traditional metaphor is even more clearly marked as a trope, because it is the criterion of the word which produces the explicit distinction between 'metaphor' and 'simile' (I shall come back to this point). A 'non-trope' metaphor is an impossibility in rhetoric; whereas in the cinema the metaphorical (or Freudian condensation) appears in the form of non-trope metaphors most of the time: and this difference serves to pinpoint the 'problem of the word', and its importance for present-day reflection on *'generalised' textuality.*

It is all the more important to react against the prestige of the word-unit and its reductive effect, in that it is further 'reinforced' by a third historical factor, which has been described very clearly in analyses by Gérard Genette[2] and Roland Barthes.[3] I shall merely reproduce here the main outline of their argument: the theory of word-based figures is only one part of the study of 'ornaments', which in turn is only one of the facets (corresponding to

elocutio or the work of 'style') of the rhetorical programme as initially defined, by Aristotle or Quintilian for example; the *trivium*
of rhetoric also included *dispositio*, i.e. the art of composition, of
'planning' the text, and *inventio* or the choice of arguments,
involving what we would see as considerations of 'content'; in addition, the *techne rhetorike* often included two more operational sections, namely *actio* (gesture and diction, the art of 'delivering' a
speech) and *memoria* (proficiency in memorising stereotypes to be
used again and again in different speeches[4]). But the *ascendancy* of
rhetoric has over the centuries continually diminished, like a
waning moon. During the Middle Ages it was gradually reduced
to *elocutio* alone. In the seventeenth and eighteenth centuries it
became increasingly confined to a study of tropes, as the result of
two converging tendencies: the critical neglect of figures other
than tropes, seldom mentioned any more (Dumarsais), and the
more or less explicit adoption of the tropological criterion for the
study of all figures (Fontanier). In other words, from being a
general theory of discourse, rhetoric has become *for us* (in the
form in which our twentieth century inherited it) a catalogue of
word-based figures, almost an appendage to lexicology and etymology.

THE RHETORICAL AND THE ICONIC

It is this predominance of the word at the expense of both the sentence and the live movement of the enunciation that inhibits the
use of rhetorical categories in the study of filmic discourse. We
must however recognise that these very precise distinctions (far
richer, in a sense, than the current metaphor-metonymy
binomial) are useful in encouraging us to refine our cinematic
classifications, and in focussing our attention on the real diversity
of the forms in which figures occur in films. Hence the interest of
studies conducted along these lines.[5] Yet the underlying principle
of such studies (the transfer of concepts from the rhetorical to the
iconic sphere) always comes up against basically the same obstacle: the filmic text (cf. the photographic text, etc.) has no units
corresponding to the word, and the figures of rhetoric, in varying
degrees, are almost all defined in relation to the word: either
directly (as in the case of tropes), or as a combination of several
words, or negatively (when the definition states that the oper-

ation in question does not apply to the word), etc. The result, in
many cases, is that in studying film the analyst discovers that
what has slipped from his grasp is the very possibility of *distinguishing* between two figures whose separation is quite clear in
rhetoric, but nowhere else. The subtlety of the classifications,
previously an advantage, can then become a problem.

I will take only one example of this, but a particularly central
and particularly striking one: do metaphors (in the rhetorical
sense) exist in films, or not? In rhetoric the term metaphor was
used only in cases where the symbolic 'work' of referential resemblance resulted in a compression, a concentration (cf. the
Freudian-Lacanian notion of condensation) within a single word
(a word actually pronounced or written), that is to say when the
vehicle, but not the tenor, was expressed in the sentence (for
instance, 'that pig' for 'that repulsive person'). When both terms
coexisted syntagmatically, it was defined as a simile rather than a
metaphor. In addition there was a whole hierarchy of intermediate cases, as Gérard Genette has shown most convincingly,[6] and
each one of these procedures corresponded to a specific 'figure',
even though they were not all isolated or given a name by the rhetoricians. In the fully-fledged simile, the 'similarity' is made
explicit in each of the stages of its journey: the statement specifies
the tenor, the vehicle, the 'ground' of comparison (the aspect
common to both *comparanda,* the way in which they are alike), and
finally the 'comparative operator' ('like', 'such as', 'resembles',
etc.). Since all these operations consist of words or phrases, the
presence or absence of any one of them can be clearly ascert-
ained, and each figure is quite distinct from its neighbour. In 'My
love burns like a flame', you have the vehicle (flame), the tenor
(love), the ground (burns) and the operator (like). In 'My love is
like a flame' (also a possible sentence), the ground is missing, but
nothing else. In 'My love is an ardent flame' (I am slightly simplifying Genette's schema) the ground reappears ('ardent') but
the operator has disappeared. In 'My love is a flame', both are
absent. Finally, after going through other possibilities which I
have omitted here, we arrive at the metaphor ('my flame'), in
which only the vehicle remains. Such is the rhetorician's mode of
procedure.

But what about the film semiologist, who will be confronted with, for example, the famous opening of Chaplin's *Modern Times*? And yet, in the entire history of the cinema, this is one of the sequences which has most consistently been defined by traditional film theory as a 'filmic metaphor'. It presents us with the image of a flock of sheep, followed by that of a crowd of people disappearing into a subway entrance. In the eyes of a rhetorician, it would not be a simile, since it lacks an operator. Nor would it be a metaphor, because the tenor (the crowd) figures on the screen. It would also be rather tricky to decide whether the ground (the *tertium comparationis,* in this instance the idea of 'flocking' together) is 'expressed' or not: it is clearly suggested in both images, and so is not 'absent'; but it is not presented as a separate entity, carried by a word which can be isolated from the others (like 'flocking'), and so it is not 'present' in its own right. As for the operator: to what extent can the juxtaposition of the two images in the film (emphasised in other examples by a visual effect: the lap-dissolve, etc.) be considered the equivalent of 'like', 'such as', 'resembles', etc.?[7]

This figure is almost impossible to define properly in rhetorical terms, once again because there are no words. The binary conception of the figural, on the other hand – and this is one of the reasons why I am taking it up, even though I intend to modify it considerably – enables us to situate the opening of *Modern Times* in terms of an analysis of referents whose subdivisions are less intricate but also more real: more real in films, but equally (there could be a possible feedback here) in written texts, provided that we look for the main symbolic trajectories rather than detailed surface-structural taxonomies, and define each occurrence in terms of the intersection of several 'deep' categories, necessarily fewer in number: indeed, on this level, where meaning becomes 'pressure', the gap between languages 'with' and 'without' words is no longer so crucial. If the metaphor-metonymy pair is clearly combined (rather than confused) with the opposition of paradigmatic and syntagmatic, the filmic figure of the flock of sheep can be defined – as I defined it on p. 189 – by its metaphorical and syntagmatic status (referential similarity and discursive contiguity). The metaphor-metonymy conception has the further advantage, which rhetoric obviously cannot provide, of having been formulated from the outset within the framework of a general semiology (merely a potential framework, but one which we can attempt to realise) extending beyond language and including images, etc., and also the advantage of legitimising some kind of articulation (although perhaps less direct than is sometimes thought) with psychoanalytic work and the concepts of condensation and displacement: an operation which would be even more difficult (and probably impossible) if we took rhetoric as our point of departure. And yet rhetoric is something we need to pay considerable attention to: not with a view to *applying* it (nothing is ever applied), but because it can help us to understand things better: for twenty-five centuries it constituted one of history's most impressive and thorough reflections of language on itself: a formidable symbolic machine.

The prospect of a direct 'match' of the rhetorical and the iconic meets with yet another complication, which has to do with both ideology and the status of the language-object. From our point of view today, the rhetorical dimension corresponds to figures which have 'set firm', those which make up a codified (and very much secondarised) nomenclature, while emerging figures are, by contrast, those which elude rhetorical classification. In actual fact this opinion is held most firmly by those who know least about what the rhetorical enterprise meant, but since nowadays almost everyone knows very little about it, it comes to the same thing. The rhetoricians themselves were, in a way, the first to endorse this view (by implication), since most of the figures their classifications dealt with were quite stereotyped, and that was what interested them. But in any case the problem is a more general one: rhetoric was developed in an age when the concept of *originality* with its attendant notions of creativity (which today arouse considerable passion, some of it totally naïve and totally blind to itself) had no existence, no ideological status. The question of degrees of emergence or stereotyping would have been meaningless to a rhetorician, that is, to someone who thought in terms of *techne* (= a set of rule-governed operations) and not of 'art'. Creativity (as distinct from real innovations, which are not usually so impatient) is an invention of Romanticism; remember Verlaine's cry of '*Prends l'éloquence et tords-lui son cou*' [Take hold of eloquence and wring its neck]. But the fact remains that rhetoric coincides to a large extent with the coded, for us today as well as for rhetoric itself.

On the other hand, many linguists consider that 'worn'

figures, to use their term, are no longer figures, that they belong henceforth to the language (I mentioned this on p. 156), and therefore that the *rhetorical moment,* the real moment of the figure, is its moment of emergence, which would make it rather more 'primary': a strange reversal! Charles Bally provides, in this connection, an explicit résumé[8] of an idea which is quite commonly held among linguists. Only when there is an effect of duality, when the literal and the figurative meaning (the first signifier 'beneath' the second) are actually perceived as separate, can we speak of a figure. When they are not (or not any more), as in '*tête*', already discussed on p. 158, we are dealing with a false figure, or else the non-figural result of something which was a figure once: at all events, with the 'ordinary' *name* that the language confers on the object in question. In fact the rhetoricians, in a different aspect of their theory and even more so in their practice, would not have disowned this view. They believed that figures (even the stereotyped ones which they had in mind) began only when they were perceived as different from the 'simple and common' forms of expression,[9] a difference which in the final analysis is none other than the difference between the literal and the figurative.

All these apparent divergences, which are also real, in fact arise because, as far as verbal language is concerned, there are (at least) three main levels of solidification, and not two: the degree zero, or genuinely emergent state (which is not yet a figure, insofar as this term implies at least some degree of stabilisation); the rhetorical codification in the strict sense ('steel' for 'sword'), which already belongs to a catalogue of more or less fixed figures, but is still felt to be genuinely figurative (the most ordinary word for a sword, even in the seventeenth century, is 'sword' and not 'steel'); and finally the linguistic codification ('*tête*'), where the figure becomes part of the language and is hence no longer a figure; where it becomes a name. Rhetoric, which in the eyes of a certain post-Romantic modernism appears as a vast graveyard, is still a principle of change when considered from the point of view of the language.

In the field of cinema, where there is no level of code that can be equated exactly with the *language-system* for spoken or written sequences, the distinction between the linguistic and the rhetorical phases disappears. As I have said elsewhere,[10] and as others have also said,[11] cinematic codifications are related to a kind of grammar and a kind of rhetoric, and it makes no difference which it is; because the very possibility of distinguishing between them arises only when the language exists as an autonomous organisation (French, English, etc.). So there will simply be, for each identifiable figuration, a complete – but single – scale of degrees of secondarisation (see Chapter 21), ranging from the state of pure emergence which startles us (in some slightly unconventional films) with the amazing, unprecedented clash of two images, to the conventional stereotype, the cliché for instance of the calendar shedding its pages to signify the passage of time, which is now a fixed metonymy but, like all banalities, was once an invention.

THE 'ISOLATING' NATURE OF THE WORD

The privilege surreptitiously accorded to the word causes a further problem. It plays an important part in obscuring, in disguising the profound affinities between the metaphorical process and condensation, and the metonymic process and displacement. This is obviously true in the case of images, but also of written texts (I will attempt to prove the point for the latter instance, proceeding as it were *a fortiori*). Condensation and displacement, being forms of psychical transfer which manifest themselves in many different ways (bringing the somatic into play in the case of hysteria), are so to speak always in transit, as 'movements' extending considerably further than the boundaries of the word-unit, even if sometimes this is where they leave their mark most obviously. Freud saw them as the typical paths of the unconscious, that is to say, of an apparatus which knows only 'representations of things' and not 'representations of words'[12] (or else treats the latter as though they were the former[13]). Lacan's position in this respect differs much less from Freud's than one might think, or than is sometimes said. Lacan believes that the unconscious is itself ruled by processes of a linguistic nature (= '*lalangue*'[14]) and it is this aspect of his teaching, more than any other, which has been taken up; many people have consequently underestimated the scope of two other ideas which are nevertheless inseparable from the first, namely (i) even if the 'mechanisms' are linguistic it does not necessarily follow that the raw materials will be, and (ii) Lacan's conception of linguistic oper-

ations is complex and wide-ranging (much more so than
Freud's), and does not in any way imply that language is reduced
to the status of a secondary phenomenon.[15] You can only accuse
Lacan of negating the primary, or of forcibly secondarising it by
turning the unconscious into a language, if your own image of
language is very secondary – a view which Lacan rightly con-
tests, and which anyway collapses as soon as you begin to look at
the real flow of linguistic signification. Condensation and displacement in Lacan's work, as in Freud's, refuse, despite constant reminders of their linguistic nature, to be enclosed within
the barriers of the word-unit (and anyway who says – what
linguist has ever said – that language can be reduced to the
word?).

Let us take one of the well-known examples that Lacan uses to
illustrate metaphor,[16] a line from Victor Hugo's *Booz endormi: 'Sa
gerbe n'était point avare ni haineuse'* [His sheaf was neither mean nor
vicious]. Jean-François Lyotard claims that this is, on the contrary, a metonymy,[17] and Gérard Genette agrees with him:[18] the
sheaf is, so to speak, the 'emblem' of Booz (Lyotard), and it has
(in the fiction) actually been harvested in his field. The objection
is undoubtedly valid, if we limit ourselves to the word (here, the
word 'sheaf'). But Lacan cites the whole sentence; nowhere does
he say that 'sheaf' is metaphorical. Personally I see nothing surprising, or even unusual, in a metaphorical movement containing a metonymic moment within it. Of course you could say that
Lacan should have been more precise. But you can't ask people
to change the way they write, and the *Ecrits* make no claim to
didactic clarity, at least in the ordinary sense (because I think
they possess another kind of clarity, profoundly didactic in its
own way: blindingly so, to the point that the reader represses it
and makes enormous efforts not to understand). The sheaf, then,
is metonymic. But the sentence is also characterised by a kind of
discontinuous line of movement which seems to me typically
metaphorical: 'his ... mean ... vicious': the possessive, evoking
the possessor, and the two adjectives, which are normally used
for people rather than things. The line is nothing more than the
observable result (the manifest content) of two representational
trajectories which have merged into one, and which themselves
remain latent (the level of production, as opposed to the

product): 'Booz was neither mean nor vicious, (the more conscious of the two thoughts) and 'Booz owned fields, harvested his
sheaves' (with various easily perceived overdeterminations: a
rich man, a patriarch, a life close to nature, etc.). It would be
possible to move further along this chain of associations and to
describe those more deeply buried segments which are nevertheless visible to anyone willing to follow up the trail: *'gerbe'* [sheaf]
is a near anagram of *'verge'* [phallus], since /b/ and /v/ are very
close in the Indo-European languages (cf. Castilian pronunciation) – and the poem is about unexpected fertility, a victory over
old age and death; meanness and viciousness are on the side of
the death instinct; but they appear in the line only to be negated
('was neither...'); and *'gerbe'*, in French, evokes all kinds of
spurting forth, etc.[19] But it is not even necessary to go this far,
and I will restrict myself to the two latent propositions which I
have just spelled out, and which people will surely not disagree
with. At their point of intersection there arises a resemblance (reinforced by contiguity, of course) between Booz' *generosity*, in
every sense of the word, and the *fertility* of his fields: when a piece
of land is unproductive, do we not use the word *'ingrat'* to
describe it in French, meaning that it does not repay our efforts?
Booz is like his harvests, he is a harvest: what could be more
typical of Hugo? The configuration as a whole is deeply, intimately, metaphorical. We would call it a metaphor presented
paradigmatically (since 'sheaf' has replaced 'Booz' in the line),
based on a metonymy presented syntagmatically ('his sheaf',
where 'sheaf' coexists with 'his', which stands for Booz).

It is also a nice example of condensation: different chains of
thought converge in a kind of terminal short-circuit – the line as it
exists – but the way in which they 'combine' is not made explicit.
It is, precisely, condensed (and I have been 'decondensing' it
with my explanations): the intermediate links have disappeared
and the result is slightly illogical (although fully characteristic of
language), having retained something of its primary force. A
sheaf cannot have psychological attributes, and if it has then it
must mean something else (this illogicality is nevertheless comprehensible: language works that way; as does the imbrication of
the primary and the secondary). The Hugo line has the structure
of a lapsus: a sentence which was planned in advance, deliberately aimed at ('Booz was neither mean nor vicious'), is disrupted by
something stronger which tears a hole in its fabric: the sheaf has

erupted into the sentence, pushing Booz out and taking his place. At the same time (as always) the secondary element has 'fought back', and won a compromise: 'his' remains in the line, and with it something of Booz: the sentence is still intelligible, whereas in the same context '*The* sheaf was neither mean nor vicious' would make no sense at all.

It soon becomes clear that a discussion like this stands no chance of coming to any conclusion (and will inevitably give the impression that 'everyone is right') as long as it is restricted to the *word* 'sheaf'. The frame of the word is too small (language cannot be equated with the word) for all the paths which intersect in its territory to become apparent within it, apparent in their full extent, or at least over a segment large enough to give some indication of what kind of symbolic operation is at work. Even so, this particular example (like some of the condensations in dreams analysed by Freud[20]) at least provides a word – i.e. again 'sheaf' – a more or less identifiable word in which, even if the backward trail of associations has been cut short, some of the threads of the operation (not all, as we have seen) are finally drawn together. An analysis based solely on the word would still allow *part* of the work of the symbolic to emerge, through metonymy: in this example, a displacement (of Booz on to his harvest, his wheat), in other words one of the displacements which together make up the condensation (cf. p. 268 below).

It is indeed a characteristic of language – and another aspect of the 'problem of the word' – that it has this constant but never fully realised tendency to encapsulate a kind of complete (but concentrated, compressed) 'argument' in every word: a tendency which is also intrinsically condensatory. Even the most ordinary word, *lamp* for instance, is the meeting-point for several 'ideas' (in the terminology of the linguist, several 'semes',[21] or 'semantic factors'[22] or 'componential features'[23]) each of which, if it were unravelled, or decondensed, would require a whole sentence: 'A lamp is a man-made object', 'A lamp is an object designed to give light', etc. This feature of language is also what enabled the movement of condensation in the Hugo line to be partially expressed at the level of the single word. In language, or in this line, the word is as it were the terminal point, not necessarily always reached, of a sort of huge turning movement which stretches far beyond it. That is why the privileged status of the word does not totally preclude an awareness of displacements behind metonymies or condensations behind metaphors.

In other cases, such an awareness is effectively precluded. Languages without words are an obvious case in point (but I do not want to make things too easy for myself). Within verbal language the phenomenon arises whenever a figural movement has hardened into a 'fixed' trope. Then the word blocks the horizon, the product makes us blind to the production, and condensation and displacement do not appear as such, but only posthumously, though it must necessarily be assumed that they have had their moment of action at some point in the past. When a man is retired and you have only ever known him in retirement, it is sometimes difficult to imagine him in his 'working life' (and yet there was a time when he did work): something rather similar happens when the deceptive dominance of the trope makes us lose sight of the links between the figural and the unconscious. The trope, in its perfected form, does not behave quite like the Hugo line or the virtual condensation inherent in any lexicon. If I say of someone that 'He's a shark' (a metaphor for 'unscrupulous and ambitious'), the process of condensation, the convergence of the two representations (the animal we fear in the sea, and the careerist we fear in society), is more intrinsically limited to the frame of the word, and that is why its 'primariness' is less apparent: it has less space for manifest action, and the various semantic trajectories which could extend it, and reveal the condensation, do not have enough room to emerge; in making itself autonomous, the word has cut itself off, thereby strengthening the hand of those who consider language to be purely secondary. The strands in the skein have, so to speak, come apart, and what is ultimately presented to consciousness is rather the mechanical and *opaque* fact of replacement, or double replacement: 'shark' has taken the place of 'unscrupulous and ambitious' (on the level of the signifier), and in the use of the word 'shark' the idea of careerism has taken the place of the idea of a ferocious animal (a corresponding switch in the signifieds): these two *jumps* are quite real, and positivist linguistics, which is specifically concerned with the code, is right to study them. It is simply that the condensation is no longer condensing anything, or not very much, and so can more easily be disregarded by those who are so inclined –

either because they don't like it and are hostile to any kind of psychoanalysis (positivism), or else because they are so attached to it they don't want to admit that it can be found in the most unpoetic places, of no interest to anybody except academic hacks (anarchism). And if condensation no longer condenses, this is obviously because of its very codification, which in turn is made very much easier by the institutionalised frame of the word.

The normal defence mechanisms (which can become neurotic) include one which Freud defined as *isolation*.[24] It acts by severing the links between representations, blocking the associative paths, and generally separating things out. This tendency belongs to the typological schema of the obsessional structure (but is not necessarily neurotic). With obsessionals, the desirable (anxiety-producing) representations, or at least very close substitutes, sometimes remain very largely accessible to consciousness,[25] but what is repressed is their link with acts of reparation (rituals) and with the production of anxiety. The repression, in short, is directed less at the forbidden representations themselves than at their association with manifest behaviour. (So there is certainly something which remains unconscious: isolation is listed as one of the defences 'other than repression', but in some respects it is a variant of repression.) Isolation also plays an important role in everyday life, particularly in the taboo against touching, or in the mechanism which ensures continuous mental concentration on a given task (something which requires us to banish 'intruding thoughts').

Every classification and every undertaking of a taxonomic nature (cf. Barthes' notion of 'arthrology'[26]) rests on a desire to separate things one from another. And this operation is necessary, up to a point, in all kinds of daily activities (it is one of the components of *clarity*). The rhetoricians, predictably, had a real mania for classification, and classification of a very detailed kind: a large number of 'small' categories, in other words maximal, galloping isolation (the obsessional, of course, is in his element *tidying up*). And here we come back to the word-unit, which in spite of its official programme rhetoric accorded a special status to, for the word (as I have just said) has remarkable powers of isolation, if only because it can itself be easily isolated. The danger of paying special attention to word-based figures is that it can make us forget the connection with the larger-scale figural movement of the sentence; it can encourage us to cut off the associative chain too soon, and disregard the action of condensation and displacement.

18

Force and Meaning

What is initially most surprising in the Lacanian reading of Freud, and which explains for example the reaction of Jean-François Lyotard at the time of *Discours, figure*,[1] is that it would seem to do away with the 'gulf' or 'barrier' which separates the unconscious from the conscious, the primary process from the secondary (and ultimately to deny the phenomenon of censorship). I shall be coming back to these terms (gulf, barrier, separation), for it is with them, with their undesirable connotations – and also with what one understands by censorship – that one might perhaps begin to shed some light on the basic reasons for the numerous disagreements and misunderstandings which have arisen in connection with these problems (much discussed in France in the last few years), as well as on the real difficulties which were partly responsible for the divergences in the first place.

Lacan tells us that the unconscious is structured like a language, he brings condensation and displacement into line with metaphor and metonymy (in language). But we have to recognise – or else we will simply be repressing the problem instead of confronting it – that for Freud condensation and displacement would seem at first sight to be 'illogical' operations of a fundamentally non-discursive nature (= 'The dream-work does not think'),[2] which pertain to the unconscious and to it alone: *pressures*, as it were, of a blind and purely instinctual kind (= the notion of 'the Id') which discharge themselves totally, by whatever means available, with no attempt at a plausible ordering of any sort (= 'free energy'), without following a planned noetic itinerary (= 'unbinding'), concerned to establish 'perceptual identity' (= hallucination, dream) and not 'thought identity'[3] (= rational reflection, the ordinary processes of waking life), incapable of sustaining a discourse (dream 'discourses' belong in fact always to the raw materials of the dream),[4] capable only of *bringing pressure to bear* (which is the distinguishing characteristic of the unconscious, and the definition of the drive) and therefore deforming, distorting, making unrecognisable: the '*Entsellung*' of the dream, a process which consists in disfiguring, as Lyotard remarks,[5] reminding us that this is the ordinary meaning of the German word (which it is).

In short, condensation and displacement, like all primary operations, far from being the cornerstone of the symbolic in one or other of its forms, would appear to be the very opposite of all thought: anti-thought operations, if you like. And since language, in contrast, is commonly held to be the most typical manifestation, the virtual definition in the eyes of many (Freud included) of the logical associations peculiar to conscious-preconscious thought, since Freud was of the opinion that representations of words were 'domiciled' in the system Pcs.-Cs. (and absent from the Ucs.),[6] will it not be the case that a conception of the unconscious as language, indeed a linguistic conception of the unconscious, will fly straight in the face of one of the most central and most permanent divisions of the Freudian apparatus, namely the separation of the primary from the secondary, the 'bound' from the 'free'?

To the extent that this opposition is understood as a principle of incompatibility, of non-penetration, of total insulation between two major types of mental functioning – for Lyotard the order of Discourse and that of the Figure, which can do each other violence, bully, fight and beat each other up, engage in mutual torsion, but never connect – the very possibility of a link-up between psychoanalysis and semiology is refused from the outset. The Lacanian position on the contrary, which of course owes a great deal to the influence of structural linguistics and anthropology, and to their repercussions on the reading of Freud, invites us to pursue in the movements of the unconscious various procedures of a discursive kind, and conversely to find the mark of the unconscious in all conscious discourses. 'The psychoanalytic experience does nothing other than establish that the unconscious leaves none of our actions outside its field.'[7] This attitude, taken to its extreme, leads us to 'semiologise' the whole body of Freudian thought (to redesign its organic structure), and in turn confronts the semiologist with the need to redefine accordingly the spaces of his own field. At the centre of all this is a huge question: how exactly do we conceive of the relations between the primary and secondary processes? That is to say, ultimately: how do we understand the phenomenon of censorship? If censorship were simply a 'barrier' (= a non-dialectical conception), the secondary and the primary would be separated, *placed apart*, as would semiology and psychoanalysis, or indeed the filmic text and its 'deep' figurative movements, by virtue of the same partitioning.

For the particular case of the cinema is situated from the outset at the heart of these difficulties and choices. One of the most obvious characteristics of film (and in this it differs from other arts) is that it combines words and images (visual images), 'representations of words' and 'representations of things', material which is directly perceived and relational orderings, so that one might expect it, in advance, to be connected centrally, and as it were via multiple points of attachment, to the most vital of the 'meshings' of the primary and secondary, and therefore to raise the central problem, or at least one of the central problems, of all semiology. It follows that there is far more at stake than just the complexities, daunting enough in themselves, which surround the notions of condensation-displacement and metaphor-metonymy. And yet these notions lead fairly directly into the vast hinterland, and this is the route that I now propose to follow.

The uncertainties we have just described stem partly from Freud's own habits of thought and writing. One rarely finds in his texts proper definitions of the major concepts he created, even more rarely a single definition (dare I say a definitive definition). Freud was little inclined towards the type of statement which exhaustively enumerates the pertinent features of a concept in the form of an explicit, independent proposition: what linguists (semanticists) call a 'definitional occurrence'. He was more interested in the phenomena than in the naming process, and his doctrinal apparatus was often only gradually put together, via a series of slips and slides (= condensations/displacements), rather than being assembled all at once and once and for all, according to a directly conceptual procedure commonly seen as the only possible form which intellectual 'rigour' can take. He has moreover, on occasion, acknowledged this freedom, and claimed it as a right.[8] Some of his concepts, appearing as they do several times in the same book or from one book to the next, are never exactly 'set out', they progress, or rather they make their way, a bit like a river in a limestone plateau, now going underground, now re-emerging, along with commentaries which, from one point of surfacing to the next, are fairly similar but not always identical, separated (and at the same time joined) by a little flurry of additions, corrections, variants, or at least by shifts of emphasis as far as the main points are concerned; and Freud sometimes neglects to consider retrospectively the ways in which these successive, semi-superimposable developments might be matched up. A 'Freudian concept' is often (as we shall see for condensation and displacement) not so much a concept as a clearing of the ground, a demonstration which proceeds in a certain direction, a kind of 'sector' which the author *shows* us, a sketch, a semantic gesture, obstinate and variable at the same time: less a watertight formula than something which has contours, which opens up as much as it closes in. One might also say: which has the elements of a definition, but not necessarily a definition.

It would in fact be interesting to reflect on the way in which Freud reflected, to take this as an object of study in its own right: it is as far as I know unique (or at least an extreme example) for the remarkable way in which it manages to combine on the one hand a reiterative stubbornness and an *esprit de système*, on the other a frequent lack of concern for formalisation, which is almost the exact opposite. An odd regime of writing: obsessional and happy-go-lucky, meticulous and inexplicit, punctilious and wide-ranging.

Among these hesitations one of the most permanent relates directly to our present topic of discussion. The whole of Freud's work, as text, is traversed by a double language and by a kind of chromatic (not diatonic) resonance which is established in the interplay of two series of words. You have on the one hand the scale of an energetics – physicalist, mechanical, 'blind' – with its pressures, its thrusts, its additional forces, its resultants, its conflicts of opposing forces, its cathectic energies, its discharges (see in particular the notions of 'the dynamic' and 'the economic'), and on the other hand, to describe the same things, you have all the elements of a fully-developed scale of the symbolic (which Lacan takes up): not only with the numerous, explicit references to linguistic problems, but especially with the terms (= figures) 'censorship' 'dream-text', 'decoding', 'translation', 'mechanisms of representation', to name but a few. This second series assumes a very structuralist air with notions like 'apparatus' and 'system', and more generally in the 'topographical' requirement posed as such (as one of the three, along with the dynamic and the economic, which the metapsychological enterprise must satisfy[9]).

Freud never unified his terminological register, and that is why the differences of vocabulary, from Freud to Lacan, are quite considerable. An author's vocabulary is what is most visible, so much so that for some readers it hides all the rest, instead of expressing it. Lacan alerts us to the fact that for obvious historical reasons Freud lacks the *reference to linguistics*: 'Geneva 1910, Petrograd 1920'[10] (in other words, and simplifying greatly, Saussure and Jakobson). When Freud was writing, the language of universal reference, or at least the dominant language, was that of mechanics. We know the durable influence that Fechner had on Freud, not only in the 'Project' of 1895, but right the way through, in every consideration of the dynamic (= successive theories of the drives), or again in the tendency, at once hesitant and persistent, to reduce the quality of the affect to quantitative phenomena of charge and discharge.[11]

But energetic relations in Freud (and this is what we shall have to explore in the rest of this study), even when stated in the terms of a mechanistic materialism – *a fortiori* when 'spoken' in the register of the symbolic – also correspond to paths of signification, trajectories of 'thought', to use Freud's term. Itineraries of discharge, whether primary, or secondarised in various ways, are very often mentioned, and this label suggests the irruption of the affect or of motor energy (their 'pressing' character). But discharge, a very general notion in Freud, is also the facilitation (another Freudian term) of a noetic path, the 'chain of representations' so often invoked. (Moreover it is worth remembering that the act of thinking, of symbolising, demands energy.) Freud was always of the opinion that thought, even secondary thought, was only another form, more or less 'bound' depending on the circumstances, of the hallucinatory satisfaction of desire.[12] And conversely, one of the points he came back to most frequently, and which he established very early on,[13] was that the 'process of thought' (of ordinary, waking thought) is a peculiarly typical example of what is understood by 'bound energy': I stress 'energy' (= thought *is* energy) so as to make plain this sort of overlapping – which you find everywhere in Freud's text – between the dimension of *force* and that of *signification*: a superimposition which is only rather tentatively expressed in the terminology, but which, as a gesture, is constant and resolute. It can be seen as one of Freud's great merits: as something resembling a materialist postulation, both 'wild' (or let us say: obstinate) and profoundly lucid even in its drastic simplifications. The dynamic and the symbolic, pressure and meaning, far from being mutually exclusive, are basically identical.

19

Condensation

Let us look first of all at condensation. It is misleading, as we shall see, to separate it from displacement, but the separation will only be temporary.

It is quite easy to pick out, from Freud's writings, various elements of a definition of condensation which seem at first sight to be very much alien to the nature of metaphor (and, more generally, any linguistic construction): they present this primary operation as, so to speak, 'a-semantic', as a physical confluence, a movement of converging forces which could never play a part in creating, in forming, the meaning of the dream, but only in *deforming* it – pulling it out of shape – through the irruption of principles which have no equivalent in waking discourse. In order to understand a dream, surely we have to *decondense* it, that is, unravel what the condensation has tied together, 'undo' the knots?

When condensation is first introduced as a key concept in *The Interpretation of Dreams*, at the beginning of the chapter[1] which is given over to it and which carries its name, it is seen as a difference of dimension, of area[2] – of 'room', almost, according to Lyotard[3] – between the (manifest) 'dream content' and the (latent) 'dream-thoughts', the first of these being somehow shorter, more cramped: as though the place in which we dream were 'narrower than the place in which we think',[4] as though it involved some physico-chemical reaction leading to a reduction in volume[5] (cf. the German word '*Verdichtung*': concentration, contraction, thickening, in the experimental sciences), and as though the 'other scene' differed from the first scene in its dimensions rather than its meaning.

But this property of contraction, which condensation undoubtedly possesses, in no way cancels out its semantic powers: on the contrary, it is what defines and explains them. Moreover, Freud first discovered condensation, along with the other primary mechanisms, in the attempt to *interpret* dreams (the meaning of '*Deutung*' in the German '*Traumdeutung*'), that is, in the course of research that deliberately concerned itself with meaning. Condensation is one of the bridging-mechanisms – '*Entstellung*', this time in the Lacanian sense of 'transposition':[6] the German '*stellen*' means 'to place' – which guarantee the transition from one 'text' to another (Freud's term), from the latent to the manifest: which do indeed deform the first text but in so doing construct (or form) the second. The circulation of meaning is a practice: in this case a physical compression, an energetic confluence. And on the other hand, meaning itself is a mechanism with its own laws (or rather, indeed, its own *figures*).

For in condensation the very fact of the reduction in area is inseparable, whether as cause or result, from specific associative paths and therefore a special kind of logic, a whole logic of *abbreviation* which compresses and ties together (cf. Lacan's 'nodal point') material which in waking thought is extended, explained and clearly ordered (hence the increase in volume). Dreams are not absurd, as Freud often reminds us, they are not evidence of a temporarily weakened or fragmented psychism, rather they demonstrate a different form of thought, that which is characteristic of someone asleep. The primary energetic of condensation is also a symbolic matrix: in order to say things more quickly, one has to say them differently and use different ideational paths (itineraries of discharge).

CONDENSATION IN THE LANGUAGE SYSTEM

The same observation can be made starting from the other end, from the waking state rather than dreams. There are some fully discursive and secondarised operations which bring into play a quasi-mechanical principle akin to that of condensation. Take for instance the *précis*, significantly renamed 'textual contraction' (which could almost be a Freudian term) in certain school exercises recently adopted in France: the précis, which no-one would claim had anything to do with dreaming, involves a transposition of the signifier as a whole, to produce a short text on the basis of a longer one according to procedures which someone like Greimas has been able to describe in technical linguistic terms.[7] Ultimately, however, it can only be defined in terms of the *criterion of extension*, the physical reduction in length compared with the original; and the semantic peculiarities of the operation (the use of 'theme-words' and 'key-words', the selection of 'classemes' at the expense of 'nuclear semes', etc.) all derive from this. The physical constraints do not exclude the symbolic dimension, they create it.

I shall not at this point consider poetic metaphor – another kind of précis and a Lacanian example of condensation, a single word with multiple resonances, the meeting-point of several distinct 'chains of thought' and hence the point at which overdetermination surfaces. For Freud, condensation was closely linked to overdetermination:[8] the condensed (manifest) element is by definition overdetermined – it is called condensed only because it 'carries', alone, more than one latent representation. (Conversely, it is when several latent chains cut across each other, and at the point where they do so, that condensation is most likely to operate, 'pushing' an overdetermined representation into the manifest dream.) Clearly, poetic metaphors behave in a rather similar fashion. But, paradoxically, they are somewhat irrelevant to my present line of argument, insofar as everyone (even those who reject a symbolic conception of the unconscious) usually acknowledges that poetic language, 'deep' language, is related to the primary process. (The problem then, of course, is conceiving the unity of language, the relation which nevertheless must exist between poetic language and 'other' language, and the very fact that poetry can be contained in words.)

It is language in the strict sense (or what is understood by this), and especially the language system, which is often denied any roots in the primary. And yet positivist linguistics, even in its most rigidly denotational and communicational form, the form least interested in the creative flights of advanced art, considers the *polysemy of the word* to be a normal and permanent phenomenon in a wide variety of idioms. Many words – all of them, in fact – have multiple and potentially divergent meanings: once the divergence becomes sufficiently great and sufficiently stable, different *acceptations* can be distinguished; but even words 'with a single acceptation' reveal a signified which is not homogeneous but open to several distinct shades of meaning. The very notion of polysemy is of course a familiar and central one in linguistic research; the term, moreover, comes from linguistics.

It is true that in each individual sentence – apart from jokes, which linguists are as interested in as Freud was – the context (Greimas' 'isotopy') determines the selection of one acceptation of the word and eliminates the others ('univocity'), whereas psychoanalytic condensation is, in contrast, characterised by the co-presence of all the semantic elements: if the condensed element were the extension of only one associative path, it would cease to be condensed. But, despite appearances, this is merely a difference of degree: the *degree of overdetermination* is probably one of the true gauges of how far secondary revision has progressed. Condensation in dreams indeed actualises several distinct 'valencies' around one manifest element, but these are not all equally accessible to consciousness; the analyst starts with those that are fully conscious, and works his way towards the others, which can only be unearthed with some effort: if they were all present and crystal-clear in the manifest dream itself, we would be dealing not with a condensation, but with an explanation. And the same situation occurs in linguistics, with the polysemy of the word: the acceptations which have theoretically been eliminated by the context do nevertheless add their particular colour and orientation to the chosen meaning (but they are less conscious): if I say that I am going to 'tackle' a job, I mean simply that I am going to get down to it (the acceptation which is retained, because of the context 'job') and I eliminate, in theory, the aggressive sense of the word (cf. 'to tackle an enemy'); but this latter, only partially 'repressed', survives in the connotation of my statement (every word is a condensation), and I have not said exactly the same thing as if I had stated that I wanted to 'get down to' the job; I have also implied that it will probably be difficult, a bit of a struggle, etc. (One of the many consequences of the polysemy of the word is to exclude total synonymy: each of the two near-synonyms, like 'tackle' and 'get down to' is distanced from the other by the pull of its other acceptations.) This set of phenomena justifies the large amount of linguistic research into connotation, into the way in which the 'affective nuance' of a word adds to its 'basic meaning', etc: so we see that the 'gulf', the 'barrier', separating off poetic creation or the fabric of dreams, ceases to be absolute. The difference is above all due to the fact that the eliminated acceptations (which are actually never eliminated: a definition of overdetermination) inhabit a zone closer to the unconscious in the case of dreaming, closer to the preconscious for ordinary polysemies, and somewhere between the two for poetic resonances: but exactly how close will vary greatly, even within each of the three registers, from one instance to another; and by working sufficiently on any one of them we would be able to progress further towards the repressed representations linked to the drive itself. It is not the fact of overdetermination which is remarkable, but the absence of its absence: it is at work everywhere, and varies only in its levels of intervention and its modalities.

For Freud – and in this he seems to be echoing in advance the linguists' position – the word (any ordinary word) was 'the nodal point of numerous ideas', which might be regarded as 'predestined to ambiguity'.[9] So although Freud situated the 'representation of the word' in the system Pcs. and the secondary process,[10] it retains even at the level of natural language, and quite apart from the overdeterminations which may result in subsequent innovation, a principle of condensation which is itself primary. Past condensations meet in each word of the language as though at a cross-roads; they have become bound and 'extinct', but the least of our dreams can rekindle and reactivate them: see for instance, in *The Interpretation of Dreams*, the famous dream of the '*Narrenturm*'.[11] In linguistics, the basis of polysemy is explained by the fact that there are more possible thoughts than words available to express them: surely this is to define the lexicon itself as the product of an enormous condensation (broken down into thousands of localised condensations)? Doesn't it look as though there is somehow *less room* in the place in which we speak (as well as that in which we dream) than in the place in which we think? 'The word', according to Lacan,[12] 'is not a sign, but a node of signification. And my saying the word "*rideau*" [curtain], for example, is not only designating, by convention, the usage of an object which can be endlessly diversified by the intentions which govern its perception by the worker, the trader, ... As metaphor, it is a curtain of trees; as pun, *"les rides et les ris de l'eau"* [the wrinkles and smiles of the water], and my friend Leiris mastering [*"Lei*RIS DO*minant"*] these glossolalic games better than I can. As a decree it marks the limits of my domain, or on occasion the screen of my meditation in the room which I share ... Finally it is an image of meaning as meaning, which in order to reveal itself must be unveiled.'

Work done in semantics, as I have said, tells us that the 'literal' and supposedly basic, non-figurative, meaning of words in the lexicon is in many cases the result of a past metaphor which is no longer really felt as such: 'worn metaphor', catachresis, etc. (see above, Chapter 11). The word then appears as a secondarised deposit – this is the *moment of the code* – forever 'positioned' between two primary forces of attraction, one of which has preceded it in the history of the language, the other (the same one, resurrected) having the capacity to 'take it back' at any moment, in poetry, in dreams, in spontaneous conversation, and set it in motion again. All these facts (and there must be many others that I have overlooked), quite ordinary facts that we sometimes lose sight of because of their very banality, invite us to conceive of the relations between primary and secondary in terms of a complex and permanent interaction (dialectical dynamism), and not in terms of some *cut* which would make each external to the other. Because there is a sense in which censorship lets everything through, and yet the price which it imposes, *secondary torsion*, is universal and very real. The existence of 'censorship' was suspected not only because something is blocked and deflected by it, but also because that something is not blocked and deflected completely: if it were, censorship would be undetectable by virtue of the very perfection of its results; no-one would have any way of telling it was active, and psychoanalysis would not exist.

SHORT-CIRCUIT, SHORT CIRCUIT

Among the various features which *The Interpretation of Dreams* attributes to condensation, there is another which, like the reduction in volume, appears at first to possess purely energetic connotations having little to do with semantics. In the psychical organisation of someone asleep, Freud tells us,[13] there are some thoughts which by themselves would not be sufficiently cathected to accede to consciousness, and it is only when several of them bring their respective intensities together in a single convergent representation (an idea which is typically Lacanian) that the latter manages to become conscious and enters into the content of the dream. This leads us to consider such things as the sum of forces (as though we were dealing with the theory of trauma and its possible effects of 'summation'), in a world of 'resultants' where the primary process begins to look more like alchemy than discourse; one might suppose (wrongly) that the various 'thoughts' in question are not affected by, indeed have nothing to do with, the movement of condensation, whose only function would be to handle the corresponding amounts of 'charge' (cf. the concept of 'quantum of affect'). In this conception, further-more, condensation is held to be inextricably bound up with sleep, which would seem to limit its field of action quite consider-ably, and to corroborate the impression of a rigid separation between the (nocturnal) primary and the (daytime) secondary.

But in a number of other passages, all of which point in the same direction (and which can be read quite easily, without any special knowledge of psychoanalysis), Freud has very noticeably enlarged the scope accorded, in this respect, to the process of con-densation. The general tendency for cathexis to weaken during sleep is still one of the extra factors which may contribute to the formation of condensatory groupings, but it is no longer a necess-ary precondition of their existence. Freud discovers condensation at work in the verbal slips and parapraxes of waking life (*Psycho-pathology*), in jokes, and in symptoms, especially those of hysteria,[14] which often consist of fragments of an original patho-genic situation, fragments which, like an imploding star, have drawn to themselves via multiple links the energy and the meaning of the whole situation.

In all cases of this kind – that is, basically, in many daytime actions whether they are ordinary or neurotic to some degree – condensation retains its quality of economic convergence, but in a more general sense which does not presuppose on the part of the convergent elements any special degree of intrinsic feebleness which might make it necessary for them to combine forces. Con-densation occurs whenever several distinct associative chains become anchored around a nodal point: several lines of force, that is, but also several symbolic trajectories. (Conversely, the movement of a semantic element seeking to 'express' itself is never purely a question of representation; it involves a thrust, a 'sthenic' aspect without which it cannot take place; you notice it when you write, even when the text is mainly a function of the transition from preconscious to conscious, and is a long way away from the roots: one has to find the word which, as they say, exactly mirrors the thought, the different directions it takes; in short, only a word which says several things at once can be 'exact'. All this takes energy, which is why writing is exhausting.)

The process of condensation in its most general outline is thus at one and the same time a kind of figure and a kind of movement – a figure in its final result, the point which is always reached, and a movement, always, in its productive principle – which can be regularly observed in a variety of semiological fields. It can be understood as a *matrix of semantic convergence* working at the intersection of several paths which turn out to be distinct as soon as they are sufficiently explored, and capable of 'forcing through' into consciousness (into the manifest text) some kind of signifying segment which brings them all together: a word, a sentence, a film image, a dream image, a rhetorical figure, etc. Condensation is an energetic phenomenon by virtue of the forcing through (the 'addition'), but it is also a major symbolic principle: a shortcircuit (a spark), but equally a *short circuit* (thereby remaining 'primary' even in its secondarised manifestations), since the superimposition it involves is never set out explicitly: the result is a particular inflection of the signifying circuit. An accumulation of intensities or a signifying configuration, depending on how it is observed: whether from the viewpoint of someone interested in the dynamics of the psyche, or that of the semiologist concerned with meaning as an operation.

CONDENSATION-METONYMY

Lacan has never said that every condensation 'is' a metaphor (even in the Jakobsonian sense), or that every metaphor is a condensation.[15] Among all the various textual occurrences we will obviously find, for instance, movements of semantic convergence in which the point of contact (the node) plays on contiguities existing between the representations involved, as much as or more than on their similarities. We will then be dealing with condensation-metonymies, a phenomenon which is by no means rare in the cinema: for example in the *Ballad of a Soldier* (1959), a Soviet film by Grigory Chukhrai, the insistent superimposition[16] in which we see the young hero crossing a gloomy winter landscape in a train, and 'on top' of this, and at the same time slightly to one side, on the edge of the screen, the face of the young girl that he has had to leave behind. The relationship between the two motifs is, on the one hand, metaphorical: the contrast between his present misery and the wonder of a few brief moments of happiness in the past. But it is primarily metonymic: it only holds together because of the link made by the plot, without which the image would be incomprehensible. The metonymy predominates and, if we think of the textual operations rather than the 'motifs', adjusts very easily to a condensatory pressure which is just as obvious in the passage, although not fully developed: there is still some duplication of the image – we can see two images, but two images tending to 'fuse', to overlap more completely. The soldier is thinking about an absent woman, he is trying to achieve 'thought identity' (and so are we), but this absent woman is present on the screen, thus implying 'identity of perception' and the hallucinatory satisfaction of desire: love abolishes distance, as condensation does, and the lovers are moving towards a real 'union'. The conscious image, as it figures in the film, is situated somewhere along this path where 'he' and 'she', happiness and sadness, past and present, might arrive at a single common expression. Somewhere along the path but, in this example, not right the way along. We can get nearer to it in other films with the (appropriately named) 'dissolve', the cinematic equivalent of the *composite structure*, or 'collective figure', as Freud calls it in the chapter on condensation,[17] the actually rather banal technique which completely superimposes the faces of the two lovers, so that the features of each are blurred by (blur into) those of the other – again a condensation-metonymy, in a different form.

In this type of example, and in many others, condensation is not a metaphor, or not exclusively. Each segment of a text combines the main productive matrices (here: condensation + metonymy

+ syntagm) in its own way. The work of analysis consists in discovering which elements in the terminal segment derive from which one of the matrices. The passage cited from the *Ballad of a Soldier* is metonymic as far as the relation between the two motifs is concerned, condensatory by virtue of the movement towards partial superimposition, the *verticality*, so to speak, of the meaning (as opposed to the horizontality of displacement) and the 'structure of the superimposition of the signifiers, which metaphor takes as its field':[18] a formula which in Lacan is applied to condensation, and from which it is clear that the latter's affinity with metaphor consists not in a distributional identity (which it does not require), but in 'taking the field'. The movement of condensation, even where it follows the paths of metonymy, retains something which is fundamentally metaphorical: a tendency to get past the censor, to make things 'come out', to push through by dint of several converging attacks, a centripetal organisation (quite different from the endless lateral pursuit which drives displacement on from one substitute to the next). In short, it is a *figure* (= in French, a face) which is more recognisably a metaphor than a metonymy, probably because metaphor, as I have tried to show, mobilises resemblances or contrasts which are much less predetermined by the 'natural' slidings from one object to the next, the already existing proximities offered by perceptual experience; resemblances or contrasts which depend more on being *noticed*, which rely more heavily on a mental act of superimposition, of juxtaposition (confrontation), and of laying one thing over another. With pure displacement, as with the pure metonymy described in Chapter 15, we remain indefinitely in the opacity of obvious connections. When several displacements converge and are thus mutually overdetermined, i.e. when condensation begins to form, things start to pile up on top of each other, creating new relationships, rather like in the work of metaphor. This is why the process of condensation often results in metaphors in the Jakobsonian sense, but it is also why it is *inherently* metaphorical, whether it results in metaphors or not.

20

From the 'Dream-work' to the 'Primary Process'

In the case of condensation and displacement, it is not only the particular elements of definition which have varied somewhat in the course of Freud's work, but their very status as concepts: hence some of the difficulties of present-day semiological (or symbolic) reflection. In Chapter VI of *The Interpretation of Dreams*, condensation and displacement are not seen essentially as manifestations of the primary process, except insofar as they contrast (in ways not fully spelled out at that point) with secondary revision. They appear above all as aspects of the *dream-work*, the concept which gives the chapter its title. This alters things more than one might think. 'Dream-work' and 'primary process' are indeed not synonymous, and the gap between them (which I shall try to show) is not simply a question of the almost 'material' difference of extension which you notice straightaway: the dream-work includes secondary revision, which escapes the primary process by definition; the dream-work assumes the economic conditions of sleep, whereas the primary process is permanently active, during the day as well.

We have to wait till Chapter VII (which deals with general problems of metapsychological theory extending in fact beyond the study of dreams) for it to be stated more clearly[1] that condensation and displacement, along with other operations, constitute the primary process. This is how they are presented from this point on in Freud's texts, and in particular in Chapter v of 'The Unconscious', entitled significantly 'The special characteristics of the system Ucs'.[2]

In the works which predate *The Interpretation of Dreams* great importance is already attached to the opposition between the primary and the secondary (in particular in the 'Project' of

1895), but the notions of condensation and displacement are not yet isolated. (Displacement has a role to play, but tends to be understood in a very general sense: it designates any form of *circulation*, the circulation of neurones, for example, in the formulations of the 'Project'.[3])

Freud's work therefore displays a kind of 3-stage progression (somewhat simplified here): in 1895 the existence of the primary process is posited, but no reference is made to condensation and displacement as identifiable figurations of a special kind. In Chapter VI of *The Interpretation of Dreams* it's the other way round. Condensation and displacement are introduced as such (and both together), but without any very visible reference to the primary process. Finally in Chapter VII, and in the rest of Freud's work, the connection is made explicit: from then on, condensation and displacement are regularly associated with the primary process; they are frequently referred to as its most typical manifestations, along with other figurations, but standing in the front rank.

From the point of view of the original development of Freud's ideas, these slides seem to me fairly understandable: what Freud first recognised, mainly in dreams, and under the as it were too particular name of dream-work, was a much broader phenomenon, the very 'presence' – or rather the *action* – of the unconscious behind and in all conscious material, the specific itineraries of this always absent presence, of this psychical substructure which never appears directly, but only in its effects. Strictly speaking this *is* the primary process, the 'figure' of the unconscious, which leaves its stamp, to varying degrees, on all conscious activities.

To the extent that condensation and displacement are too narrowly interpreted in relation to the dream-work and nothing else, their actual field of operation – and their semiological status, for the purposes of my argument – are liable to be considerably underestimated. It is not a coincidence that currents of thought which tend towards surrealism or anarchism, which are hostile to a 'linguistic' conception of the unconscious and reckon on its dissociation from the conscious, are more interested in dreams than in the primary process as a whole, in its permanent and very varied modes of intervention.

It would indeed seem at first sight to be true that the dream-work, as Freud often reminds us, does not create meaning. Or to be more precise, of the operations which constitute it, the only one which makes a 'positive' contribution to the final content, which *adds* something, is secondary revision,[4] by definition outside the scope of my argument. Its other elements, including therefore condensation and displacement, look much less like principles of formation than principles of *deformation*: they are orders of torsion whose essential function is to deceive the censor; which play only a very small part in the internal constitution of the true meaning of the dream (= latent content), which strive, on the contrary, to mutilate it, to distort it and make it unrecognisable, and which, therefore, must shoulder the bulk of the responsibility for the very fact that an interpretation is necessary.[5] It strikes me, in this connection, that various Freudian formulations point very much in the direction of Jean-François Lyotard's reading, beginning with the whole section of *The Interpretation of Dreams* (VI. F) where everything in the manifest dream which would appear to be of the order of thought (chains of reasoning, judgements, numerical calculations, etc.) is attributed to the pre-existing, latent dream-thoughts, to the raw materials on which the dream-work operates, and with which (Freud is quite emphatic) it is not to be confused. Its intervention, here, will consist precisely in turning these 'intellectual' elements away from their meaning so as to make them into fanciful and illogical figurations.

In a more general way you could say that the whole of Chapter VI of *The Interpretation of Dreams* carries, as if in suspension, the possibility of an 'a-symbolical' interpretation of condensation and displacement. It seems to me to lead to nothing in the end, but it would be wrong to ignore it. In fact I would like to formulate it a little more explicitly than Freud himself did, possibly even hardening it slightly (but without caricaturing it). The account would go something like this: once the dream has been deciphered, its 'true' meaning consists in a set of thoughts (focussed around a wish) whose internal articulations are in no way strange or irrational, and can be resumed (as the book itself shows, by one example after another) in a succession of sentences of an entirely secondary kind, conforming to the waking laws of the preconscious. In short, the content of the dream is not at all dream-like. The essence of the dream is in the dream-work. This does not result in the creation of meaning, but in its destruction or mutilation. The role of censorship, in the dream, is above all a negative one (as indeed the term suggests): it jumbles everything up so that the end-product cannot be recognised. A given sequence of the manifest dream will appear absurd because it is the result of condensation,[6] but as soon as the work of interpretation has broken it down sufficiently into its constituent elements (= decondensation) each of the chains of thought will be transparent and easy to understand, easy to situate in the biography of the dreamer: they are only incoherent and absurd because they are telescoped (because they are subject to the condensatory principle itself). To sum up, if you wished to parody the semiological notion of the 'principle of intelligibility' you might try to argue that condensation and displacement are *principles of unintelligibility*. And the reason for this is that they are the result of censorship, and this is how the censor 'wants' them to be.

This kind of view of the dream-work, which is in fact fairly widely accepted by tacit agreement, indeed dominant, seems to me to enter into contradiction with several of the constant features of Freudian thought. To begin with, if you think carefully about it, it cannot be applied to the whole of the latent content. The 'meaning' of a dream, once established by the analysis, divides into two zones which, in the dream, tend to mingle, but which otherwise remain separate: on the one hand you have the day's residues in the broadest sense (= all the preconscious material which 'comes back' in the night), on the other hand the unconscious wish or wishes. This is the famous distinction, carefully maintained by Freud, between the 'entrepreneur' of the dream (who can be preconscious) and its 'capitalist' (always unconscious[7]), or else between the wishes in the dream and the dream-wish.[8] Although it is true that the very effectiveness of dream production implies that they will meet at a given moment (a moment which Freud later describes as 'the preconscious dream-wish'[9]), the fact that this meeting has to take place, and the numerous occasions on which it does not, are proof of their essential duality.

Insofar as the content of the dream relates back to preconscious thoughts, the dream-work can obviously be seen as a blind force of distortion: we are dealing with procedures which are initially more or less 'reasonable', and which in the end have ceased to be so. Freud is moreover quite explicit about this:[10] if the day's residues undergo this distortion, it is because they are not transmitted directly from the Pcs. (the site of their provisional origin) to the Cs. (the final site of the dream); before reaching their destination they make a regressive detour via the system Ucs. into which they are drawn by the dream-wish. In other words, among the dream elements there are certain representations which have remained in the system Pcs.-Cs. throughout (or, to be more precise, which only left it to return straightaway), and which have been modified mainly in the sense of suffering a loss of meaning: in relation to such materials, condensation and displacement exhibit above all their deforming, 'disfiguring' quality (while in other contexts they are much more than this): they represent censorship at its crudest, a principle of suppression, mutilation, obliteration.

But in the dream there also, and above all,[11] intervenes the unconscious (infantile, repressed) wish. Which was unconscious before the dream, before any dream, in order for something like dreaming to be possible. A semantic element, now, of a quite different kind, and of which you cannot exactly say that it has undergone the censorship of the dream, since its very existence, its internal particularities and configurations, result from an older and more permanent censorship, a censorship which the dream can only reactualise, and even then in a weakened form: a censorship which, in the last analysis, relates back, step by step and via the 'return of the repressed', to the primal repression. It is possible to think, as Freud sometimes seems to have done, that the function (the only function) of the dream-work is to get round the censor – which without going any further would make the primary one of the conditions of the conscious – but this interpretation is more difficult to maintain for those of the dream constituents which have undergone the same censorship at a much earlier stage. Through the pull they exercise at the moment of the dream's elaboration (= the transference of the dream[12]) they submit the day's residues to a primary lamination which is for them (the day's residues) a new and violent misadventure, an alien irruption, a de-semanticisation. But the actual dream-wish, being unconscious, is not modified by condensation and displacement, still less mutilated by them. It consists already in a set of condensed and displaced affects and representations, and the question of becoming primary does not arise: it is primary of its very nature, and has always been so. For it, condensation and displacement are not late or accidental contingencies, factors of deviation, but the immanent itineraries which go to make it up: not deformations but *formations* (hence the Freudian notion of the 'formation of the unconscious').

I have now, I hope, made clear the extent to which 'primary process' and 'dream-work' are two divergent concepts (not only by virtue of the obvious differences of extension mentioned on p. 245, but for reasons which go deeper), even if Freud, in one of the stages of his discovery, recognised the one through the other, the primary in the dream. The dream-work, if you disregard secondary revision, is so to speak a *process of primarisation* (in comparison to waking life it puts us closer to ourselves): its action is therefore only 'mutilating' for that part of the raw material which in advance of the dream was more or less secondarised; for the remainder, obviously the main part, the dream-work does not bring about any really specific change: the modifications of the unconscious, its perpetual turns, occur just as much outside the dream; the latter being only the dynamic reactivation – one among many others which also have their ebbs and flows – of condensations and displacements that already belonged in this sphere, and defined it as such.

If Freud first presented as deformations what he subsequently, and more and more clearly, conceived as the fundamental semantic trajectories of all psychical work, this is partly because Chapter VI of *The Interpretation of Dreams*, although so central in the psychoanalytic edifice, can be seen from another point of view, and without it being immediately obvious, to be in a rather unusual position and a little out of line in relation to the Freudian enterprise of exploration as a whole. Freud's aim in this chapter, as in the earlier chapters of the book (but not in Chapter VII or in the later texts), consists on the one hand of interpreting dreams *in terms of their signified*. Anxious to reject current views on the absurdity of dreams, he is forced to proceed by demonstration (and it is always difficult to adopt this approach without overdoing it); he is more or less obliged to set out explicitly, for the various dreams he takes as examples, a reasonably clear and convincing 'meaning', which inevitably gives the impression of being definitive, 'final'. Many passages,[13] on the other hand, show that Freud was sceptical about the whole possibility of tying up the signified, even provisionally, in this way: a further interpretation can always be found, overdetermination does not at any point cease to operate, the demands of the cure mean that a dream is never followed up as far as it ought to be, etc.

And yet, the didactic intention, the desire to establish a new science, a whole strategy, meticulous and profound, for the management of the published discourse – motivations which are rarely absent from Freud's detailed formulations – impel him to offer, as he interprets the various dreams, and even when the interpretation is 'revised' from one passage to the next, a kind of *finished version* (or several successive ones...), rather like a translator who is forced in the end, sensitive as he may be to the infinite possibilities of language, to deliver a manuscript to the publisher. And then, there is something else, Freud's self-analysis. The dreams which figure in *The Interpretation of Dreams* are often his own, and this circumstance greatly encourages the stops on the signified. It does so for two opposite and yet convergent reasons: firstly because all of us, when it's a question of ourselves, are interested in content at least as much as in figurations (even if we profess the contrary in our theoretical studies), and secondly because Freud, cautious as always, had worked out pretty exactly what he was going to say or not say about himself, so that he had to have a dream signified to publish which stopped somewhere, which was *terminable*.

It is above all in the context of these necessarily rather static 'interpretations' that condensation and displacement appear as deformations. If you are going to work out on paper (or in your head) a version X (doctored to point Y) of the meaning of a dream, the very movement of the primary process also has to be stopped, it has to be taken as if against the grain (the signified then challenges the meaning), it must be apprehended in one or other of its results, which as such is precisely no longer primary: in short you have to work *against* it even in your efforts to name it. This is what happens to everybody: to me, for instance, at the moment, as I write this text.

To the extent that you wish to spell out a signified, you have to 'untwist' the primary (you have to flatten it): so you only meet it, you only experience it, as a principle of torsion. A serious error of perspective: it takes on an appearance which is conferred on it in part by its enemy (its analyst). In short, it appears as a deformation, and if there is a risk of our losing sight of its formative character, this is because the interpreter (well named in all the senses of the word) subjects it to a *contrary deformation* in trying to translate it, whereas, as the principle of production of all subsequently translatable phenomena, it is in itself the only thing that cannot be translated. In a sense it is the secondary which deforms the primary, and not the other way round: there is censorship also on the other side (I shall be coming back to this), and the ego is indeed, as Lacan has argued, the site of the imaginary (of the a-symbolic) and of misrecognition [*méconnaissance*].

21

'Censorship':
Barrier or Deviation?

When you begin to notice how many of the problems raised in the last chapter are actually problems of *translation*, the notion of 'censorship' and its exact status becomes quite central to the semiological enterprise. If censorship between the unconscious and the preconscious were in fact (as it is sometimes pictured) a kind of watertight and concrete obstacle (a dike, a barrier, a wall, a trench, a gulf, etc.), the primary process and the secondary process, on either side of this iron curtain, would be deprived of any conceivable interaction; each would reign in isolation over a separate kingdom. You would have a non-dynamic topography, a *line* of censorship, but not one resulting from two opposing forces (which bend it constantly because they alone are what create it); you would have on the one hand the fief of the primary with, notably, condensation and displacement, on the other the fief of the secondary, with the different formalised logics, mathematics, languages, and therefore among other things metaphor and metonymy, with the one exception of their particularly 'poetic' occurrences (but as you see, this very widely accepted reservation already supposes that the wall has a few holes in it).

Semiology would then be faced with a choice: either it could think of itself, as it usually has done up to now (without being sufficiently conscious of the fact), as a science of the secondary (to which Freudian discourse could contribute nothing of any real relevance), and claim this position as of right; or else it could subdivide into two semiologies which, except for their name, would cease to have anything in common, a 'semiology of the secondary' which would draw on linguistics, and a 'semiology of the primary' which would draw on psychoanalysis. We should note, moreover, that these choices – however superficial or even absurd they may seem when you think about it, or perhaps in fact because of this – are precisely the ones that semiology is driven back against (wishfully, dramatically, in the sphere of the imaginary) by those who have not understood what is at stake, or who, on the contrary, have caught a glimpse and taken fright.

The need to make the choice simply doesn't exist: only a certain conception of censorship could lead us to argue that it does, and this conception of censorship is impossible to maintain. The peculiarity of censorship, and one of its most noticeable characteristics – in the absence of which we would never be able to grasp its existence – is that things are always managing to get past it, to 'get round' it, you could go even further and say that it consists only of countless swirling movements, twists and turns: still a 'bar' of sorts, but rather like the sluices you sometimes see at the mouths of rivers, where the water gets through one way or another.

UNCENSORED MARKS OF CENSORSHIP

I would now like to take up and develop in my own way one of Freud's most common comparisons on the question of censorship, the parallel with censorship of the press. (In the word 'censorship' in the analytical sense this comparison became a metaphor and in the end a literal term.) If censorship of the press under a given political regime (one can think of a number of more or less blatant examples) were really absolute, no one would ever know it existed. It would not leave the term 'Censored' (which would be an uncensored term) on the blanked out rectangle of the newspaper, obviously. Nor would it tolerate the blank itself: as a blank, this would also be an uncensored mark of censorship. It would bring together the remaining lines and paragraphs till the empty space was filled, and nothing more could be got on the page. Moreover it would take care that the end-result of this 'bringing together', this stretching out of convergent elements, should not be to make the text incomprehensible, since any manifestly incoherent, poorly articulated passage would again tell us that censorship was *present*, that it was therefore uncensored.

Now in the conscious productions of human beings, the equivalent here of the newspaper page, what we observe from day to day is rather different from this extreme case where things are shut out as it were hermetically, and we know nothing at all; and this is precisely what makes it possible to recognise censorship. Censorship is the name given to the 'agency', to the set of psychical forces which *would wish* to establish this perfect barrier, which try to do so: for example, the active permanent anticathexis which maintains repressions once they have occurred;[1] or, in the last topography (and the 'second theory of anxiety'), the unconscious part of the ego as a reservoir of anxiety and the place of infiltration of the super-ego (see *Inhibitions, Symptoms and Anxiety*). But at the precise points along the front where it achieves its aim fully, even the psychoanalyst would not recognise it, would not *see* it. All we ever know of censorship are its failures. But the reverse is equally true, and perhaps more important: the failures of censorship establish the knowledge we have of it, so that (since Freud's discoveries) we do after all know something about it.

I was saying a moment ago that the censor does not print the term 'censored' on the newspaper: this is of course the idea you find constantly in Freud[2] that the repressive agency is itself unconscious (it is the unconscious part of the ego and the super-ego). But these same forces, considered in other aspects of their permanent and varied action, are also the distant source of self-imposed repressions and more or less conscious and deliberate renunciations: and this corresponds to the blank with the term 'censored' printed across it.

The censor does not leave an obvious blank on the page: nor do our mental processes, since they proceed ordinarily, as the hours and the days go by, from one conscious action to the next (according to a 'timetable' for example, or simply in their use of time). The conscious is not used to finding holes in the stuff it is made of. And yet, on other occasions, it glimpses interruptions, minor chasms, it suddenly ceases to understand what is happening to it:[3] a fairly common experience, which is already a knowledge of censorship (and therefore a localised failure of censorship), a consciousness of the unconscious:

> *C'est bien la pire peine*
> *De ne savoir pourquoi*
> *Sans amour et sans haine*
> *Mon coeur a tant de peine*[4]

> (Verlaine, *Romances sans paroles*)

The press censor is careful to match up the uncensored passages to make them appear logically coherent: the very definition of secondary revision in dreams,[5] and more generally of all rationalisations. But these procedures are peculiar in that they fail just as much as they try not to fail, and with the same regularity, the same obstinacy. Secondary revision often does not prevent the dream-text from exhibiting an incoherence which can be seen straightaway. Rationalisation also is always trying its luck (as for example when we seek motives for our anxiety, to reassure ourselves), but only rarely is it fully successful in discharging its function: if this were not the case, it would not be so often seen for what it is, it would not tend to be unmasked as a rationalisation (and therefore as irrational); it would not leave behind, in the wake of its efforts, that irredentism, that feeling of dissatisfaction which everyone has experienced, that persistent lack of conviction, that new upsurge of the very anxiety it had set out to quell. We would no longer be dealing with rationalisation, but with rationality (or else psychosis). In the last analysis, in spite of all the efforts of the censor, the newspaper page doesn't give the impression of being very coherent:[6] it represents the failure of censorship, you can *see* the censor.

GETTING PAST OR NOT GETTING PAST: THE GAP BETWEEN THE CONSCIOUS AND THE UNCONSCIOUS

Censorship is at one and the same time, and without it being possible to make a clear distinction, the place things *cannot* get past (which is how people usually think of it) and the place things *can* get past (but it's the same place). A psychical element is not said to be unconscious because it does not appear at all (if that were so it would be something which did not exist), but on the contrary because it appears *in a particular form*: in a different guise and as it were one step removed from itself (= 'displacement' in the very general sense). It is obviously possible to suppose, i.e. to infer indirectly (as Freud does when he talks for instance of 'construction'[7]), that there does exist something which never gets past the censor at all: the unconscious in its primitive, unaltered state (a mythical, or rather asymptotic, postulation which every analytic advance brings us closer to, but also causes to recede, like a walker his shadow): the 'root-stock' as opposed to the 'shoots'; something quite close to the primal repressed, and the actual representative of the drive. But when the work of association (of working through) has reached the point of being able to throw some faint light on this place of mythical beginnings (mythical and yet necessary as a base which is itself mobile), the fragment we see of it ends up by suggesting a set of psychical formations analogous to those which have always remained conscious: for example images charged with desire, memories haunted by fear, the unavoidable pairing of visions which constantly summon each other up, etc.; in short, psychical formations like those we come across daily (only the sequences are different); and it is for this reason that psychoanalysis (paradoxically) asserts the unity of mental life[8] (the unconscious *is* 'psychical': no less so than what would automatically be described as such).

At the other end of the productive operation, at the arrival end, so to speak, the unconscious formation always results in some conscious phenomenon (for example the return of the repressed): it can therefore be said to 'become conscious' (in its twisted, deflected consequences): something of it has got past. But has not got past, since a deviation was necessary: some aspect of it, some fragment, has stayed back, has broken down. Censorship is therefore not linear: it is not a barrier of the kind you get at level crossings, which stops some vehicles and lets others through (an agency which would involve two quite separate and well defined positions, as on electric switches): there is no associative path which entirely escapes its action, but equally there is none which its action can completely annihilate.

The unconscious is what we have to suppose exists between one conscious and another. Manifest behaviour, with the meanings it gives itself, always demands a more or less symptomatic reading through its incoherences, its side-slipping, its frequent infidelity to the very principles it has itself announced: whether someone is being discreet, has made a mistake or is telling a lie, the real point is always elsewhere.[9] And on the other hand, everything that analysis can suppose or imagine to account for these daily mysteries will take the form of another set of images, ideas, memories, affects.[10]

Censorship is not linear, I repeat, it is not a line which divides the territory into two spatially distinct areas. It belongs in another topology, that of *refractions*: it is a point of deflection, a modifying principle. The modifications we ‘observe are not what it does, what it results in (as if we knew it in other contexts), they are all we know about it. Looking at manifest behaviour, we can say that censorship is what differentiates it from (and unites it to) the background which we have to reconstruct to understand it: censorship is the fact that there *is* a background, and that in order to decipher the façade you have to *go round*. If on the other hand you think of this background as reconstituted by the work of analysis, censorship – still a deviation, and the same one, but seen now from the opposite direction – is the fact that a particular latent element is not identical with its conscious manifestation, that the background, in order to come into view, first had to be sensed as a break in the manifest chain, as a crack in the façade, and therefore once again as part of the façade.

The unconscious only appears in its conscious results, the conscious is only made intelligible by its unconscious interpolations, is only made coherent by its incoherences. Nowhere do we find two provinces side by side, or a frontier. Each is ‘in’ the other and the other in it: the other of the other. What unites them is the same as what separates them (as in the principle of the paradigm, which is not related to metaphor for nothing): this is censorship, which is basically – since it separates and unites at the same time – a form of *translation*, as Freud was fond of saying. A translation which is *possible* (= the principle of union), but one which is also *necessary* (= the principle of separation). A translation, moreover, which is unusual in that it operates in both directions at once (like the *Janus bifrons* of the Romans, or a prose which is also an ‘unseen’): there is of course the ‘interpretation’ which goes from the conscious to the unconscious, but any interpretation is also a reconstruction, which tries to ‘show’ us the route from the unconscious to the conscious. A genuinely different topography, which subverts the relationship between the ‘upstream’ and the ‘downstream’ elements (while nevertheless preserving the two terms): a river where the journey upstream can only be made by imagining what the journey downstream was like, where this process of imagination travels up the river (= analysis), while making it possible to travel down again by other routes (= the ‘cure’).

The various processes which get round the censor, and in particular condensation and displacement, are the only traces of its existence, so that censorship circumvented is the only form of censorship. They get round the censor, and in so doing assert its existence. They bear witness, in one and the same gesture (i.e. 'getting round'), both to its relative efficiency, since this detour was necessary, and to its relative inefficiency, since the detour is effective.

A dialectic of two mutually opposed and indistinguishable operations, but between which the relation of forces is not always the same: the coefficient of *transition*, of a successful clearing of the obstacle, is higher for condensation than for displacement, on account of the force of penetration which is generated at the energetic confluence (see pp. 240–2). The coefficient of *evasion*, of side-stepping, of non-transition, is more obvious with displacement than with condensation, since the same overdetermining concentration does not occur in a displacement which is only a displacement (a displacement which is not tied up with a condensation). For Lacan, as we know, metaphor leans a little more to the side of the symbolic, metonymy a little more to the side of the imaginary,[11] even if both are essentially symbolic. Metaphor partakes more of revelation, metonymy of disguise,[12] although they can both only reveal by disguising, and disguise by revealing. Freud was making a very similar point when he attributed to displacement the more specific function of getting round the censor,[13] while also admitting (and quite rightly not seeing any contradiction) that this function was a characteristic of the dream-work as a whole, and therefore of condensation among other operations.[14] These difficulties have to do with the notion of 'getting round', as when you speak of 'getting round the censor'. To get round it is to win a victory of sorts over it which is also a sure defeat (you can get round it, but you have to get round it): for anyone considering the operation as a whole, the relative importance of these two movements, the proportions in which they are present, will vary appreciably from one case to another.

Censorship is not the frontier between the conscious and the unconscious: for that to be so the conscious and the unconscious would first have to exist independently of it, and then it would be a question of situating the dividing line. It is the name given to the fact that they are distinct, as well as to the fact that they are perpetually intertwined; to the index of deviation, the mark of transition and non-transition which indicates the continuity and discontinuity through which their strange relationship is defined: unity of the 'psychical' and division of the 'subject'. In Freud's writing one can find at least one passage (perhaps others, which have escaped my attention) in which this idea of censorship as an index of refraction is fairly explicit: 'Everything that can be an object of our internal perception is *virtual*, like the image pro- duced in a telescope by the passage of light-rays. But we are justi- fied in assuming the existence of the systems (which are not in any way psychical entities themselves and can never be access- ible to our psychical perception) like the lenses of the telescope, which cast the image. And, if we pursue this analogy, we may compare the censorship between two systems to the refraction which takes place when a ray of light passes into a new medium.' (*The Interpretation of Dreams*, vol. v, p. 611).[15]

PRIMARY/SECONDARY: REFRACTION

The primary process and the secondary process, similarly, are not two principles holding sway on either 'side' of the frontier. They are not *situated* on either side of the censor: it is the fact that they are separate (that they deviate, once again) which creates censorship, which is censorship. From the point of view of the conscious (obviously the point of view we adopt most fre- quently), the primary process is not what we have to go looking for behind the barrier, it is the barrier, or at least what stands in its place: if we are 'censored' that is because it is difficult for us to consciously explore the workings of the primary. And from the viewpoint of the unconscious, the viewpoint adopted for instance in some psychoanalytical work, the barrier (still not really a barrier at all) – censorship – merges with the secondary process itself (and not with some mythical dividing line): if the primary organisation of unconscious elements carried over into their con- scious development, the fact is that there would be no such thing as censorship; and if such a thing exists (if there is something we call censorship) that is because our initial impulses only accede to consciousness by consenting to adopt a minimally logical appearance: to pass through a secondary milieu: so, for them, censorship is the secondary, whereas for the person who analyses, censorship is the primary: according to the direction you have come from, you experience censorship as one or other side of the gap which defines it anyway.

For it is important to remember that so-called primary operations cannot be described as such, can only be defined at all to the extent that so-called secondary thought analyses them and dismantles them. When conscious reflection struggles to say something about condensation and displacement, it takes on a task which is strictly speaking impossible, since the primary is by its very nature what it cannot grasp, since its otherness resides precisely in the processes which characterise it (and basically in them alone), so that *talking about it* is the last thing the secondary is capable of doing. Conscious reflection can only gesture towards its radical 'other' (but this much it can do: its radical other is *its* other, and therefore not radically other): it can try to point to it, in the way people might indicate a direction in space, vaguely and yet precisely. With every new word it discovers to describe it, it destroys it just as surely. As it closes in on its object it causes the object to disappear (but the reverse is also true: it's by causing the object to disappear that it closes in on it).

Let us consider displacement, in its primary form. It is commonly defined by the fact that its psychical charge is transferred entirely from one representation to another. But this definition – how could it be otherwise? – rests from the start on an insurmountable internal contradiction. It pretends to believe (and sometimes it believes, which is more serious) that somewhere between these two representations there exists a 'real', authentic relationship, consisting precisely in the fact of their duality. And so it runs the risk of making displacement look like some absurd extra operation, something faintly comical, a kind of optical illusion which 'sees' one object only (or at least some radical and substantive transitivity between two objects) in a situation where there are two quite separate objects. But *where* do these two quite separate objects exist, except in secondary thought, which conducts the whole argument as both judge and counsel? The characteristic of displacement is that in its eyes (for it can see, or rather it partakes of vision) 'one' and 'two' are not mutually contradictory: if a dream I have displaces my particular set of maternal images on to another person, a friend (the figure of my mother being more or less repressed, or itself displaced on to some other point of the dream), 'censorship' is what has *forced* me to substitute one person for another, and it is at the same time what has *allowed* me to proceed in this way: the question of whether my friend and my mother are separate or not does not arise, displacement plays on its irrelevance, on the fact that the specific virtue of the friend-figure (the arrival point of this particular displacement) is that it is my mother *and* is not my mother: take away this characteristic and you are left with no displacement, or at least no displacement on to the friend.

Let us imagine for a moment (absurdly) that the primary process has been given the job of drawing up a definition of conscious thought and its characteristic operations (which would therefore include non-displacement). The primary process would come to the conclusion (a funny way of putting it...) that non-displacement is a somewhat bizarre operation involving the fabrication of two objects, the friend and the mother, where in fact there is only one, or to be more exact a mode of duality entirely compatible with oneness: the primary might be surprised (?) to come across a 'milieu' where people like to complicate the simplest things. In short, if analytical research chooses to isolate condensation, displacement and the other primary operations this is because, in analytical research as in every other kind of research, it's the secondary process which is doing most of the talking. If the situation were reversed the operations to be listed and described would be the absence of condensation, the absence of displacement, etc. Such a reversal is of course utopian (at least in its complete version) since the usual abode, the *habitat* of human beings is the conscious or the preconscious, with the unconscious as a breach (and not the other way round). My only reason for bringing it up was to show how any definition of the primary process is in fact *a definition of the difference between the primary process and the secondary process*: we are dealing with an unusual, and perhaps unique, case where it is impossible not to end up defining something different from what one wanted to define, and where this second definition is the only form that the first can take. In the same way that the unconscious is, literally, beyond our grasp since we can only grasp it by making it conscious, so no one can 'get hold of' the primary process since to do so would involve reducing it entirely to secondary formulations. That is why it is something we *point to* (rather than define) in phrases which are essentially deictic, in negative and relational terms, as a kind of *desecondarised secondary*. It is characterised for instance by the 'absence of the principle of non-contradiction' (Freud) but in order to be able to pick up this absence you also have to have some idea of what it means for the principle of non-contradiction to be present, and in a world where it was really absent (as in the primary process, precisely) the task of making explicit this absence would be both absurd and impossible (these two adjectives being themselves contradictory...).

The horizon of the 'primary' is only the dialectical other of secondarisation: its limit, its point of disappearance, and at the same time its work, its creation. The primary is the name secondarisation gives to the holes in its fabric.

CONFLICT, COMPROMISE, DEGREES

And so – taking all this into account – we should not really be surprised if the primary and the secondary are always interacting in these very strange, very common ways, which we observe daily and which never cease to surprise – whether it's their strangeness which is the most striking thing about them or their banality would be hard to say. The primary, it is true, is still the opposite of the secondary, it carries within itself a force of disruption and madness (= 'unbinding' in Freud) capable of putting paid to any logical sequence. But at the same time, and in contradiction with this, the most reasonable of our mental operations are permanently feeding on a more or less distant primary source. The primary and the secondary do not exist in a pure state, they are only tendential entities extrapolated on the basis of an observed *compromise*, the only thing that can be observed, and the more or less universal regime of all psychical operations. The fact of psychical conflict, which we observe constantly and which is so striking, leads us to hypostatise as 'primary' and 'secondary' the both mythical and real figure of the two adversaries. There is no such thing as the primary, no such thing as the secondary, there are only secondarisations, with their degrees and modalities.

Condensation: a little *mise-en-scène*: I have a dream about Mr X (someone I know) and I see a rhinoceros. I'm quite sure that it's

Mr X, and I'm quite sure that it's a rhinoceros: two certainties I shall retain when I wake up. But my dream had a third: it knew this was one and the same being, the obvious oneness of the dream-figure was not threatened in any way by the fact that Mr X and the rhinoceros are separate entities, a fact which the dream also established quite clearly. *That* is the thing I will no longer understand the following day: the fact that one does not have to choose between these two solutions: and that is the heart of the matter, the primary inner core. And yet, insofar as my dream did in fact 'distinguish' two ideas (Mr X and the rhinoceros) in its own way (its condensing way), it was already showing evidence of a certain secondarisation. And conversely, my waking state does not abolish all the links between Mr X and the rhinoceros: I am amazed at the fact that they have come together, so the fact that they have come together does not escape me. The relationship persists, but at a 'higher' level of secondarisation: to understand what has happened I have to manipulate a somewhat laborious kind of explanation, which would go essentially: 'In my dream it was a *single* figure, but I can remember that it was *both* Mr X *and* the rhinoceros'. The words I have just underlined are like the visible traces of the mutual torsion of the primary and the secondary: by indicating that something is surprising which was not surprising in the dream (i.e. something which violates the principle of non-contradiction), they show that the 'I' who speaks has now migrated into the realm of the secondary; but simply by expressing it, even in the register of surprise, they bear witness to something like an understanding which has been preserved: preserved in an oblique kind of way, redirected, made strange: transition, non-transition. Between the night and the morning censorship has grown one degree stronger, the secondary has gained ground: my dream is not getting through. But it *is* getting through, well enough for me to be surprised by it.

And then, the 'ladder' of secondarisations has more than just the two steps which figured in my example. During the day I may also be 'struck' – this is Freud's '*Einfall*' – by some resemblance between Mr X (the real Mr X) and a rhinoceros. This time it isn't a dream any more, nor is it the half-dream in which one remembers a dream (especially in the morning): I am walking down the street, I have my mind on what I am doing. The power relationship (primary/secondary) is again modified (but, we shall see, *this is the only thing that is*). What prevails now is the basic and indisputable evidence that Mr X is not a rhinoceros, that no rhinoceros could be Mr X. A logical requirement which is, however, less absolute than it seems. My thoughts may indeed be 'bound', but not to the point of closing the road which links Mr X to the rhinoceros (a road which is, itself, of a primary nature, and the very one which my dream followed). I take the road: it is what is usually called an association of ideas (such a good name): isn't it true that Mr X *looks like* a rhinoceros? It had never occurred to me before, and yet (today) it strikes me. I could also say (in French or in English): 'Mr X has got *something of a rhinoceros* about him' (= a formulation which is slightly more primary). At all events, I'm at the stage of making comparisons, which is not very logical: '*comparaison n'est pas raison*', as we say in French. If it seems logical, it's through sheer force of habit (= codification). In every comparison one can detect a transitive force, a 'jump' in attention, which directs us necessarily towards the unconscious – there are too many perceptible (possible) resemblances: why choose this one? – a thrust which tends towards assimilation, and which preserves something of condensation. The act of comparison is itself a compromise: I ratify the bringing together of Mr X and the rhinoceros, I admit it into my consciousness, but I attenuate its impact (I am not dreaming any more), I am careful to make quite clear – *to whom* if not to myself, since no one is contradicting me? – that it is precisely nothing more than a '*rapprochement*', and this word expresses (*for* me, since that is its meaning in my language) the twin idea of material separation and, in a second gesture, bringing together: I am safely anchored, as you see, protected on all sides. Comparison: I state an association, but I keep it at arm's length; I let it get through, and again, I stop it getting through. The explicit operators ('like', 'as', 'to look like', etc.) are specially assigned to this defensive function, but a more diffuse context can be enough in other cases: as long as it's more or less clear that what is being said is just a 'manner of speaking' – as if all discourse were not a manner of speaking! – I can lower my defences by a notch. Mr X is still going round in my head (if that's the case, I can't like him very much); in fact *that rhinoceros* is beginning to get on my nerves: metaphor.

22

Displacement

'Displacement' in the psychoanalytic sense (cf. p. 155) is a broader concept than the way it is used would sometimes suggest. It is readily seen as a kind of localised shift, as a path from A to B (which it also is), at a pinch as a 'device' which could be made to coincide exactly, without spillage or surplus, with certain precise segments of texts (literary texts, film texts, dream texts, etc.): in such and such a dream, you will hear people say, this image 'is' a displacement (and this other image 'is' a condensation): a restrictive, 'realist' conception, which reduces the phenomenon to one of its results, i.e. what is more accessible to immediate observation, or to one of the stages of the journey.

Displacement, in the basic sense of the term, is the most general principle of all psychical activity, the expression of the energetic and economic hypothesis which lies at the heart of analytic thinking.[1] It is the ability to *move across* (= to 'displace energy', as Freud says), to pass from one idea to another, from one image to another, from one act to another. It is also, more obviously than condensation, censorship itself. On this point Freud[2] and Lacan[3] are quite emphatic. If our initial impulses travelled in a straight line to full consciousness (instead of proceeding via a series of displacements, in zigzags, from one substitute to another), there would be no censorship. The 'instinctual vicissitudes' which Freud has studied (reversal into the opposite, turning round upon the subject's own self, etc.) are all displacements, as their name already shows, and Freud defines them moreover under the heading of defence,[4] as defence mechanisms which are not the same as repression, but which preserve something of its character

266

insofar as the initial element of the displacement is always obscured, or hidden, by the displacement itself.

When it first appears as a title in *The Interpretation of Dreams*[5] displacement is not defined as a slide of meaning between two given dream elements, but as a global shift of emphasis, of focus,[6] as a redistribution of intensities[7] characterising the 'transition' from latent dream-thoughts to manifest content: dreams, according to Freud, are 'differently centred'[8] from their thought-material. Moreover it is not only the representations which can be displaced, but also the affects.[9] And then the transition – again the transition – from abstract words to corresponding concrete words which precedes and encourages the audio-visual staging of the dream (= 'considerations of representability') is presented as yet another form of displacement.[10]

More than once, in the texts written after *The Interpretation of Dreams*,[11] Freud characterises the general mechanism presiding over the formation of the phobic substitute as a displacement of an 'internal danger' towards an 'external danger'. Or again, he considers 'displacement on to something . . . indifferent' as one of the striking features of obsessional neurosis,[12] with its absurd rituals and its pathetic attention to detail.

As early as the 'Project' of 1895, the primary process and the secondary process are both conceived as displacements of energy (neuronic energy in the 'Project'), which is in line with the fact that they are called processes. But whereas the secondary process only displaces limited and controlled quantities of energy (necessary, however, in all discourse for getting from one idea to the next) the primary process, with every step it takes, displaces, at least potentially, all the available energy; hence the complete transitivity of primary displacements, the asymptotically absolute equivalence they establish between terms, and the propensity of the 'first' of these terms to become less conscious (= the mechanism of substitution and defence, once again).

MEANING AS TRANSIT, MEANING AS ENCOUNTER

This list of reminders could be extended, but it is long enough already, it seems to me, to establish (once more) how broad a notion displacement really is, something which is sometimes forgotten in the concern with localised dream itineraries, and which explains in particular one of the peculiarities of the relationship between condensation and displacement. This has been pointed out by Freud himself, by certain commentators[13] (and by me in passing, pp. 172, 202, 244, 259, but not always clearly enough or with sufficient emphasis.

When, like the author of *The Interpretation of Dreams*, you are proceeding demonstratively, and trying to give striking examples of condensation and displacement, you obviously tend to avoid cases where the two operations are intertwined in a particularly complex way. What you aim to do, if you can, is to produce one series of examples in which only condensation comes through strongly, and another in which displacement enjoys the same didactic advantage. (This is one of those *intrinsic mishaps of discourse*, which are actually very frequent and which, if they were more commonly perceived as such, would undercut certain polemics: in the process of trying to make one point clear you often end up obscuring another.) Chapters VI. A and VI. B of *The Interpretation of Dreams*, dealing with condensation and displacement respectively, inevitably produce a diptych effect, and a quick reading can leave the impression that here are two symmetrical sets, related externally (rather like the verb and the noun in grammar), and that the field of occurrences is simply divided up between them.

On the contrary, one of displacement's most notable virtues is that it encourages condensation, and even *enables it to occur*. These two figures do not exist side by side, although their provisional products sometimes do. They are 'situated' so to speak the one in the other. The one in the other, but not the other in the one. A one-way relationship: every condensation implies displacement, without the reverse being true. Displacement is a more general, more permanent operation, of which condensation is, in a sense, a particular case (which avails itself of the more ordinary path, and sometimes *turns it back* against censorship). Condensation always requires displacements (at least two), not as subsidiary adjuncts or optional variants, but for its very formation, that is to say, to exist at all: a representation has to settle at the confluence of a number of others, and these must therefore, in the process, all be 'displaced' in its direction.[14] In fact condensation *is* a displacement (a directed set of displacements). And yet we are right to use the term 'condensation' whenever it's a question of drawing attention to one aspect of the global process, the convergence of displacements (their nodal configuration, their intersecting pattern) rather than the displacements themselves. Similarly, we tend to say 'displacement' when the displacement is not accompanied (or only slightly, or not immediately) by a condensatory grouping, or when it is provisionally the only one, or when its convergence with other displacements is not what we are interested in, etc.

A one-way relationship, as I have just said. Am I quite sure about this? Or to be more exact, doesn't the relationship also go one-way in another direction, the opposite direction, so that a potential condensation would appear 'behind' (in) every displacement? We are not dealing with a return journey, with a reciprocal arrangement, since the journey out and the journey back follow different routes. The relationship is a remarkable one: it is two-directional, but non-reversible; it goes *one-way both ways*.

Displacement substitutes one object for another: in so doing it separates them, but it also tends to assimilate them, to *identify* them, to see them as equivalents, all the more completely the more primary it is (= the *total* charge is then transported). For Freud identification was a kind of condensation.[15] Displacement of course refuses this identification at the very moment it outlines it (points to it): a refusal – a flight – which sets it in motion, which pushes it on, which makes it a displacement (whereas condensation accepts the identification, and establishes it). Displacement keeps us a good distance away from the truth of the unconscious, it proceeds via substitutes.

'Condensation' and 'displacement' are surely the names given to the two sides of a single, immense movement (showing/ hiding), the use of one or other term depending on whether a particular occurrence tips over, more or less decisively, on to one of the sides or the other. In cases where we speak of displacement the potential condensation which persists is the (rejected) tendency towards identification, and displacement proper appears in the fact of moving on (of rejecting). Condensation on the other hand is invoked when the meeting of the paths is more important than the paths themselves.

Condensation, i.e. the 'presence', in the dream or in the text, of several chains of thought upstream from a single manifest element: there is always meaning behind meaning, *discourse always reinforces discourse*[16] (if it did not, it would simply never emerge as such), no sentence, no image is capable of saying everything that is said in it, nothing can occur to us which is not summoned up from several directions at once (as in the 'dual anchoring' of neurotic symptoms), every utterance is a bit like a spark – it would never have occurred if for a brief instant, the only really productive one, various distinct impressions had not come together in such and such a way. Condensation, in short: a vast set of displacements.

This description does not work the other way round. The dissymmetry remains. The only condensatory thing about displacement is the fact that it assimilates backwards. Condensation is something *more* than displacement (and this is also why it needs several of them).

In truth, displacement and condensation are not 'qualities', still less 'devices' of meaning. They are meaning itself (Kristeva's '*signifiance*'). Displacement is meaning as transit (as a flight from meaning), condensation is meaning as encounter (as meaning rediscovered for the space of an instant). The horizontal and the vertical dimensions of meaning. And Jacques Lacan's two formulae[17] which spring to mind again, inevitably: Condensation: 'the structure of the superimposition of the signifiers, which metaphor takes as its field'. Displacement: 'that veering off of signification that we see in metonymy'.

DISPLACEMENT-METAPHOR

I remarked earlier on (p. 244) that condensation is inherently metaphorical, and that this results in two opposite consequences, one of which is quite well known, the other seldom pointed out: condensation often results in metaphors (in the Jakobsonian sense), but it preserves something metaphorical when it results in metonymies; hence the notion of 'condensation-metonymy' which I proposed in the same passage.

The situation is somewhat comparable for displacement, with its inherently metonymical quality. Displacement can be observed in metonymy (see 'types' 3 and 4, p. 190, but it also takes the road of metaphor. There is (basically) nothing surprising about these non-correspondences, since metaphor and metonymy are defined solely on the conscious (manifest) level, the reference being to the 'logical' relationship between two terms (a static relationship) rather than the movement which unites them.

A few words, then, on *displacement-metaphor*. Its action can be pinpointed, in the cinema, whenever the filmic text, as it proceeds, enters into what is clearly a transitional action, connecting (displacing) one motif *on to* another, in a movement which has more to do with translation, in the physical sense, than with convergence or a possible 'encounter', and when, in spite of this, the two motifs are related by similarity or contrast, because there exists no plausible referential 'contiguity' between them, or none to speak of beyond an initial conjuncture. You then have an interesting 'hybrid', a metaphor by virtue of the type of relationship between the terms, a displacement by virtue of the type of *transit* which leads from the one to the other.

The old editing schemes of traditional cinematography gave ample space to montage by 'similarity', by 'association', by 'contrast', etc., in short by metaphor in the modern sense, the metaphor being more or less 'pure' depending on the extent to which it refused the pretext of some nearby element of plot. I would add that montage in the strict sense (collage) is for me, in this context, just one of the modes of realisation of displacement, along with camera movements or optical procedures such as the dissolve, the wipe, etc.

It is true that metaphorical associations of this kind can result from a condensatory operation, insofar as a superimposition in depth encourages the release of a more or less unconscious pressure. There is a sequence in *Citizen Kane*, the film by Orson Welles,[18] in which Kane's former butler is getting ready to tell the investigator about the sudden departure of the hero's second wife, Susan. He has just said: 'Yeh, but I knew how to handle him. Like that time his wife left him.' An ultra-rapid dissolve ushers in the close-up of a shrieking cockatoo (a little textual trauma: nothing had led us to expect it) which immediately flies away from the verandah where it was perched, revealing Susan who is crossing it hurriedly to leave Xanadu (the metonymic pretext, as you see, is extremely thin). It is the metaphor of flying away – which applies to Susan also, as when you say that 'the bird has flown' – of a sudden, cacophonous, compulsive soaring, over-compensating in the idea of something completely unpremeditated (= the gesture of the bird) for the long years of weakness and of putting up with it which the film has previously evoked: a real syntagmatic jolt for the spectator, as for the husband whom we see shortly afterwards, after a moment of reeling confusion, in an attack of impotent rage, wrecking the room of the woman who has left. And then the cockatoo, although it looks stupid (like Susan again) seems through the bad-tempered violence of its cry to be wanting to provoke Kane, and taunt him; it is something of the hero's very power, of his capacity to dominate, which has just flown away: a discreet surfacing of the phallic resonances which our culture associates with the theme of the bird. Via this multiplicity of superimposed associations (I have mentioned only a few), the metaphor accomplishes something of the work of condensation.

But in many other cases it merely designates a conscious resemblance, which proceeds from the manifest to the manifest, without any special resonances. In Jean Vigo's *A propos de Nice*[19] there is a famous metaphor which provides a good example of this, actually quite common, type of sequence. The face of a ridiculous old lady is followed immediately on the screen by a shot of an ostrich carrying its head and neck in a way which suggests irresistibly the comic, faded dignity of the *comme il faut* winter visitor. A simple, unambiguously horizontal displacement which has something intrinsically metonymic about it, and which nevertheless in its textual literalness flows into a metaphorical course (the metaphor, in this example, is even particularly 'pure' since it is not part of the narrative).

One might obviously be tempted, so as to 'salvage' the correspondence between displacement and metonymy on the level of occurrences, to try and show that such metaphors can in fact be interpreted as metonymies. A tactic which has on occasion been outlined.[20] But it seems to me (as I have already said) that surface correspondences are not absolutely necessary to the 'deep' homology, and particularly that the idea of a deep homology would be weakened very considerably if the notion of 'metonymy' were to be fashioned on the exact model of psychoanalytic displacement (= a tautological procedure) and in contradiction with the principles of rhetoric, traditional rhetoric as well as the Jakobsonian variety, for which (even if its definition of metonymy has varied a good deal in the course of history) images like the one of the ostrich will never be metonymic, and will always be assigned a place in the vast province of 'similarities'.

23

Crossings and Interweavings in Film: The Lap-dissolve as an Example of a Figuration

When we speak of a 'figure' in film, any figure, what are we talking about *in the first instance*? We are talking about the bringing together of two motifs in shot 43, or the unexpected cut between shots 13 and 14, or the superimposition which occupies the screen at a given moment and can also be 'minuted': in other words, a fragment of text. There are of course figures which are more complex and more diffuse, like the figure of the harps and the Mensheviks in Eisenstein's *October*, which I was commenting on, following Marie-Claire Ropars, on pp. 191–3 but these are still fragments of texts. The difference is that there are several of them, and also that any one of them does not necessarily involve all the filmic material which appears with it: the harp and the instrumentalist will be part of the figure, the décor of the room which we see simultaneously will not. (This qualification, however, also applies to a number of simple figures: in a superimposition, the figure proper consists in the fact that the images are superimposed, and not in the content of the superimposed images.)

At all events, we are dealing with localisable fragments we have extracted from manifest film sequences. Now a textual fragment – whether it's long or short, continuous or broken into sections, whether or not it coincides with a global unit like the shot: in brief, however the analyst may have chosen to isolate it, whatever the segmentation procedure – a textual fragment is a kind of perceptual block, visual and/or auditory, which has already undergone the effects of this isolation and is *circumscribed* within a given space.

By contrast, the symbolic matrices, the major categories whereby meaning is produced (like the principle of the para-

274

digm, that of condensation, the tendency towards secondarisation, etc.), are all movements *and not 'units'*, movements which are not contained even in the units whose form they assume in passing.

Any figure which is relatively easy to isolate in the flow of a film, and recurs with relative frequency in several films (that is to say which has been coded in a genre and in a period) can be thought of as the temporarily solidified result of more extensive semantic trajectories which preceded it and brought it into being, which will disperse it and create others. And, even venturing beyond those cases which lend themselves to 'cataloguing' more easily than others, there is no reason to suppose, in a general way (contrary to an unspoken expectation which is nowadays very common, no doubt because it would make classification easier and quicker), that a filmic element which is materially separate, an image, a sound, the linking of an image and a sound, the collision of two motifs, an optical procedure, etc. should correspond to a single principle of figuration, or that it could 'be' a metonymy, or a displacement, or a metaphor.

To establish bi-univocal correspondences (of the kind people rely on too often for sorting out the problem of cinematic figures) it is necessary, in whatever field, to have two instances alike in their internal structure (= isomorphic) and separate in their substantive reality, since these one-to-one parallels result from a kind of projection. The ordinary words for the same thing, like 'correspondence' or 'parallel', contain both ideas simultaneously. Neither condition is satisfied in the problem on hand, where the instances we are studying are the production and the product, the figuration and the figure, as such fundamentally dissimilar in their structure, and actually linked in the process of textual generation.

It seems to me that real progress could be made (at the present time) if critics were to undertake the task of situating filmic figures in relation to four independent axes: any one figure is secondarised to a greater or lesser extent; closer to metaphor, or closer to metonymy, or a clear mixture of the two; manifests condensation especially, or displacement especially, or an intimate combination of the two operations; is syntagmatic or paradigmatic.

The positions on each axis are numerous and complex, intermediate cases very frequent; the axes are bipolar (with the
exception of paradigm/syntagm where the two terms are exclusive and cannot appear in differing combinations). The way in
which the axes intersect are more varied still, thus bringing us
closer to the particular features of actual texts (we could never of
course hope to exhaust them).

It is also necessary to remember that a 'mixed' or 'intermediate' position (the words are in fact highly inaccurate) does not
mean a vague position. It is always possible to explore *what it is*,
in the figure as a whole, which manifests one of the poles, and
what it is which manifests the other. Neither of the two elements
in the mixture is itself mixed. I shall try to illustrate all these
points.

The lap-dissolve interests me now for more than one reason:
because it offers the ('tactical') advantage of being relatively easy
to circumscribe; also because it is common in the films of a
certain period, and therefore a characteristic of these films; and
especially, because it is a *'transition'* and so gets me to the heart of
my subject; forcing the point a little, you could say that at the
moment of the lap-dissolve the film exhibits nothing other than
its textual progression, its mode of operation in the virtually pure
state.

Condensation or displacement? What you notice first of all is
displacement. The lap–dissolve allows us to watch, more closely
and for a longer time than images (or its opposite, the cut), the
actual movement whereby the film passes from image 1 to image
2: the moment of travel is emphasised and expanded, and this
already has the value of a meta-linguistic commentary. Moreover, by *hesitating* a little on the threshold of a textual bifurcation,
the text makes us attend more closely to the fact that it performs a
weaving operation, to the fact that it is always adding something.

But the condensatory process is not absent; it is simply *somewhere else*, though still 'in' the figure. It resides in the (momentary, fleeting) co-presence of two images on the screen, in the
short instant when they become indistinguishable (see the 'collective figures' which Freud mentions apropos of condensation[1]).
It appears as an incipient condensation, unusual in that the
beginning is more like something residual, something which has

always been residual. We speak, in French, of 'nascent' figures, but the lap-dissolve in its condensatory aspect is a dying figure, a figure which is dying right from the start (that is where it is different from the stable and prolonged superimposition): two images go to meet one another, but they go backwards, turning their backs on each other. If a condensation begins to take shape, it does so en route towards its progressive extinction. As image 2 becomes clearer, as it 'arrives', image 1 becomes less so, it 'goes away' – like two billiard balls which meet only to send each other off again, so that meeting and separation become the same thing. And yet there is a moment when they do really 'touch'. The condensation we observe is in the process of being undone.

Is the lap-dissolve primary or secondary? There is straightaway something fairly secondary about it: it is the path between two manifest boundary-marks, image 1 and image 2, both taken at the moment when they are not mixed up, when they stand alone and are clearly readable (= the beginning of the dissolve for image 1, the end for image 2). Another secondary feature: the dissolve is often very highly codified, in 'film punctuation' particularly,[2] and the code focusses the spectator's attention arbitrarily on a stable signified, a cause/effect, before/after relationship, with a 'time jump', etc.: something it extracts from an overall meaning which is always more complex.

The primary aspect: it isn't only the boundary-marks that we are dealing with, but the path itself. Two successive paragraphs in a book can be linked (and at the same time separated: so far exactly as in the dissolve) by an expression like 'on the other hand' or 'the next day', etc., as well as by a blank (a new paragraph), a blank which is a segment in the same way as the expressions: could you imagine the end of paragraph 1 and the beginning of paragraph 2 being printed on the same lines, the typographical characters overlapping and getting mixed up? And yet that is what happens in every lap-dissolve. The device doesn't simply plot out some relationship between two segments on the level of the signified, it combines their signifiers physically, exactly as in the Freudian definition of the 'means of representation' which characterise dreams[3] ('means of representation' reads '*figuration*' in French, and this word suggests a kind of primary rhetoric). Thus it suggests to us a kind of relationship (whatever its official description may be: causality, etc.) which has to do with the fusion of elements, magical transmutation, mystical efficacy (= the all-powerfulness of thought). The images may be ordinary, the path which links them is not entirely so. Or rather, there are two paths, the ordinary one, publicised by the code, and the other one or ones. In short, and considering it only as a displacement, the dissolve is already a combination of movements secondarised to varying degrees. The fact that two villages are linked by a road with signposts does not mean that the paths and shortcuts which also run between them cannot be negotiated: it's a bit like the associations grafted on to the account of a dream in psychoanalysis.[4]

Anyone who invokes the regimented nature of the dissolve and the total obviousness of what is going on (both of which are undeniable) so as to rule out or underestimate a primary component is only speaking the language of defence, of resistance: primary sequences, through their overdetermination, tend to confer great strength and consistency on associations which will appear only in their secondary aspect, so that a certain vigour of the secondary is often evidence of the primary (which explains the fact that the dissolve was used for such a long time, and so frequently). To argue the point about clarity too strongly is to confirm in spite of ourselves, as much by the heatedness of our reaction as by our reluctance to look any further, the very reality of this magic transitivity which operates under cover of rationality.

Syntagmatic or paradigmatic? The lap-dissolve is a syntagmatic marker, and this time wholly so; no 'mixing' occurs. It produces syntagmatic sequences (that is why it is there), it even produces two at once: a simultaneous syntagm, in space (a variant of the superimposition), and a consecutive syntagm, in time, since the superimposition does not last, it is finally resolved into a succession, image 2 comes 'after' image 1 (hence my numbers). The definition of the dissolve – one of a number of devices for linking two images present in film – excludes the paradigmatic dimension. The dissolve forms a paradigm with other 'transitions' (the cut, etc.), but its own functioning is not paradigmatic.

Metaphor, metonymy, or both? It all depends, here, on the relationship between the initial image and the final image. Insofar as they come together for reasons to do with the plot, or on the basis of some stable proximity known both to the film-maker and the spectator, the movement forward is metonymic; if it plays on a similarity or a contrast, it is metaphorical. It is often both, and not by accident: two objects can exist side by side and at the same time be alike, the two criteria are not exclusive, the categories they designate are not complementary but cut across each other to a considerable extent (and yet they are separate, as in set theory). Here I refer back to Chapters 14 and 15.

What must now be added is that the lap-dissolve, though it isn't purely metonymic, shows a remarkable *capacity to metonymise*. It tends (if I can put it this way) to create a pre-existing relationship after the event. (In fact it is the displacement 'behind' the dissolve which brings this about, but the result is the same). Metonymy brings together two objects which stand in a relationship of referential contiguity; and the force of transitivity which characterises the dissolve, as well as the textual contiguity which it does actually effect (and which it underlines by its slowness and its gradual nature) restrict the spectator's freedom to think that the two elements it associates might *not* be contiguous in some referent. Perhaps that is why editing and metonymy are often confused (see p. 183). The dissolve would seem able to make the purest metaphors appear metonymic. And so it offers us a kind of magnified image of the functioning of metonymy in language (p. 154): the latter chooses one contiguity from a number of other possible ones, all equally 'referential', but the force of the metonymic act predisposes us to find this contiguity more contiguous than the others, more remarkable or more important in reality itself. The dissolve acts in a similar way. And on a bigger scale: because it reveals its itinerary (it differs in this respect from metonymy in language) and also because possible contiguities, in the cinema, are more numerous, so that to choose between them becomes even more arbitrary.

The lap-dissolve is a banal procedure. Other more unusual filmic figurations would lead us into a more complex labyrinth of operations. I wanted to proceed *a fortiori*. It is as important to identify the primary, or original elements, or productivity, in places where they are never seen as in places where their presence is obvious. Also, the code is relentless: when it is underestimated it returns as the repressed, and in our concern with originality we are more banal than we think.

The example of the lap-dissolve shows that every fragment in the fabric of film, however small and simple, requires several movements of the loom. The temptation to be avoided is making out that the dissolve fits immediately into one compartment and one alone (= the taxonomic illusion). It appears on the contrary as a good example of what psychoanalysts would call gain formations, the only ones which are fairly lasting, because they 'answer' with a single gesture to multiple motivations: they are anchored several times over, the knot 'holds' for a good long time. If we wish to 'classify' the dissolve, or simply to get a more precise idea of the way it works, we must take into account several registers at once, as well as the fact that they intersect.

24

Condensations and Displacements
of the Signifier

Since Lacan's various pronouncements on the matter, which are all too often interpreted in an over-simplified way, there has sometimes been a tendency to think of the relationship between condensation and metaphor, and between displacement and metonymy, in terms of a simple equivalence of occurrences, every condensation being a metaphor and conversely, every metonymy being a displacement. In this study I have repeatedly emphasised the crossing over, the non-correspondence of categories drawn from different fields (linguistics, rhetoric, psychoanalysis), and my purpose in spending such time as I have done in discussing revealing 'hybrids' like condensation-metonymy or displacement-metaphor was to situate the homology between the two primary movements and the two figures of modern rhetoric on another level: that of *operational affinities*, of resemblances in the meaning process. Condensation has something metaphorical about it, and displacement something metonymical, in their very principle, in the trajectories they describe, and not because they result in a certain number of figures we define as metaphors or metonymies. Condensation and displacement, as I have already said, stand in a 'prototypical' relationship to metaphor and metonymy, as when Freud saw mourning as the prototype of melancholia, or the affect as that of hysteria; and yet the affect is not always hysterical, any more than mourning is always melancholic.

This amounts to saying that manifest examples do not have to coincide exactly, or at least not in every case, for there to be a deeper similarity, which can be inferred directly from the theoretical study of the mechanisms.

And yet, there is a point (which I have said nothing about so far) at which these affinities themselves reach a limit, a kind of *overspill zone* where condensation and displacement operate in a way which cannot be attributed to metaphor or metonymy in any of their definitions, even the most extensive ones, like the binary conception of our own day. I am thinking of all those cases where condensation and displacement act directly on the signifier and affect it in its material substance.

This assertion will perhaps appear surprising, if it is read too quickly: are we not constantly reminded by Lacan (who has done more than anyone to impose the homology between the two primary trajectories and the two 'super-figures') that condensation and displacement, metaphor and metonymy are above all activities of the signifier, as in the word-plays he himself adopts so readily? Didn't Freud always take an interest in jokes, quite apart from the work he devoted to them specifically? Did he not continually emphasise that particular form of condensation which acts on the phonetic substance of words (= 'representations of words' treated as 'representations of things'[1])? Did he not observe, apropos of the associations grafted on to the account of a dream, in psychoanalysis, that the link between two elements often accedes to consciousness, at least initially, via a purely physical similarity (pronunciation, spelling) between the corresponding verbal formations?[2] In short, is it not the case that condensation and displacement, metaphor and metonymy, are *always* figures of the signifier?

ON THE NOTION OF THE 'OPERATION OF THE SIGNIFIER'

The fact is that this frequently invoked notion can mean (at least) two quite different things, which sometimes tend to be confused: either it applies generically and is a characteristic of *all* movements of signification, or it refers to something much more specific, much less widespread.

Semantic trajectories are always operations of the signifier, in two senses (which are really only one, seen from two complementary angles). Firstly, as Lacan has noted in insights of crucial importance, because the signified is never a given, because it is simply something which is indicated, in much the same way that a general direction in space might be by a gesture (meaning is always *deictic*), because the signifier, in the journeys and provisional halting points of meaning, is the only instance which is in some way 'presented' to us, and whose form and dispostion are, up to a point, beyond dispute, or at least amenable to some form of verification. Modern linguistics has always held the view that one of the major differences between the order of the signifier and that of the signified arises from the 'concrete', perceptual nature of the first in contrast to the fleeting insubstantiality of the second: of these two 'sides' of the Saussurean sign, the side of the signified is automatically the one we must reconstruct, or go looking for, the one which partakes of *the hidden*, which escapes the register of the manifest as of right.[3] It is strange that linguists, who as a rule are not very concerned with the unconscious, should have been able to say this kind of thing, to be sensitive in their own way to the 'vanishing' of the signified, to its fundamental absence, even if what they have in mind is essentially the latency of the preconscious. Every figure of meaning is a figure of the signifier in the first instance, because the signifier and its orderings are the only concrete element we are given.

Conversely, the thrusts of meaning (even if we observe them from the shores of the signified) always appear as disturbances, or else on the contrary as temporary forms of organisation which involve a certain number of signifiers. If I change my mind I also change the words I use, and if I try to clarify my ideas (to 'fix' my ideas, as the French puts it so well), again I find myself engaged in an effort to *nail down* my words. Synecdoche perceives or creates some equivalence between '*la voile*' [sail] and '*le navire*' [boat]: the physical constitution of the signifying chain, whether spoken or written, is immediately affected, and '*voile*' takes the place of '*navire*'. Eisenstein wishes to compare the demobilising speeches of the Mensheviks to soothing music: the text of the film, in its visual aspect, is straightaway enriched with images of harps and balalaikas. The least of our propositions concerning the signified inevitably brings us up against particularities of the signifier. This is once again something which linguistics has been well aware of, since it tends to think of 'form' as the only thing which guarantees the linguistic character of a phenomenon:[4] for example, in languages where there exists only one past tense for verbs there is no reason to assume a permanent semantic distinction between the continuous past and the past definite; and if such a distinction can be proposed for languages like French, the reason is that their signifier includes two separate formations, the imperfect and the preterite, recognisable aurally as well as in writing. To this extent it can be said that every trait of meaning is a trait of the signifier, because it results in differences in the signifier. (In reality, it's the other way round, of course: the differences are what we see first of all, and from them we infer something about the meaning.)

There is, on the other hand, a phenomenon which is neither permanent nor coextensive with the operations of meaning: when a semantic trajectory *brings about an alteration*, however slight or localised, in a previously constituted and stable unit of the signifier. Brings about an alteration in it, or begins (threatens) to do so: it is no longer now simply a case of modifying the arrangement of the signifying chain while respecting the internal form of its basic segments, words for example.

This is what condensation and displacement do in certain cases, which allow us to think of them as 'directly' affecting the signifier (more directly, and differently from the way they do this permanently). For condensation, an amusing and well known example of Freud's springs to mind[5] (there would be dozens of others). A man offers to take a woman home (a polite gesture, but the fact of the matter is that he finds her attractive). Addressing himself to her, a slip of the tongue makes him say '*begleidigen*'. This is a German word which does not exist, a little monster of the signifier, which can be read as the condensation of a conscious proposal ('*begleiten*', to accompany) and a less clearly recognised desire, 'beleidigen', a German verb which means 'to insult', not without sexual connotations in the circumstances. In cases of this kind, which abound in the literature of psychoanalysis, condensation is no longer content to act on the signifier of an utterance, as in Hugo's '*pâtre-promontoire*' [shepherd-promontory], or to modify the distribution of lexical signifiers diachronically, as when an object changes its name through a metaphor which subsequently loses its original force; it is no longer content to *set the signifier in motion*, if need be to push it around a little, to make it function in a particular discourse or in the evolution of the code itself: condensation now attacks its very substance, undertakes to redefine its familiar forms, to get right inside it so as to bring about its disintegration. A process which is altogether more primary (even if a number of intermediate cases would more than likely appear to anyone who took the trouble to look). So that, short of a step-by-step analysis, the manifest result of formations of this type is on average less intelligible than in other forms of condensation. In the famous dream of the *Autodidasker*,[6] the (German) reader unacquainted with Freud's explanations is simply faced with an absurd word, whose manifestly hybrid character – this at least is perceived immediately, proving incidentally that the order of the signifier is not entirely destroyed – whose manifestly hybrid character, striking as it is, offers no very obvious clues.

Displacement can also take this form. I remember a dream I had recently, at a time when I was thinking about the ideas I am putting forward in this chapter. It was a dream already corresponding to a wish in that I needed examples of dreams for the points I was going to make, and sure enough, I managed to come up with some (there is no one so obliging as oneself, as the saying goes in French). In fact I have forgotten many elements of this dream, but I have remembered – hardly a coincidence – the passage where this wish is directly realised: I was in the process of reflecting on *The Interpretation of Dreams* (the *Traumdeutung*),[7] and in my dream the title was the *Zusammen* (the German adverb meaning 'together'); I was in no doubt that this word referred to Freud's work, and that this was always its meaning; it didn't surprise me at all; and also, I had lost all recollection of the real meaning of '*zusammen*' in German. It was when I woke up that the signifiers '*Traumdeutung*' and '*Zusammen*' fell back into their objective positions in the apparatus of language, and that the substitution of the second for the first struck me as a typical, and strongly primary displacement (which I have not, in fact, analysed at all exhaustively; '*Zusammen*', I think, was a reference to an amorous episode which figured in the same dream, and which I can hardly remember; I would guess that the function of the dream, looking at it more as a whole, was to 'say something' to me, this time through condensation, about my position *vis-à-vis* my work, my investment in it).

The displacement on to '*Zusammen*' does not change the perceptual substance of the signifier; the word was pronounced 'correctly' in my dream. But what it does attack, and this is just as important (just as *compromising*, in the literal sense) are very stable and long since codified associations between units of the signifier and units of the signified. Of course, you could simply say that it 'modifies the meaning' of the word '*zusammen*', but it doesn't do so in the same way as the synecdoche which modifies the meaning of the word '*voile*' [sail] to make it mean '*navire*' [boat]. With '*voile*' the innovation is merely an extension, a limited slide, the gaining of a strip of territory; that is why the new meaning can be understood fairly quickly, and without a lot of explanation. There is indeed a change but, although it could never be predicted with any certainty, it is authorised, at least to some extent, by the state of the code before the change: of the different elements which go to make up a boat, the sail (like the hull, for example – in French '*la coque*') is one of the most obvious, one you would tend to think of as fairly characteristic of the whole boat. Synecdoche can give '*voile*' (or '*coque*', the pleasure-boating term), but something like '*taquet*' [cleat] for instance would scarcely be possible (and yet that is also a part of the boat). The displacement of '*Traumdeutung*' on to '*Zusammen*' is even more unexpected, more primary, since the two terms it unites (and separates) stand in a much looser logical relation than 'cleat' and 'boat' – looser, you could say, to the point of being to all intents and purposes non-existent. No conceivable diachronic evolution could bring the German word '*zusammen*' to mean 'interpretation' or 'dream' or both; no German sentence could possibly exist (except in a dream) which would permit the substitution of '*Zusammen*' for '*Traumdeutung*' without becoming instantly unintelligible for anyone who did not know about my dream.

And so, when the relation between units of the signifier and units of the signified is modified beyond a certain point the change cannot be assimilated by the code, and its effect is no longer to make it evolve, but to subvert a fragment of its dominion. Displacement is then no longer the driving force of language, or of discourse, as in the examples which I discussed in Chapter 11, but a potential cause of the disintegration of the signifier, even if this is not physically affected.

CONDENSATION/METAPHOR, DISPLACEMENT/METONYMY: OVERSPILL

These particularly 'strong' forms of displacement and condensation, which are only part of a much wider phenomenon, are the ones which would point most clearly towards the position of

Jean-François Lyotard in *Discours, figure*, which consists in postulating a separation, an incompatibility, the existence of a kind of perfect barrier between the primary and the secondary, the unconscious and language. A position which is not my own, for more general reasons which I have indicated along the way. But in some respects I shall come close to it on one point, and a fairly important one: when condensation and displacement affect the signifier directly they begin to differ from metaphor and metonymy in their very principle, and no longer simply because of non-correspondences on the level of occurrences, which do not seem to me to compromise the homology.

It is still true, even in these particularly primary manifestations, that the telescoping we observe in the condensation (*begleidigen*) has something in common with the semantic convergence which characterises metaphor; similarly the transfer which the displacement effects (*Zusammen*) is reminiscent of the 'veering off' of metonymy. But the *operation as a whole* (that of condensation and displacement), while thus retaining, even in this form, some elements of metaphor and metonymy, has become further removed from the operation of the two major rhetorical figures, because it now also involves the direct alteration of the signifier, and this is alien to the work of metaphor or metonymy.

The primary and the secondary stand in polar opposition to one another, allowing for all the intermediate cases of varying economic combinations and relations of forces; here we touch on the important question of secondarisation (the degrees of secondarisation). Condensation and displacement are formations which are primary in the first instance (which are found in dreams, and not in discourse), but which can be more or less secondarised; metaphor and metonymy are formations which are secondary in the first instance (which are found in manifest texts, and not in the unconscious), but which can have primary resonances and overdeterminations. These four operations move towards each other, in pairs, depending on the degree to which they are secondarised or 'primarised' respectively (that is what I have tried to show up to now). But on the other hand, as condensation and displacement assume more primary forms, so they move away from metaphor and metonymy, in a movement which is opposite and symmetrical to the one I noted in Chapter 11 apropos of strongly secondarised figures in which condensation has ceased to condense, and displacement to displace, where both operations only appear in their posthumous state, in the form of an inert residue.

At this point it is necessary to recall that metaphor and metonymy, although they always shift the signifier around, are referential operations (cf. Chapter 14). Lacan, who is interested above all in their movement, in the typical status of the trajectories they describe, which is indeed so striking, has attached little importance to the nature of the terms between which these paths are established. But this is also important. For centuries, rhetoric has gone on and on discussing the question of how far you can stretch a link like similarity (does it include contrast or not, etc.?), or else contiguity (does the unilateral inclusion which defines synecdoche belong under the heading?). But the links themselves have always been thought of as links between aspects of the referents which the figure mobilises, and not between aspects of their signifiers. This point of theory, which has never been contradicted (and which reappears in Jakobson with the notion of 'semantic' similarities and contiguities), belongs along with others to the definition of metaphor and metonymy which would obtain over and above the historical vicissitudes. There hardly exists a concept of metaphor or metonymy in which these figures affect the phonic or graphic element of words. You go from '*navire*' to '*voile*' as you do from 'love' to 'flame' by virtue of considerations which (however illusory and overdetermined the official versions of a paralysing metalanguage may appear) still concern, even if in the imaginary, the boat-object and the sail-object, the love–'object' and the flame-object, and not the three phonemes of '*voile*' and the five of '*navire*' or the place of the /m/ in the spelling of '*flamme*' compared to its place in '*amour*' . . .

Traditional rhetoric did, it is true, define several figures directly involving the signifier. Thus *alliteration*, already mentioned on p. 214 the repetition of phonemes, and more particularly consonants, at close intervals over a short segment; or *apophony*: same definition, for vowel qualities rather than consonants (e.g. '*Il pleure dans mon coeur comme il pleut sur la ville*'). But we can see from these examples that figures of this type are precisely the hardest to link up with metaphor or metonymy. The present-day partisans of the binary approach have moreover never attempted to make the connection; alliteration, apophony and the like are simply not mentioned. The task was in any case impossible, not because of the late emergence' of some secondary obstacle, but because these figures never have anything to do with the referent, whereas metaphor and metonymy are defined in relation to it. For the same reason, but working in the opposite direction, metaphor and metonymy become progressively further removed from condensation and displacement as the latter intervene more directly in the signifier.

Further removed, I would emphasise. No more, no less. For even the physical undermining of the signifier will not necessarily prevent condensation and displacement from *also* continuing to engage representations, affects, signifieds. In the '*begleidigen*' example you have a telescoping of phonemes, but also , and inseparably from this, the telescoping of two intentions, and two wishes, hence in some sense of two referents: the courteous intention, on the part of the author of the Freudian slip, to take the woman he is speaking to home, and the less avowable desire to submit her to some vaguely imagined insult. In other words you have the convergence of two 'chains of thought', a convergence which is metaphorical for that reason. But over and above this there is an operation which has nothing to do with metaphor, a specific thrust whose end-result is the installation at the very heart of the signifier of this encounter and this superimposition. When cases of this kind are taken into account (and the others should not be forgotten), the relation between condensation and metaphor appears as dissymmetrical and so to speak unilateral: condensation is *more* than metaphor, without the reverse being true; in all its forms it has something of the metaphorical process about it, but in some of them something which cannot be contained by it, which *spills over*. The same could be said of the relationship between displacement and metonymy.

THE SPILLING OVER OF THE IMAGE

The medium of film, or more generally of images, also involves movements of condensation and displacement whose action extends inside the coded units. The experimental cinema would supply numerous examples[8] corresponding moreover, in part, to its stated aims, its programme being to subvert and enrich perception, to put it in closer touch with the unconscious, to 'decensor' it as far as possible.

Up until now, in examining a certain number of metaphors and metonymies in film, I have been dealing with configurations in which one image takes the place of another or else, on the contrary, combines with it on the basis, or pretext, of some figural link between the corresponding objects. But in all these examples the object (the iconic object, the recognisable object, the relevant unit of the iconic signifier in the analogical code), the object remained intact, instantly nameable (the code of perceptual identifications is inseparable from linguistic designations[9]). In Chaplin's *Modern Times*,[10] although the relations between the flock of sheep and the image of the crowd going into the subway must be stated precisely, and are different from other instances suggested by their own counter-examples, the fact remains that shot 1 quite clearly represents a flock of sheep (and nothing else), shot 2 an urban crowd.

And yet, I have already had occasion to point out[11] (particularly with the lap-dissolve, even the classical lap-dissolve, which mixes two images physically) filmic figurations where the work of meaning goes so far as to scramble the internal element of the signifier. I have noted their primary appearance, their striking resemblance with some of the 'means of representation' in dreams, in the Freudian sense, which consist of expressing an associative link between two elements by their very arrangement, and if need be by the amalgamation or deformation of the corresponding signifiers: hence the 'direct transformation of one image into another'[12] as an allusion to some causal link (whether real or magic) between the referents: the resemblance with the mechanism of the lap-dissolve is obvious, but other filmic figurations (and other figurations in dreams) take the disintegration of coded iconic units a stage further. For in this example of Freud's, although the sudden eviction of one image by the other has something miraculous about it (=displacement), the images themselves remain identifiable and unadulterated; and in the lap-dissolve, which jumbles them up rather more towards the middle of its development, a certain unambiguous clarity is preserved at the start and at the finish, when each of the two images is no longer (or not yet) contaminated by the other.

The disturbance of the iconic signifier by primary trajectories can be more serious than this. I shall take an example which is certainly not the strangest or the most disquieting that could be found (indeed, when all is said and done, it is fairly 'tame'), but which has the advantage, for my argument, of having been subjected to detailed analysis within a rhetorical/semiological perspective by 'Group μ' of the University of Liège,[13] whose important *Rhétorique générale*[14] is widely known. It's a poster designed by Julian Key, an advertisement in the form of a drawing for a Belgian brand of coffee, '*Chat noir*'. The drawing represents a strange and manifestly hybrid object, which is nonetheless stylised, clearly outlined and instantly recognisable as the combination of a cat and a coffee pot. The linguistic equivalent, suggest the authors (rightly, I would say), would be a word like '*chafetière*' (= *chat* + *cafetière*) (we are not very far from '*begleidigen*' and '*Autodidasker*'). The strange effect comes from the amalgam of elements, or more precisely, as the authors insist, from the persistence of this amalgam alongside something else which is also obvious: the fact that there is only one object (the style of the drawing contributes to this in the poster). Here, precisely (although the article does not have recourse to psychoanalytic notions) we see the work of condensation: in this possible coexistence of one and two, which I mentioned earlier on,[15] which belongs to the Freudian definition of *composite structures*,[16] in this violation of the principle of non-contradiction – a violation in this case of a rather good-natured and inoffensive kind.

The article attempts to specify how such an image is related to the metaphorical process, and how it differs from it. Of the usual features which permit the iconic identification of the cat-object in everyday representations, some figure on the poster (pointed ears), other not (whiskers); similarly for the characteristics which in the normal way allow us to recognise a coffee pot. Underlying the drawing, as in metaphor, are the features common to the two objects (the foundations of the 'similarity'); in logical terms, the zone of intersection between the two sets: thus the same graphic contour on the poster can be interpreted as the tail of a cat or the spout of a coffee pot (in the same way, what love and the flame have in common has to do with burning). Other features of the drawing, on the contrary, escape this double usage; the cat's eyes, for instance, do not correspond to anything for the coffee pot; this is the zone of non-intersection, the equivalent of the semantic features which apply to love and not to the flame (like non-concreteness), to the flame and not to love; in the composite structures of dreams the equivalent would be the various features thanks to which the more or less conscious impression of duality is maintained at the very heart of the condensation.[17]

The '*chafetière*' is therefore metaphorical insofar as it answers to the schema of the two intersecting sets (that is to say insofar as it is based on an encounter between like and like). But, the article goes on (p. 45), in metaphor this intersection only concerns the features of the signified (taken, I would add, from the real or imaginary referent) whereas in this particular case, as has just been said, it affects two 'perceptual forms' (p. 45) which belong to the signifier in its physical aspect. Such an operation remains outside the province of metaphor (pp. 44–7). For instance, some of the features which stand in a relationship of exclusion (i.e. are not common to the two objects, have nothing to do with the similarity, like the cat's eyes) nevertheless *coexist* with the others in the figure as a whole (pp. 46–7).

The interest of this study for me, apart from its precision, is that, without having sought to do so, it links up with the idea that condensation, in some of its forms which act directly on the signifier, extends beyond the work of metaphor, while retaining something of it.

25

Paradigm/Syntagm in the
Text of the Cure

This study, which I am now coming to the end of, will have been travelling from start to finish between four *contact points*: metaphor-metonymy, primary-secondary, paradigm-syntagm, condensation-displacement. These, I notice, do not all stand in the same relation to the psychoanalytic field; the differences in distance are striking: 'paradigm/syntagm' plays little part in the reflections of psychoanalysts, even those among them who have assimilated the heritage of structural linguistics; the two terms hardly ever appear in their writings. 'Metaphor/metonymy' on the contrary figures prominently, at least since Lacan, and in the work which follows his lead: the notions are initially rhetorical but are in the process of becoming psychoanalytic. 'Condensation/displacement' and 'primary/secondary', for their part, have always belonged within psychoanalysis, since it is Freudian theory, in the person of its founder, which produced them.

It strikes me that the absence of 'paradigm/syntagm' (the only one of the four axes) in the body of analytic theory is in no way accidental, and is worth examining. Psychoanalysis proper (= the practice and theory of the cure) forms a horizon in which 'paradigm/syntagm' *disappears*, completely, *behind* 'metaphor/ metonymy'. Why?

The semiotic/psychoanalytic study of literature, of the cinema, of cultural productions in general, is always dealing with concrete texts, texts which have become objects in the external world. It is for this reason that its procedures can never coincide exactly (nor should they try to) with those which inform genuine psycho-

analytic research, whose proper object is a set of mental processes: this is something psychoanalysts never forget, even when
they are talking about something else (the 'arts' for instance); the
cure is their daily work, and it is never far away.

The reality of the distinction between paradigm and metaphor
on the one hand, and between syntagm and metonymy on the
other, can only be preserved by keeping the discursive and the
referential dimensions separate, and recognising the shifts
between them (see Chapter 14). But for this to be possible in the
first place, it is necessary for discourse to be *closed off*, and
inscribed in some physical space (the page of a book, the cinema
screen). When you focus on the psychical processes themselves,
rather than 'works' of one kind or another, metaphor and paradigm – and metonymy and syntagm – tend to come together.
What links them, i.e. the movement of 'similarity' or that of contiguity, begins to be more important than what separates them.

Two filmic elements, as I have said, can be united, or rather
united-and-separated (so far, just as in psychoanalysis) by a
thrust which tends towards substitution, without this tendency
necessarily being brought to the point of realisation in a given
passage of a film one is analysing: one of the motifs is 'trying' to
expel the other from the text, but the possibility remains of determining whether it has not, as yet, managed to do so (so that the
motifs are both still present in the film and form a syntagm) or
whether it has indeed evicted the other one by absorbing it,
'swelling up' at its expense, and creating a paradigm.

The words of the analysand form a discourse of another kind,
which has no limit, which is constantly correcting itself and can-
celling itself out, a discourse *which cannot be located* (hence its force)
and which, moreover, must constantly be placed in a varying relation with the manoeuvres of an unconscious. No text is completely immobilised, but that of the analysand is less so than any
other: the 'cure' doesn't only consist in the fact that the analysand talks about what is happening to him, but just as much in
the fact that new things are happening to him while he talks (cf.
the difference in Freud between remembering and reproduction[1]). If one of two signifiers in transference is unconscious (too
close to the drive in one or other phase of the cure), its conscious
substitute will stand in a paradigmatic relation to it, since it
represses it, and at the same time in a syntagmatic relation, since
they coexist in the psychical apparatus (see the horizontal bar in

the well-known Lacanian formulae[2]). And what about the different 'offshoots' (whose reactivation brings about the cure) which are constantly driving each other out, but only so as to present themselves more effectively and end up appearing side by side? What remains, since there is no longer any *ring* around the text, since the inside and the outside become more totally embroiled than elsewhere, since this discourse is nothing other than its own perpetual re-establishment, what remains is the movement of superimpositions and translations in its metaphorical and metonymic principle: which makes it even more difficult to find a 'segment' which will stay reasonably still, the only possible basis on which to decide whether or not the representations are co-present, whether they form a syntagm or a paradigm.

On pp. 174 and 183 I made the point that present-day discussions often obscure the paradigm/syntagm distinction, or even drop it altogether in favour of metaphor/metonymy. A situation which doesn't make for clarity, but which reflects a certain state of affairs. It isn't simply carelessness (on the contrary: the re-establishment of all the divergences demands close concentration).

We can now see that the root-cause of this frequent 'oversight' is itself double: there is the structural homology of each of the two conceptual pairs, which is very real and fairly complex (cf. Chapters 13 and 14) and which makes the confusion too tempting for it to be always easy to avoid. But there is also an implicit pressure which comes from the psychoanalytic field, where the very existence of a difference between paradigm and syntagm is ·of minor importance and extremely hard to pin down. It is really surprising in this connection, indeed I find it odd that no one else (so far as I know) has made the point, that analysts like Lacan and his followers, who are so concerned with linguistic theory, hardly mention paradigm or syntagm, do not consider them as potentially useful tools.

And yet, the difference between the cure and bona fide texts is in a sense only one of degree. In rhetoric and in linguistics (cf. pp. 176 and 209, we have also, for instance, come across a kind of 'force' emanating from simile (syntagm) and impelling it to change into metaphor (paradigm). But the semiotician has 'corpuses' – the irreducible difference must indeed have to do with the text's mode of inscription – so that he is better placed to decide the exact stage – a stage which will be provisional, but not totally so – which the process will have reached at any one point of the chain.

The unconscious is a text without frontiers, which leaves no *external deposit*, whereas film is 'recorded' (on celluloid), a book 'printed' (on paper): these words speak for themselves. Memory traces are inscriptions too, as Freud was fond of saying, but ones which are inaccessible to the sense organs. Also (but it's the same point) the book does not change the order. of its pages as the semiotician comes to study it, the film does not mix up its reels while its analyst is looking at it.

In short, when you pass from the text proper to the text of the analysand, it is the relative strength or importance of the discursive dimension (= paradigm/syntagm) as against the referential dimension (= metaphor/metonymy) which shifts perceptibly in favour of the latter, even if this in its turn is conceived of in symbolic terms (Lacan); especially in fact when this is the case, in spite of the apparent paradox, since the referent, itself apprehended as a discourse, will account for all discursive phenomena.

Hence a double movement: the divergence between syntagm and paradigm loses some of its force, the notion is no longer of any great use; but on the other hand, whatever discursive elements may remain in the speech of the analysand can be expressed theoretically through initially referential notions which have been 'drawn' towards discourse.

Metaphor, in this way, assumes the global heritage of 'similarity' and absorbs paradigm which has become too vague. Metonymy swallows up syntagm and takes care of all contiguities.

We should not allow ourselves to be deceived: the process of analysis is necessarily 'referential' (even if this word has a bad reputation nowadays): there is a patient to be modified, the stakes are high, the talking is not about nothing. But it is precisely towards this horizon that the discourse as a whole, with its *positions*, has moved: paradigm and syntagm are less absent than they appear to be. The territory established by the relationship of analysis is perhaps the only one of which you can say that the referent is entirely *transported* into discourse (you talk, and nothing else) but where, conversely, discourse itself constitutes the only real referent (you talk about discourse, and nothing else), although not in a negative way (the cure is not an avant-garde text: something we forget because both are fashionable): where discourse, in short, constitutes the referent *fully*, in all the senses of the word.

Notes and References to Part IV

CHAPTER 11: 'PRIMARY' FIGURE, 'SECONDARY' FIGURE

1 'I shall choose ...': already the problems that this text will discuss are raised on a small scale. This was pointed out to me by a member of my seminar, a psychoanalyst, Pierre Babin. For why have I chosen 'Bordeaux' from the hundreds of other examples which would equally well have suited the conscious topic of my paper? So here I am forced to illustrate what I shall be claiming by my own mode of procedure. There is no beginning, and things are never cut and dried.

2 As early as the 'Project for a Scientific Psychology', 1895; later, for instance, in The Interpretation of Dreams (vol. v) pp. 564–7 and 602–3, the 'Formulations on the Two Principles of Mental Functioning' (1911: thought as a 'reality testing activity'), The Ego and the Id (vol. XIX) p. 45, etc.

3 Cf. particularly The Interpretation of Dreams (vol. v) pp. 602–3.

4 Freud frequently remarks that the most basic as well as the most mysterious characteristic of mental functioning is that it relies entirely on various kinds of quantitative masses of intensity ('quantities of excitation', 'energy', 'charges', 'cathexes', etc.) whose mobility accounts for the vagaries of human behaviour. See for example The Ego and the Id (vol. XIX) pp. 43–5 ('desexualised narcissistic libido'), or Beyond the Pleasure Principle (1920) (vol. XVIII) pp. 30–1: we simply do not know what a 'psychical excitation' actually is; it is like an x which we have to incorporate into all our argumentation, etc.; also, p. 7 of the same work (on the economic mystery of pleasure/unpleasure).

5 Figures III (Ed. du Seuil, 1972) p. 23 (in 'La rhétorique restreinte').

6 Antoine Meillet, 'Comment les mots changent de sens', L'année sociologique, 1905–6 (reprinted in Linguistique historique et linguistique générale, Paris, 2 vols, 1921 and 1938).

7 Notably in Le Langage et la vie (a collection of articles), Payot, 1926 (expanded third edition, Geneva: Librairie Droz, and Lille: Librairie Giard, 1952).

8 And yet, as some members of my seminar (Régine Chaniac, Alain Bergala) have pointed out, this spontaneous act of naming is still likely to owe a great deal to a sort of coded field which surrounds it like a dotted line. The pneumatic drill is often used as a symbol of modern industrial noise; you could almost say that it has a typical 'nuisance-value'. Also, it suggests building sites [chantiers de construction], and it disrupted my work when this text was 'en

298

chantier' [in the process of being put together] (a banal metaphor). Etc.

This had not occurred to me. I had arrived at the idea of the pneumatic drill by other, truly spontaneous paths which I have begun to explore in these pages. A nice example (even nicer than I thought) of the interpenetration of primary and secondary. Not unlike what we found with *'Bordeaux'* (see p. 154 and note 1), but this time the other way round. Associative paths are always both more and less 'personal' than one thinks at first.

9 These remarks do not apply only to metaphor and metonymy, but also to the paradigm and the syntagm. The two pairs of concepts do not coincide with each other, and I shall have to consider at some length the implications of this disparity (see ch. 14). But their behaviour is similar in that they may be secondarised in greatly varying degrees, ranging from the 'solidification' more or less identical with the *code* to the properly *textual* emergence. The possibility of variations along this axis is a very widespread phenomenon, common to all symbolic elements or units of discourse, one which does not concern either metaphor or syntagm (etc.) specifically. Basically it is the problem of the code and the text, and it is indissociably 'linguistic' and 'psychoanalytical'. The linguistic aspect of the question was already very central in my book *Language and Cinema*.

On the screen as elsewhere, syntagm and paradigm, insofar as they are well and truly established by tradition (because emergent paradigms and syntagms do exist), become largely conventional configurations, consumed in immediate 'communication', and implicated in a particular cinematic code or sub-code. But syntagms and paradigms do not become fixed right away; like 'figures', they have their moment of emergence, of more or less primary incandescence. Alternating editing is now very common, it is one of the 'normal' signifiers of filmic simultaneity (and one of the most stable of cinematic syntagms); but when it first appeared in early films – and something of this still remains in films of our own time – it was a kind of phantasy of 'all-seeingness', of being everywhere at once, having eyes in the back of your head, tending towards a massive condensation of two series of images, itself proceeding in a succession of displacements to-and-fro between the two series.

10 In *Le Langage et la vie*, already cited.

CHAPTER 12: 'SMALL-SCALE' FIGURES, 'LARGE-SCALE' FIGURES

1 *Ecrits*, trans. Sheridan, p. 177, note 20; also p. 298.

CHAPTER 13: RHETORIC AND LINGUISTICS: JAKOBSON'S CONTRIBUTION

1 A member of my seminar, Guy Gauthier, who works at the *Revue du Cinéma –Image et Son* and at the *Ligue Française de l'Enseignement*, has also commented that in the sixties, when semiological ideas were first beginning to gain currency among film specialists, the terms 'paradigm' and 'syntagm' met with

special resistance, made people laugh, etc., whereas at the same time and in the same circles 'Signifier/Signified', 'Denotation/Connotation' or 'Metaphor/Metonymy' 'went down' more easily.

2 This essay constitutes the second part of *Fundamentals of Language* (The Hague: Mouton, 1956), a book by Roman Jakobson and Morris Halle, and is reprinted in *Studies on Child Language and Aphasia* (Janua Linguarum. The Hague: Mouton, 1971) pp. 49–74.

3 Gérard Genette states on p. 25 of *Figures III* (in 'La rhétorique restreinte') that the binary conception of the figural, organised entirely around the metaphor/metonymy pair, had already appeared in 1923 in Boris Eikhenbaum's work on Anna Akhmatova, and then in 1935 in Jakobson's own article on Pasternak's prose. One could add, for the cinema, Jakobson's article of 1933, published in Prague (see later, pp. 193–6, in which the metaphor/metonymy binomial is already fully operational. But its large-scale diffusion dates from the 1956 article.

4 Gérard Genette, *Figures III*, p. 23.

5 (vol. v) p. 463: the affect is dissociable from the representation, and can be 'introduced at some other point in the dream ... Such a displacement not infrequently follows the principle of antithesis.'

6 This is one of Freud's dreams. He is a naval officer. His superior suddenly dies, after telling him about his worries for his family's future (worries which are in fact those of the dreamer). But Freud, at the time, feels neither emotion nor anguish. These affects are displaced on to another episode of the dream, which comes slightly later, when the enemy warships approach (*The Interpretation of Dreams* (vol. v) pp. 463–4).

7 *Ecrits*, trans. Sheridan, p. 156.

8 'Two Aspects of Language and Two Types of Aphasic Disturbances', pp. 69, 70 and 71 in the 1971 edition.

9 S. Ullmann, *Précis de sémantique française* (Bern: Ed. A. Francke, 1952), pp. 285–6.

10 *Figures III*, pp. 26–8 (in 'La rhétorique restreinte').

11 See the whole of the first part of *Sémantique structurale* (Larousse, 1966), or 'La Structure élémentaire de la signification en linguistique' (*L'homme*, IV, 3 (1964) 5–17). One of Greimas' examples in this article (p. 9): the opposition *big/small* postulates the semantic axis 'measurement of the continuous'.

12 'Les oppositions significatives' (*Cahiers F. de Saussure*, x (1952) 11–40), especially pp. 11, 26, 27, etc.

13 'Two Aspects of Language and Two Types of Aphasic Disturbances', p. 61 in *Fundamentals of Language* ('... in a substitution set signs are linked by various degrees of similarity which fluctuate between the equivalence of synonyms and the common core of antonyms').

CHAPTER 14: REFERENTIAL, DISCURSIVE

1 See pp. 68–9 (1971 edition) and in particular the sentence which begins: 'In manipulating these two kinds of connection (similarity and contiguity) in both their aspects (positional and semantic) ... an individual exhibits his personal style, etc.'

2 I refer the reader to my *Essais sur la signification au cinéma*, vol. I, pp. 130–1 (*Film Language*, trans. Taylor, pp. 129–30) and vol. II, pp. 111–37.

3 *Theory of the Film* (London: Dennis Dobson, 1952) ch. 6, pp. 46–51. This is the phenomenon of the 'creative camera'; by means of the editing (and also the close-up, etc.) the camera fabricates a fictional geography, even a spectator who had been present at the shooting, standing beside the camera, could not have 'seen' this 'place'; only on the screen does it begin to exist.

4 [The 'vehicle' is the metaphorical element and the 'tenor' the literal element which it replaces: terminology proposed for literary criticism by I. A. Richards – see *The Philosophy of Rhetoric* (New York, 1936) pp. 96 and 120–1, and *Principles of Literary Criticism* (London, 1925) p. 240.]

5 *The Interpretation of Dreams* (vol. IV) pp. 307–8 and (vol. V) 339–40.

6 'Fonction de la métaphore dans *Octobre* d'Eisenstein', *Littérature*, 11 (1973) 109–28. This article studies a good many of the figural operations of Eisenstein's film in the details of their textual development; for the purpose of the present discussion, I shall only be referring to one of them, the 'theme of the harps'. As many readers will know, the author has been working for several years now, as part of a research team, on a very complex study of *October* which is to appear in several consecutive volumes; the first was published in 1976 (Marie-Claire Ropars-Wuilleumier and Pierre Sorlin: *'Octobre' – Ecriture et idéologie*, Editions Albatros, Collection Ça/Cinéma).

7 Page 113.

8 In fact, this 'metonymic origin' (p. 113) strikes her as being more indirect in this example than in other metaphors in *October*. But what interests me here, leaving aside the question of variants for the moment, is the very process whereby metonymy 'gets diverted' to metaphorical ends (p. 114). It is an important phenomenon (cf. pp. 130–2), and one which the author is right to explore in some detail.

9 Page 114. Cf. also (on the same page) the 'reduction [of metaphor] to the metonymic order'.

10 Either through the establishment of a sort of ideal diegesis in which the figures become the only reality (pp. 112–14), or because a metaphor which at first seems 'pure' turns out afterwards to have been borrowed from an element of the representation (p. 113, with the example of the china dog).

11 Pages 113–14.

12 'Two Aspects of Language and Two Types of Aphasic Disturbances', p. 78 in *Fundamentals of Language*.

13 'Upadek filmu?', in *Listy pro umñí a kritiku* (periodical Prague) 1 (1933) 45–9. French translation: 'Décadence du cinéma?', in Roman Jakobson, *Questions de poétique* (Ed. du Seuil, 1973) pp. 105–12; or in the *Revue d'Esthétique*, 2–3–4 (1973) special number entitled *Cinéma: théories, lectures*, pp. 69–76.

14 'Conversazione sul cinema con Roman Jakobson', a cura di Adriano Apra e Luigi Faccini, *Cinema e film*, 1–2 (1967) 157–62.

CHAPTER 15: METAPHOR/METONYMY: A DISSYMMETRICAL SYMMETRY

1 See my *Essais sur la signification au cinéma*, vol. I, pp. 112–13; *Film Language*,

trans. Taylor, pp. 109–10.

2 J. Mitry, *Esthétique et psychologie du cinéma*, vol. II, *Les formes* (Editions Universitaires, 1965) p. 447.

3 The same tendency exists at the moment in literary studies and in research on rhetoric itself, as Gérard Genette has pointed out at greater length in 'La rhétorique restreinte' (*Figures III*).

4 L'oscillation métaphoro-métonymique', *Topique*, 13 (1973) 75–99. This article has the particular merit of showing the importance of *both* the major figural paths and their mutual interconnections. Moreover it gives a very interesting account of the dissymmetry attaching to their status, which this chapter will discuss. Cf. especially 'the metaphorical organisation which rests on that of metonymy while opposing it' (p. 75), 'the high frequency of metonymies' (p. 82) and also (p. 80): 'We therefore posit that metaphor exploits metonymy, and is based on it. It will therefore not be surprising to find a metonymy behind every metaphor.' (I would not perhaps go quite so far.)

5 The notion of the symbolic (symbol, symbolise, etc.) is not only common to the metaphorical and the metonymic; it also applies to the paradigmatic, and the syntagmatic, and many other things as well. It is a general concept denoting any *meaning operation*, any 'play' involving a signifier and a semantic force (with or without a fixed signified); ultimately it denotes meaning itself, meaning as an operation, the effect of signification. It follows that the different figurations which this study is attempting to define are all symbolic.

This perhaps needed to be made clear, insofar as people are tending more and more, on the basis of a vague impression or as a kind of reflex, to associate the idea of the symbolic solely with metaphorical operations. It is worth noting in this connection that the word 'symbol', in its Greek etymology (*sumbolon*) itself derives from a metonymy or synecdoche. It denoted any object cut in two so that later on it could serve as a means of identification.

For Jacques Lacan, metaphor and metonymy are the two great principles of the symbolic order; a term he thus uses in the widest possible sense, covering the production of meaning in general. But an older tradition has consistently used the concept in just as general a sense: for instance, when psychologists or neurologists speak of the 'symbolic function' (which covers all the operations of the signifier), when sociologists study different kinds of symbolic institutions or actions independently of their internal semiotic mechanisms, or again in traditional literary and art criticism, which defines an element as 'symbolising' another whenever there exists between them a relation (of any kind) involving evocation, or suggestion, or equivalence – in short, a semantic circuit. So in fact the broadest definition of the 'symbolic' is also one of the most common.

In the field of classical semiology, 'symbol' has often been defined more narrowly, in particular when it is used to mean a '*motivated*' signifying link (as opposed to the 'sign' in the Saussurean tradition) or on the other hand, in C. S. Peirce's system, an 'arbitrary' one, in contrast to 'icon' and 'index'. These distinctions, while I do not contest them, will not play a great part in the present text.

6 On the one hand in *Totem and Taboo* (1912) (vol. XIII) p. 85, on the other hand in *The Interpretation of Dreams* (vol. v) pp. 538–40 (I discuss this passage on p. 202.

7 This is rather like what tends to happen in certain passages of Eisenstein's *October*. Marie-Claire Ropars, in the article I have already commented on (pp. 191–3, analyses this process whereby a kind of ideal diegesis is established, in which the figures become the sole, or at least the principal, reality. André Bazin had already pointed out that in Eisenstein the ideological discourse constructed by the concatenation of images/signs formed a kind of secondary plot, superimposed on the narrative diegesis proper. ('L'évolution du langage cinématographique', *Qu'est-ce que le cinéma?*, vol. I (Ed. du Cerf, 1958) p. 133). To the extent that this is so, one can indeed claim that the metaphor turns into a kind of 'symbolic' metonymy (M.-C. Ropars, p. 114). But the formulation would seem to be a little dangerous in that it uses 'metonymy' in a metaphorical sense (deliberately, of course, but one wonders how many readers will notice this), and so risks adding to the confusion between metonymy and syntagm, which is all too common as it is.

As for the other case of metaphors becoming metonymic which M.-C. Ropars analyses, it is not altogether relevant to my present topic. It involves metaphors which when they first appear in the film seem to be 'pure' (non-diegetic) but which later turn out to have been borrowed from an element of the representation. M.-C. Ropars analyses one of these in *October* (p. 113): a close-up of a china dog suddenly replaces a close-up of the face of a member of the Provisional Government, slumped in an armchair, passively awaiting the Bolsheviks' attack; only later, the author notes, do we guess that the dog must be part of the furnishings of the room the character is in; at first we are struck simply by the metaphorical link, the resemblance between the dog and the face. If we follow the order of the text, this is indeed a metaphor which becomes a metonymy. But seen in a wider perspective, it is also a metonymy which becomes a metaphor, and not the reverse; so that it follows a fairly common pattern, with however a less common inversion on the *syntagmatic* (but not the referential) axis. In fact M.-C. Ropars herself comments: 'We note however that the order of editing reverses the direction of this relation' (p. 113).

8 *Ecrits*, trans. Sheridan, p. 160 (displacement as 'the most appropriate means used by the unconscious to foil censorship'). Also on p. 164 the 'formulae' representing metaphor and metonymy by two different arrangements of the signifier S and the signifier S': 'maintenance of the bar', as the author says, in metonymy, and 'crossing of the bar' with metaphor. See also p. 158: 'what does man find in metonymy if not the power to circumvent the obstacles of social censure? Does not this form, which gives its field to truth in its very oppression, manifest a certain servitude inherent in its presentation?'

9 Pages 538–40 (vol. v).

10 *Précis de sémantique française*, p. 285.

11 'Métonymie chez Proust' (the article as a whole), *Figures III*, pp. 41–63.

12 In collaboration with Albin Grau. A German 'expressionist' film made in 1923. Original title: *Schatten* ('Shadows').

CHAPTER 16: FIGURE AND SUBSTITUTION

1 Examples include a passage from Lacan (*Ecrits,* trans. Sheridan, p. 157): '*One word for another*: that is the formula for the metaphor ...' In fact, it is the definition of the trope in general, and of the metonymic trope among others (see the end of this chapter) – a point which has already been made by Genette (*Figures III,* p. 32, note 4).
2 'Two Aspects of Language and Two Types of Aphasic Disturbances', pp. 76–7 in *Fundamentals of Language.*
3 See especially the two formulae given in *Ecrits,* trans. Sheridan, p. 164. Metaphor and metonymy both mobilise the signifier S and the signifier S'.
4 *Figures III,* 'La rhétorique restreinte', p. 23; and especially 'La rhétorique et l'espace du langage', *Tel Quel,* 19 (1964) 44–54.

CHAPTER 17: THE PROBLEM OF THE WORD

1 A technique familiar to the comic Latin authors, especially Terence, which consists for instance in taking two Greek comedies by Menander and using them as a basis for a single Latin play.
2 'La rhétorique restreinte' (the first part of the article).
3 'L'ancienne rhétorique' (the whole article), *Communications,* 16 (1970) 172–229.
4 All these divisions can be seen to relate to *eloquence,* to the 'genre of oratory' with its three initial sub-types: deliberative (political), judicial, epideictic (ceremonial). Rhetoric in fact originally covered all the techniques of coded acts of utterance, and reached its limit only in 'poetics' (cf. the opposition in Aristotle between the two treatises so titled). Poetics was the theory of the fictional (usually *written*), as opposed to that of public speeches in real life situations. In the French classical period this barrier comes down and 'poetry' itself comes under the jurisdiction of rhetoric. And this is why the rhetoric taught nowadays in schools and colleges is a written exercise as much as (or more than) an oral one.
5 There are in fact a number of studies, often solid and illuminating, which analyse the figures of the cinema – or more generally iconic figures, with reference especially to advertisements – in terms of the 'small-scale' classifications of traditional rhetoric (which does not necessarily exclude, in certain cases, the Jakobson type of binary conception). I am not familiar with all of them, but the following should be mentioned:

　　Ekkehard Kaemmerling: 'Rhetorik als Montage', *Semiotik des Films,* a collection of articles edited by Friedrich Knilli (Munich: Hanser Verlag, 1971) pp. 94–109.

　　Gui Bonsiepe: 'Visuelle Rhetorik', *Zeitschrift der Hochschule für Gestaltung-Ulm,* 14–15–16 (1965 or 1966) 22–40; also in Italian: 'Retorica visivo-verbale', *Marcatré,* 19–22.

　　Alberto Farassino: 'Ipotesi per una retorica della communicazione fotografica', *Annali della Scuola Superiore delle communicazioni sociali,* 4 (1969) 167–90.

　　J.B. Fages: 'Les figures du conditionnement', *Cinéthique,* 5 (1969) 41–4.

Jacques Durand: 'Rhétorique et image publicitaire', *Communications,* 15 (1970) 70–95.

Jacques Durand: 'Les figures de rhétorique dans l'image publicitaire: les figures disjonctives', *Bulletin de Recherches-Publicis,* 6 (1969) 19–23.

Geneviève Dolle: 'Rhétorique et supports de signification iconographiques', *Revue des Sciences Humaines,* 159 (1975) = *Le Cinéma en savoir,* special number edited by Jacques Morin, pp. 343–57.

6 *Figures III,* 'La rhétorique restreinte', pp. 28–31.

7 This kind of problem is briefly discussed, following on the work of Jean Mitry, in ch. x of my 'Problèmes actuels de théorie du cinéma', published as an article in 1967 and reprinted in vol. II of *Essais sur la signification au cinéma.*

8 See in particular the end of his article 'La pensée et la langue', *Bulletin de la Société de Linguistique de Paris,* XXIII (1922).

9 Gérard Genette, 'La rhétorique et l'espace du langage', pp. 47–8. Cf. also Roland Barthes, 'L'ancienne rhétorique', p. 218.

10 *Essais sur la signification au cinéma,* vol. I, pp. 111–21 (*Film Language,* trans. Taylor, pp. 108–19) and vol. II, pp. 75–86.

11 Notably Pier Paolo Pasolini ('Le cinéma de poésie', *Cahiers du Cinéma,* 171 (1965) 55–64) and Jean Mitry (*Esthétique et psychologie du cinéma,* vol. II, especially p. 381: the idea of connotation being no different from denotation in its formal definition).

12 See especially 'The Unconscious' (vol. XIV) p. 201 and *The Ego and the Id* (vol. XIX) p. 20.

13 *The Interpretation of Dreams* (vol IV) p. 296 sq., 'The Unconscious' (vol. XIV) pp. 198–9.

14 [Lacan uses this term when he wishes to emphasise the *primary* element in language.]

15 For example *Ecrits,* trans. Sheridan, p. 160: 'What distinguishes these two mechanisms [condensation and displacement], which play such a privileged role in the dream-work (*Traumarbeit*), from their homologous function in discourse? Nothing, except a condition imposed upon the signifying material, etc.'

16 *Ecrits,* trans. Sheridan, pp. 156–7.

17 *Discours, figure* (Klincksieck, 1971) p. 256.

18 *Figures III,* p. 32, note 4.

19 [It can mean shower, spray, etc.]

20 Thus in the famous dream of the botanical monograph' (*The Interpretation of Dreams* (vol. IV) pp. 282–3 the associations are certainly numerous and varied, but they can nevertheless be fairly well expressed on the level of two words, *monograph* and *botanical* (hence the name given by Freud to the dream).

21 French terminology.

22 Soviet terminology.

23 American terminology.

24 See especially *Inhibitions, Symptoms and Anxiety* (vol. XX) pp. 120–3.

25 Repression' (vol. XIV); p. 157; *Inhibitions, Symptoms and Anxiety* (vol. XX) p. 117.

26 *Elements of Semiology* (Cape, 1967) p. 57.

CHAPTER 18: FORCE AND MEANING

1 Ed. Klincksieck, 1971. Especially pp. 239–70, in the chapter entitled 'Le travail du rêve ne pense pas' [The dream-work does not think]. This passage had been published separately in 1968 (under the same title) in the *Revue d'Esthétique*, XXI, 1, pp. 26–61.

2 See note 1 above. This formula, which Lyotard has made famous, may be found in Freud, *The Interpretation of Dreams* (vol. v) p. 507: 'The dream-work does not think, calculate or judge in any way at all; it restricts itself to giving things a new form'.

3 Cf. in particular *The Interpretation of Dreams* (vol. v) pp. 602–3.

4 This is the idea developed in Chapter VI F of *The Interpretation of Dreams* entitled 'Some Examples – Calculations and Speeches in Dreams'.

5 *Discours, figure*, pp. 241–3.

6 See in particular 'The Unconscious' (vol XIV) pp. 201–2; *The Ego and the Id*, (vol. XIX) pp. 20–1.

7 *Ecrits*, trans. Sheridan, p. 163.

8 See for instance 'On Narcissism: an Introduction', (vol. XIV) p. 77 (Psychoanalysis is not a speculative discipline, it is based on the interpretation of observed facts; so the concepts it uses are not the foundations of the building but rather its 'roof': it can be modified without the building falling down; research may progress via concepts which from a purely philosophical point of view might sometimes seem to be 'nebulous, scarcely imaginable', etc.).

9 See in particular 'The Unconscious' (vol. XIV) pp. 173 and 181.

10 *Ecrits*, trans. Sheridan, p. 297.

11 See for example *Beyond the Pleasure Principle* (vol. XVIII) pp. 7–8 and 63, *The Ego and the Id* (vol XIX) p. 22, or 'The Economic Problem of Masochism', 1924, p. 288 in the French translation (in *Névrose, psychose et perversion*, ed. J. Laplanche, P.U.F., 1973). André Green's book *Le Discours vivant (La conception psychanalytique de l'affect)* (P.U.F., 1973) is largely given over to this problem.

12 *The Interpretation of Dreams* (vol. v) pp. 602 ('All thinking is no more than a circuitous path, etc.') and 567 ('Thought is after all nothing but a substitute for a hallucinatory wish'). 'A Metapsychological Supplement to the Theory of Dreams' (vol. XIV) pp. 230–1, and *The Ego and the Id* (vol. XIX) p. 21: the calling up of memories, meditation, and so on also involve a regressive process, the difference with the dream being that they stop short of hallucination.

'A Project for a Scientific Psychology' (1895): thought as a bound form of the 'displacement of energy'.

'The Unconscious' (vol. XIV) p. 202, and *The Interpretation of Dreams*, (vol. v) p. 544: the activity of thought, of relating things, is in itself unconscious. Etc.

13 See ch. 11, note 2.

CHAPTER 19: CONDENSATION

1 Chapter VI A, 'The Work of Condensation'.

2 See especially vol. IV, p. 278: 'Dreams are brief, meagre and laconic in comparison with the range and wealth of the dream-thoughts. If a dream is written out it may perhaps fill half a page. The analysis setting out the dream-thoughts underlying it may occupy six, eight or a dozen times as much space'.

3 *Discours, figure*, pp. 243–4 and 258–9.

4 *Discours, figure*, p. 259.

5 *Discours, figure*, p. 243.

6 *Ecrits*, trans. Sheridan, p. 160.

7 *Sémantique structurale*, p. 72 sq. This is the passage on 'expansion' in linguistics (for example: going from a word to its complete definition) and on its opposite which Greimas, significantly, calls 'condensation'; the final stage of condensation is *denomination* (p. 74), which summarises a set of properties in a single word (see above, p. 225).

8 *The Interpretation of Dreams* (vol. IV) pp. 283–4. Overdetermination is not only one of the major forms of condensation (alongside omission pure and simple, composite formations and those which result from compromise), it is in fact linked to condensation in every case.

9 *The Interpretation of Dreams* (vol. V) pp. 340–1.

10 See p. 306 note 6.

11 Vol V, pp. 342–3. This was a dream of one of Freud's friends, a woman who had been in love with a musician whose career had been interrupted by mental illness. The dreamer sees a great orchestra playing. In the middle of the orchestra is a high tower culminating in a platform surrounded by an iron railing. The conductor is rushing around on the platform, running in all directions like a *madman*, a madman *enclosed* by the railings. The conductor represents the musician the dreamer loved (i.e., she would have liked him to be able to conduct, and appear in public). In her view he 'towers over' the other musicians. At the same time, the platform and especially the railings are allusions to the real fate of the unfortunate man. The link between these various associations is provided by the old German word *Narrenturm*, which designated the lunatic asylum but whose literal meaning is 'tower of fools'.

12 *Ecrits* (Editions du Seuil, 1966) pp. 166–7. [This passage has not previously been translated into English.]

13 See especially *The Interpretation of Dreams* (vol. V) p. 507 and p. 596.

14 'Repression' (vol XIV) pp. 155–6, 'The Unconscious' (vol. XIV) pp. 184–5. *Inhibitions, Symptoms and Anxiety* (vol. XX) pp. 111–12.

15 Lacan and Jakobson are sometimes seen as being in disagreement on this point. ('Two Aspects of Language and Two Types of Aphasic Disturbances', p. 81 in *Fundamentals of Language*). They both connect displacement with metonymy. But for Jakobson condensation (like displacement) would appear to be one of the figures of contiguity: if not a properly defined metonymy, at least a synecdoche, whereas for Lacan it is metaphorical.

I think we should not overestimate the extent of this disagreement. In Jakobson's case it was a purely incidental comment, which he does not develop and which he might not wish to stand by: when asked by his translator, Nicolas Ruwet, above the discrepancy with the Lacanian positions, Jakobson merely replied that 'condensation' was a rather imprecise notion in the Freudian texts, covering cases of metaphor *and* synecdoche.

However, it is true that the process of condensation, in one of its aspects, substitutes the 'part' for the 'whole': one manifest element represents a larger whole, itself latent or unconscious, it is a form of overdetermination (cf. above p. 237 and note 8) and can be found in hysterical condensation (p. 241 and note 14). Condensation definitely has an element of synecdoche. But I do not see how this would exclude its metaphorical aspects. Not only because it is a complex skein into which many threads may be wound, but also for a more specific reason: the fact that condensation brings to consciousness the 'part' of a 'whole' still tells us nothing about the nature of the relation which links this part to the other parts of the same whole: it may be resemblance (you then have a metaphor-synecdoche), which is a classic phenomenon in psychoanalysis, when a subject unconsciously reactivates parental images in connection with someone involved in his present life, someone who lends himself to this purpose by virtue of his appearance, character, age, function, etc.; this person becomes the metaphor-synecdoche of a whole, much more diffuse parental 'line of ancestry'.

Jakobson also suggests, in the same passage, that the psychoanalytic equivalents of metaphor and other figures of similarity could be 'identification' and 'symbolism' in the Freudian sense (rather than the condensation which Lacan proposes). All the same, we should remember that Freud saw identification as a form of condensation (*The Interpretation of Dreams* (vol. IV) pp. 320–1): so that Jakobson is closer to Lacan than it might seem. As for the allusion to symbolism, it is so brief that it is difficult to interpret. *Symbolism* is used by Freud in the ordinary sense of the word, which is very general (see above, p. 302, note 5); he does not associate it specifically with either condensation or displacement. When Freud uses the word in a more technical sense, as in ch. x of the *Introductory Lectures on Psychoanalysis*, it means something quite different: Freud then reserves the term 'symbol' for those dream signifiers which have a fixed cultural meaning common to a large number of dreamers; he contrasts them with individual signifiers, whose scope can be estimated only through 'free association' involving the individuality of the subject who has had the dream. Clearly it is not a question here of condensation as opposed to displacement; it is presumably not this passage of Freud that Jakobson had in mind. But as he does not go into details, we cannot proceed any further.

16 Which struck me in 1971, at a time when the idea of a psychoanalytic semiology was (vaguely) dawning in my mind. I had begun to look at this sequence from Chukhrai's film in *Essais sur la signification au cinéma*, vol. II, pp. 182–3 and 185–7.

17 *The Interpretation of Dreams* (vol. IV) p. 293.

18 *Ecrits*, trans. Sheridan, p. 160.

CHAPTER 20: FROM THE 'DREAM-WORK' TO THE 'PRIMARY PROCESS'

1 See in particular vol. v, ch. VII E, entitled 'The Primary and Secondary Processes – Repression'.

2 On pp. 186–7 (vol. XIV) these characteristics are grouped under four head-

ings: indifference to the principle of non-contradiction, indifference to time, indifference to reality, and extreme mobility of cathectic intensities (= free energy) given as a synonym of the 'primary process', and of which the two forms mentioned are condensation and displacement: 'I have proposed to regard these two processes as distinguishing marks of the so-called *primary psychical process*' (p. 186).

3 Vol. I.

4 See in particular *The Interpretation of Dreams* (vol. v) p. 489.

5 See in particular *The Interpretation of Dreams* (vol. IV) pp. 277–8 and (vol v) 506–7.

6 This is the theme of condensation as being 'mainly responsible for the bewildering impression made on us by dreams' (cf. especially *The Interpretation of Dreams* (vol. v) p. 595.

7 *The Interpretation of Dreams* (vol. v) p. 561.

8 'A Metapsychological Supplement to the Theory of Dreams' (vol. XIV) p. 226.

9 Ibid.

10 Especially in 'A Metapsychological Supplement to the Theory of Dreams' (vol. XIV) pp. 226–8.

11 See in particular *The Interpretation of Dreams* (vol. v) p. 561, which is very emphatic on this point.

12 *The Interpretation of Dreams* (vol. v) p. 594 ('The energy which belongs to the unconscious wish is "transferred" onto certain preconscious elements, the latter being so to speak "drawn into the unconscious"').

13 For instance *The Interpretation of Dreams* (vol. IV) pp. 279–80.

CHAPTER 21: 'CENSORSHIP': BARRIER OR DEVIATION?

1 'Repression' (vol. XIV) pp. 148–9 (= 'repression proper' or 'after-pressure') and 151 (repression as a 'persistent expenditure of force'); 'The Unconscious' (vol. XIV) pp. 180–1 (anticathexis); *Inhibitions, Symptoms and Anxiety* (vol. XX) p. 157 sq. (relations between resistance, censorship and anticathexis); etc.

2 'The Unconscious' (vol. XIV) pp. 66 and 198, *The Ego and the Id* (vol. XIX) pp. 17 and 49–50 (on the 'negative therapeutic reaction'), *Inhibitions, Symptoms and Anxiety* (vol. XX, in particular pp. 159–60), etc.

3 In a way this is a milder version of the impression of being 'lived by unknown and uncontrollable forces' which Freud notes in passing (*The Ego and the Id* (vol. XIX) p. 23) without stopping to consider its concrete phenomenology or its frequency, and attributing the point to Groddeck (*The Book of the It*, trans. V.M.E. Collins, London: Vision Press Ltd., 1969).

4 [Literally: 'The worst pain is not knowing why, with no love and no hate, my heart is in so much pain'.]

5 *The Interpretation of Dreams* (vol. v) p. 490.

6 Hence the status of the unconscious as a 'necessary assumption' (see for instance 'The Unconscious' (vol. xiv) p. 166), necessary because otherwise we would not understand the data of the conscious.

7 A more indirect and more 'interpolating' analytic technique than interpret-

ation proper (which stays close to the given). Freud was of the opinion that we ought not to be too proud to have recourse to it when analysis is lagging too far behind its ideal objective, which remains anamnesis, as total as possible (cf. 'Constructions in Analysis', 1937).

8 See for example 'The Unconscious' (vol. xiv) pp. 167–8: it is useless to suppose that latent material is somatic and non-psychical since physiology in its current state of play does not allow us to study it in any respect, whereas it lends itself as well (or as badly) as conscious material to being described in terms of 'ideas, purposes, resolutions and so on'. (I would add that this remains the case if the psychical *as a whole* is considered to be a manifestation of the somatic, a position which Freud partly adopts, especially from 1920 on.) Cf. also *The Ego and the Id* (vol. xix) p. 15 (the latent is not 'psychoid' in character, but fully psychical).

9 As Lacan says, 'The mistake made in good faith is the most unforgiveable of all (*Ecrits*, Editions du Seuil, p. 859, not previously translated into English).

10 Cf. note 8 above. The concept of the *drive* in psychoanalysis is, as we know, 'a borderline concept between the psychical and the somatic', only approached via its 'representatives': its *ideational* representative and its *instinctual* representative, hence psychical formations analogous to those which exist in the conscious.

11 *Ecrits*, Editions du Seuil, in particular pp. 70 (metonymy) and 708 (metaphor).

12 See p. 303, note 8.

13 *The Interpretation of Dreams* (vol. iv) p. 308, (vol. v) pp. 449 (twice on the same page) and 507.

14 See for instance *The Interpretation of Dreams*, (vol. iv) p. 322, the passage which ends: 'thus, by making use of dream-condensation, I have satisfied the claims of the dream-censorship'.

15 A passage from the *Introductory Lectures on Psycho-Analysis* also springs to mind, although it corresponds less closely to the point I am trying to make. Here Freud compares the distance between the unconscious and the conscious to that between a negative of a photograph and the photograph itself (vol. xvi, p. 295). Freud's repeated use of the *optical metaphor* to represent the psychical apparatus ought to be studied more closely. Jean-Louis Baudry has begun to do this and set out the problems very well ('Le dispositif: approches métapsychologiques de l'impression de réalité', *Communications*, 23 (1975) 56–72).

A member of my seminar, Patrice Rollet, who is well acquainted with psychoanalytic theory and whose various contributions have been especially useful, points out quite rightly that here we come up against a topological problem, which is not simply a metaphorical one: it concerns, rather, the 'model' to be adopted (topology is a branch of mathematics): in what type of logical space can we represent the unique relations between the unconscious and the conscious, the primary and the secondary? Quite apart from Freud's allusions to optics (or indeed his very concept of the topic') there is also Lacan's constant interest in topology proper and the abundance of spatial figures in his work, in particular the privileged reference to the Moebius strip.

CHAPTER 22: DISPLACEMENT

1 See p. 298 notes 2 and 4.
2 See p. 310 note 13.
3 See p. 303, note 8.
4 'Instincts and their Vicissitudes' (vol. xiv) p. 126 ('Bearing in mind that there are motive forces which work against an instinct's being carried through in an unmodified form, we may also regard these vicissitudes as modes of *defence* against the instincts').
5 Ch. vi B.
6 '... It could be seen that the elements which stand out as the principal components of the manifest content of the dream are far from playing the same part in the dream-thoughts. And, as a corollary, the converse of this assertion can be affirmed: what is clearly the essence of the dream-thoughts need not be represented in the dream at all' (*The Interpretation of Dreams* (vol. iv p. 305).
7 *The Interpretation of Dreams* (vol. iv) p. 307 ('transference and displacement of psychical intensities'), (vol. v) pp. 339 ('displacements of intensity between .... elements'), 507 ('*displacement of psychical intensities* to the point of a transvaluation of all psychical values'), etc.
8 *The Interpretation of Dreams* (vol. iv) p. 305.
9 *The Interpretation of Dreams* (vol. v) p. 463: the affect is inseparable from the representation, it can be 'introduced at some other point in the dream .... Such a displacement not infrequently follows the principle of antithesis'. See also p. 300 note 6.
10 *The Interpretation of Dreams* (vol. v) p. 339 ('We have not yet referred to any other sort of displacement. Analyses show us, however, that another sort exists and that it reveals itself in a change in the *verbal expression* of the thoughts concerned ... a colourless and abstract expression in the dream-thought being exchanged for a pictorial and concrete one').
11 Especially in *Inhibitions, Symptoms and Anxiety*; but already in 'Repression' (vol. xiv) p. 155, 'The Unconscious' (vol. xiv) p. 182 sq., etc.
12 See for instance 'Repression' (vol. xiv) p. 157.
13 Guy Rosolato puts it very well (in 'L'oscillation métaphoro-métonymique', already mentioned on p. 302 note 4: 'the organisation of metaphor which depends on, and is opposed to, that of metonymy' (p. 75).
14 This point is made very clearly in the following passage: 'The displacements we have hitherto considered turned out to consist in the replacing of some one particular idea by another in some way closely associated with it, and they were used to facilitate condensation insofar as, by their means, instead of *two* elements, a single common element intermediate between them found its way into the dream' (*The Interpretation of Dreams* (vol. v) p. 339.
15 *The Interpretation of Dreams* (vol. iv) pp. 320–1.
16 Cf. the cases of practical 'cooperation' between a conscious statement and an unconscious movement which Freud called 'reinforced tendencies' ('The Unconscious' (vol. xiv) p. 195).
17 *Ecrits*, trans. Sheridan, p. 160.

18 USA, 1941.
19 Made in collaboration with Boris Kaufman. France, 1929–30.
20 For example in Guy Rosolato's valuable article 'L'oscillation métaphoro-métonymique', mentioned on p. 302. I am thinking here of the opening passage, from which I shall quote the following sentences: 'And so, what dominates in this definition [of metonymy] is the total obviousness of the relation, and of course its existence; you never need to refer to an unconscious chain because the link with the missing terms is perfectly clear, and interpretation easy ... This conception of metonymy, as we see, embraces all possible figures, provided that their relational mechanism is exposed' (pp. 76–7). Or further on (pp. 81–2): 'For metaphor reduced to a single circuit functions as metonymy, or disappears as a "figure" in comparison with other figures'.

Such an approach poses the problem of Lacan's intervention very directly, the problem that is to say of the homology between the operations of the unconscious and those of rhetoric. This correspondence acquires its full force only if established between instances which remain genuinely autonomous; one cannot modify the rhetorical definitions to bring them in line with the Freudian distinction between condensation and displacement.

CHAPTER 23: CROSSINGS AND INTERWEAVINGS IN FILM: THE LAP-DISSOLVE AS AN EXAMPLE OF A FIGURATION

1 *The Interpretation of Dreams* (vol. IV) p. 293 ('... uniting the actual features of two or more people into a single dream-image').
2 I refer the reader to my study entitled 'Ponctuations et démarcations dans le film de diégèse' (reprinted in *Essais sur la signification au cinéma*, vol. II, pp. 111–37).
3 Ch. VI C of *The Interpretation of Dreams*, which carries this title. Freud asks how the dream expresses various logical links, succession, causality, opposition, etc. And the fact is that it does not mark them out separately, and explicitly, like language which has its 'whens' and its 'althoughs' (p. 312, vol. IV. It 'expresses' them (or at least the analyst can reconstruct them) in another way: through the arrangement (possibly the telescoping) of the sum total of elements, and not through a logical marker which would link them up and be additional to them: dreams 'disregard all these conjunctions, and it is only the substantive content of the dream-thoughts that they take over and manipulate' (p. 312, vol. IV). For example (p. 316, vol. IV): the causal link between two elements appears as 'the direct transformation of one image into another': almost a lap-dissolve. Resemblance appears as identification or composite transformation, which are forms of condensation (p. 320 sq., vol. IV); etc.
4 *The Interpretation of Dreams* (vol. V) pp. 531–2 (Between two given elements several associative links may exist; the first which occurs to someone telling a dream is sometimes off the mark, improbable, more or less absurd, but it points to others which are being held back from consciousness by censorship).

CHAPTER 24: CONDENSATIONS AND DISPLACEMENTS OF
THE SIGNIFIER

1 *The Interpretation of Dreams* (vol. IV) p. 296 sq., 'The Unconscious' (vol. XIV)
pp. 198–9, etc.

2 *The Interpretation of Dreams* (vol. V) pp. 530–1, and in particular this sentence,
which the author underlines: 'Whenever one psychical element is linked
with another by an objectionable and superficial association ['joke', 'play on
words', 'assonance', as it says a bit earlier] there is also a legitimate and
deeper link between them which is subjected to the resistance of censorship'.

3 This viewpoint is formulated very explicitly in an article by Luis J. Prieto,
'D'une asymétrie entre le plan de l'expression et le plan du contenu de la
langue' (*Bulletin de la Société de Linguistique de Paris*, LIII, 1957–8). The 'asym-
metry' which the title refers to is precisely the one I am commenting on, and
the aim of the article is to explore some of its consequences for the technical
work of the linguist. The signifier is 'manifest', says the author, the signified
'non-manifest', purely 'psychical', a theme which is moreover constant in
the whole linguistic tradition of Saussure and Hjelmslev.

4 This corresponds to the title André Martinet gave to one of his studies: 'La
forme, garantie du caractère linguistique' (in *Eléments de linguistique générale*,
trans. E. Palmer: *Elements of General Linguistics*, London: Faber and Faber,
1964).
  Antoine Meillet was a frequent proponent of the idea – which all linguists
are familiar with.

5 *The Psychopathology of Everyday Life* (1901) (vol. VI) p. 68.

6 *The Interpretation of Dreams* (vol. IV) pp. 298–9.

7 [In the original French text of this book Metz often refers to *The Interpretation
of Dreams* by its German title; he speaks of 'le *Traumdeutung*'.]

8 One such example, *Appétit d'oiseau*, a cartoon by Peter Foldès, has been
closely studied from a semio-psychoanalytic point of view by Thierry
Kuntzel in an extremely interesting article: 'Le défilement', *Revue d'Esthétique*, 2–3–4 (1973) = *Cinéma: théorie, lecture*, special number edited by Dominique Noguez, pp. 87–110. I can do no more than refer to this text which
demonstrates very effectively how condensations and displacements affect
the very identity of the 'objects' represented, and how processes of recognition, and of naming, are called into question.

9 I refer the reader to my study entitled 'Le perçu et le nommé' (*Pour une Esthétique sans entrave – Mélanges Mikel Dufrenne*, 10/18, 1975, pp. 345–77; reprinted in *Essais sémiotiques*, Klincksieck, 1977).

10 See above, pp. 189, 219.

11 Pp. 277–8

12 *The Interpretation of Dreams* (vol. IV) p. 316. In another passage (vol. V. pp.
595–6) Freud makes the point that these primary figurations in which
thought acts on the signifier in its material aspect can also be found in
certain commonplace (secondarised) procedures, for instance the habit of
using italics, or bold type, for words or phrases deemed to be important.

13 'La *chafetière* est sur la table...', *Communication et langage*, 29 (1976) 36–49.
The article is signed by Jacques Dubois, Francis Edeline, Jean-Marie Klink-

enberg and Philippe Minguet.

14 Larousse, 1970. By the same people, plus Francis Pire and Hadelin Trinon.

15 P. 263 sq., apropos of my 'rhinoceros' (!)

16 *The Interpretation of Dreams* (vol. IV, p. 320 sq.). Freud makes the point that composite structures, unlike identification which usually concerns people, apply more to things.

17 *The Interpretation of Dreams* (vol. IV) p. 320.

CHAPTER 25: PARADIGM/SYNTAGM IN THE TEXT OF THE CURE

1 The analysand is not, or not yet, at the stage of being able to consciously recognise such and such a childhood memory (which the analyst would have preferred), but he relives it in the present 'with undesired fidelity', without experiencing it as a reproduction, in the form of biographical or affective changes brought about by the transference process of the cure itself, which to this extent does not simply analyse material, but brings in fresh material (see *Beyond the Pleasure Principle* (vol. XVIII) pp. 18–19, and *Inhibitions, Symptoms and Anxiety* (vol. XX) pp. 159–60, etc.).

2 *Ecrits*, trans. Sheridan, pp. 149 and 164. On this point see Jean Laplanche and Serge Leclaire, 'L'inconscient, une étude psychanalytique', *Les Temps Modernes*, 183 (1961) 81–129, in particular pp. 113–14.

Index

In this index references to films have all been listed under 'films discussed', and technical rhetorical terms and examples, excepting a few terms originating in rhetoric but now fairly extensively naturalised in other discourses, under 'rhetoric, technical terms and examples'.